A CONEY ISLAND READER

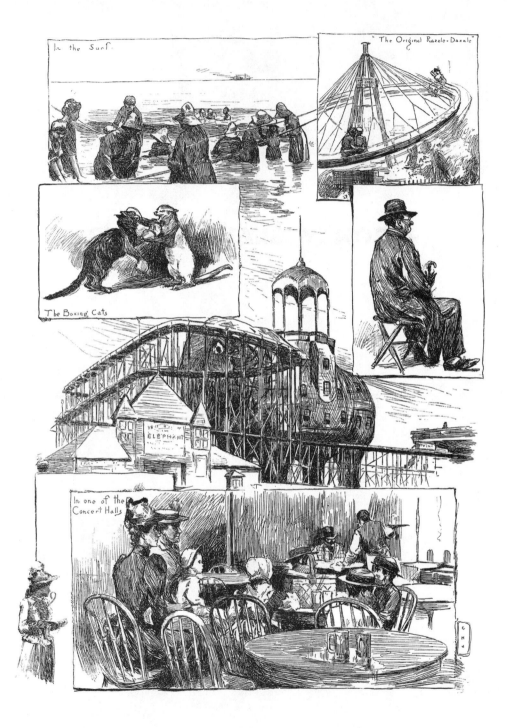

In the Surf.

"The Original Razzle-Dazzle"

The Boxing Cats

In one of the Concert Halls

A CONEY ISLAND READER

Through Dizzy Gates of Illusion

★ ★ ☆ ★ ★

EDITED BY **LOUIS J. PARASCANDOLA**
AND **JOHN PARASCANDOLA**

COLUMBIA UNIVERSITY PRESS ♔ NEW YORK

COLUMBIA UNIVERSITY PRESS

Publishers Since 1893

New York   Chichester, West Sussex

cup.columbia.edu

Library of Congress Cataloging-in-Publication Data

A Coney Island reader : through dizzy gates of illusion /
edited by Louis J. Parascandola and John Parascandola.

    pages   cm

    Includes bibliographical references.

    ISBN 978-0-231-16572-3 (cloth : acid-free paper)

    ISBN 978-0-231-16573-0 (pbk. : acid-free paper)

    ISBN 978-0-231-53819-0 (e-book)

1. Coney Island (New York, N.Y.)—Literary collections. 2. Amusement parks—New York (State)—Coney
Island—History. I. Parascandola, Louis J., 1952– editor. II. Parascandola, John, 1941– editor.

    PS509.N5C66 2015

    808.8'03274723—dc23

2014022522

Columbia University Press books are printed on permanent and durable acid-free paper.

This book is printed on paper with recycled content.

Printed in the United States of America

C 10 9 8 7 6 5 4 3 2 1

P 10 9 8 7 6 5 4 3 2 1

FRONTISPIECE: Charles H. Johnson, "A Visit to Coney Island," *Harper's Weekly*, September 12, 1891.

48–49: "Brighton Beach." (Photograph published by Bain News Service, New York. Library of Congress,
Prints and Photographs Division)

80–81: "Bowery by Night on Coney Island, N.Y.," ca. 1912. (Postcard published by American Art Publishing
Company, New York. Photograph by lawcain, Bigstock)

168–169: "Municipal Baths and Beach, Coney Island, N.Y.," ca. 1912. (Postcard published by American Art
Publishing Company, New York. Photograph by lawcain, Bigstock)

248–249: Cyclone, Coney Island. (pedrosala, Bigstock)

COVER DESIGN: Philip Pascuzzo

BOOK DESIGN AND TYPESETTING: Vin Dang

COVER IMAGE: Coney Island beach and boardwalk scenes, ca. 1898. (Color lithograph published
by Strobridge Lithographing Company, Cincinnati and New York. Library of Congress, Prints and
Photographs Division)

FOR THE BITTERSWEET DREAM TO BE
WITH THE SUPPORT OF FIGURE FOUNDATION

CONTENTS

ILLUSTRATIONS

FOREWORD
Kevin Baker

"I THINK I KNOW ENOUGH about Coney to say that it won't work out the way anybody's saying it will," Richard Snow, Coney Island's most perceptive chronicler, told me once, referring to the proposal of the Department of City Planning to rezone Coney Island—the latest in a long series of attempts to cover the island with respectable people doing respectable things.

What Snow understands is what a very complicated place Coney is. It's easy to lose one's direction out there, amid the surf and the sand and all the amusements. Coney changes constantly, as barrier islands do, but to try to make those changes adhere to a particular human scheme is something else again. You might as well try to plan the sea.

Louis and John Parascandola bring that realization home in this splendid and important compilation of writings on Coney. Putting all these diverse observations—fiction and nonfiction, verse and journalism, and memoirs and official reports—between two covers is a critical achievement, for only in this way can we see what a chimera Coney is, how it shifts and vanishes and re-forms right before our eyes.

Those who visit Coney with preconceived notions about it tend to fare badly. Revolutionaries, especially, have trouble with Coney. One would like to have heard what Sigmund Freud really thought about the place after his visit in 1909. Referring to the genteel, bourgeois park of his native Vienna, he remarked only that Coney Island was "a magnified Prater," which it most certainly was not.

José Martí, in exile from Cuba, dreaming of poetry and plotting revolution, gives us almost a parody of the melancholy poet in his dispatch to a Bogotá newspaper. He manages to condemn in the same sentence both those American mothers who take their young children to stroll along the summer beach—"concerned only with their own pleasure and never fearing that the biting air will harm the child's natural delicacy"—*and* those "ladies who abandon their babies in hotel rooms to the arms of some harsh Irishwoman."

Maxim Gorky is funnier but no less disdainful. "Hell is very badly done," he tells us of one Dreamland exhibit, and claims that he is unable to find "even the suggestion of beauty" in the great parks, concluding that "one thing alone is good in the garish city: You can drink in hatred to your soul's content, hatred sufficient to last thruout [sic] life, hatred of the power of stupidity!"

In the end, both men returned home to die for their revolutions. The people whom Martí disapproved of so thoroughly erected a very poetic statue of him, falling from his horse after being shot, at the entrance to another one of their pleasure groves: Central Park. And, almost despite himself, Martí wrote of Coney as "a town of stars—and of orchestras, dances, chatter, surf sounds, human sounds, choruses of laughter and praise for the air, hawkers' loud cries, swift trains and speedy carriages, until it is time to go home."

How romantic! And how romantic to think of his audience, the newspaper readers of Bogotá, dreaming of Coney Island in 1883, high in the mountains of Colombia. More than twenty years later, Gorky put aside his hate to render his own description, as quoted in Peter Lyon's "The Master Showman of Coney Island": "With the advent of night a fantastic city all of fire suddenly rises from the ocean into the sky. Thousands of ruddy sparks glimmer in the darkness, limning in fine, sensitive outline on the black background of the sky shapely towers of miraculous castles, palaces, and temples. . . . Fabulous beyond conceiving, ineffably beautiful, is this fiery scintillation."

It's not surprising that they should have been so confused, because, of course, it's the nature of Coney Island to confuse. Even Coney's own revolutionary, Frederic Thompson, inventor of Luna Park, the most glorious amusement park ever created, seems befuddled, insisting that fun must be "manufactured" and that he builds only for "that ninety-five per cent of the American public [that is] pure and good." The plasterboard heads of leering clowns and wolves and pigs that he mounted all around his park told a different story. So did the fantastic, disorienting architecture of Luna Park, which was not any real architecture at all but his own, surreal invention.

Coney Island is a carnival, and, as at any carnival, the Lord of Misrule runs away with all of us, even the pure and the good. Everything is on edge or turned upside down; everything is unsettled.

It is at Coney where Delmore Schwartz cries, "Don't do it!" at his own parents' courtship, and Henry Miller laments, "Everything is sliding and crumbling, everything glitters, totters, teeters, titters." It is where James Huneker marveled a hundred years ago that "humanity sheds its civilisation and becomes half child, half savage." Where Giuseppe Cautela tells us, "You are shown all the punishments of sin and all the rewards of virtue. You become forgetful of both, and your body, taking on wings, flies through the air with the speed of a meteor."

It is where Colson Whitehead reminds us, "Everything disappears into sand." Where a young Isaac Bashevis Singer collapses into a deep sleep and finds "the secret of time, space, and causality. It seemed unbelievably simple, but the moment I opened my eyes it was all forgotten. What remained was the taste of something otherworldly and marvelous."

Even the most marvelous of Coney's manmade attractions were and are cheap, flimsy things, as *Fortune*'s anonymous correspondent reminded the magazine's readers in 1938: "At close range, in the hard early morning light. . . . Shoddy shows through the tinsel. . . . At six in the morning Coney Island is like the stage of a very old theatre before the audience arrives."

Coney has always needed people to animate it, give it romance, meaning, dread. Why they should arrive at all is enough to baffle Huneker, who claims that he can't understand the place's allure: "Why, after the hot, narrow, noisy, dirty streets of the city, do these same people crowd into the narrower, hotter, noisier, dirtier, wooden alleys of Coney?"

Yet come they did, and come they always would.

Sex was an attraction, of course. So, too, was Freud's other great human instinct. Richard Le Gallienne ventures the thought that "death, or at least the fear of it, as always, still holds a foremost place in popular amusements," and no doubt he was at least partly right. Death was there in 1910, when the motorman-operated Rough Riders roller coaster failed to negotiate a turn, sending four cars and sixteen passengers flying into the air, thirty feet above Surf Avenue. Four of them died that day—which bothered everyone so much that the Rough Riders rode on to kill three more passengers in 1915.

Pondering the same question about Coney Island in the era of the great parks (1897–1911), I wondered why it was that people who lived in constant fear of fire in ramshackle, deathtrap tenements should want to see spectacles such as Dreamland's exhibit Fighting the Flames, in which just such a building is set ablaze for every performance. It occurred to me that it was the same reason why they came to gape at the tableaux of the Johnstown Flood or the eruption of Mount Pelée on Martinique, why they came to watch the U.S. Navy battle all the nations of the world or the incubator babies struggle for breath, or why they came to gawk at even the gilded electrical plants that powered the parks. They were there to see the pageant of their lives, and their time, played out before them.

Or maybe it was the sea or the cotton candy or the hot dogs. Maybe what William Henry Bishop describes as the "regiment of charlatans [who] detain you, one after another." Or, as Reginald Wright Kauffman's observes, "Of course, you are probably quite as ridiculous at all times as you are at Coney, but at Coney you are a little more egregiously and much more merrily ridiculous."

Indeed. And yet still they come. The Colson Whiteheads and the Katie Roiphes, in the footsteps of Henry Miller and Lawrence Ferlinghetti, still trying to climb inside that Coney Island of the mind. "South," Whitehead commands us, "to the beach where a broom of briny air sweeps away this miserable funk . . . to the bottom of the subway map, settling there like loose change in various denominations."

It is where Roiphe hears "not the sleek modern sound of speed" but "speed from another era" aboard the Cyclone, where she becomes "nothing but stomach, air, and fear" but "wonder[s] woozily why I feel so good." (José Martí would agree, in his way.)

Near the very end of this volume, you will find the latest determination of the other city, the city of power and wealth that looms just over the horizon, to bury once and for all the carnival in Coney. To turn it into one more place full of seaside condos, to make it safe for the pure and the good, or at least the solvent and the well insured. You will find as well the small, futile protest raised by some of us who love Coney Island.

I suspect that Richard Snow is right and that the island will ignore us both. All the grand plans for "redevelopment" will never come to pass, like so many other grandiose undertakings of the past.

Or perhaps, in this era of rapid climate change, Coney is saving its greatest trick of all for last: to disappear. Once it is carbuncled with condominium towers, it will simply sink beneath the water, clutching its last attraction, a drowned city, under the waves—a reef full of shiny-eyed fish, winding their way through all the bright enamel fixtures and the marble kitchen counters. It will be the perfect exit, turning all that people did there and all that they planned for it into an illusion.

"Never was there a time better fitted than yesterday," Walt Whitman writes, and never was yesterday better fitted anywhere than to Coney Island.

ACKNOWLEDGMENTS

THE GENESIS OF THIS BOOK was a time of great sadness for us, the loss of our parents and the serious illness of our two sisters: Maryann and Judy. We wanted to work on a project that reminded us of the closeness of our family and the memories of better times, when we were all together. In quick order, we decided that our youthful excursions to Coney Island could provide the seeds for this bonding source. The first incarnation was the development of two Honors' courses taught on Coney Island at Long Island University. We would like to thank the co-directors of Honors, Cris Gleicher and James Clarke, for approving these classes. And we would also like to thank the students in those classes for their feedback and enthusiasm. When compiling material for the courses, we noticed that while much has been written on Coney's storied history, no one work collected the various reactions to it. This book attempts to fill that gap. In writing and editing this book, we would like to thank the following for their assistance:

Louis's graduate assistants Mary Walker, Rajul Punjabi, Chris Iverson, and Asja Parrish (one of those Honors Coney Island students) for their help in typing the manuscript, researching material, and proofreading, and for their advice and support.

Tiani Kennedy, Pat Palmieri, Tim Milford, Lara Vapnek, Vidhya Swaminathan, Dohra Ahmad, and Yani Perez for reading parts of the manuscript and offering their encouragement and helpful suggestions.

Gary Racz for his suggestions on García Lorca.

Sapphire for her suggestions on the opening section of the introduction.

Our editor at Columbia University Press, Philip Leventhal; editorial assistant Whiney Johnson; and the two reviewers of our manuscript for their guidance and judicious advice.

Irene Pavitt for her close attention to detail and for her helpful suggestions as a copy editor.

Marisa Pagano for her jacket, marketing, and publicity copy.

Philip Pascuzzo for the wonderful jacket design.

Dean David Cohen for providing LIU Developmental Funds, and LIU Brooklyn Provost Gale Stevens Haynes for financial support from her budget.

(Mayor) Fred Courtright of the Permissions Company for helping us obtain permissions. Also the many permissions agents who generously allowed us to reprint writings and images, in addition to several of the authors—such as Valentine Miller (daughter of Henry Miller), Edwin Torres, Katie Roiphe, Donald Thomas (Donny Vomit), and Maureen McHugh—for kindly corresponding with us directly.

Charles Denson, Michael Immerso, John Kasson, Dick Zigun, and the staff at Coney Island USA, and Nicole Robinson-Etienne, Community Outreach Coordinator, and the rest of the staff at the Coney Island Development Corporation for their groundbreaking work and their ceaseless support of projects on Coney Island.

Kevin Baker for coming to our Coney classes and for writing the foreword.

Our brothers-in-law, Robert Barbieri and Ben Bilello, for the love and devotion they have given to our sisters.

The memory of our parents, Louis and Ann Parascandola. Thanks for taking us on those early trips to Coney Island and so much more.

And, finally, we wish to express our sincere gratitude and convey our love to our wives, Shondel Nero (Louis) and Randee Parascandola (John), for their endless support, encouragement, and patience during the process of preparing this volume. It is a debt we cannot repay.

A NOTE ON THE TEXT

IN THE INTRODUCTION, the titles of the selections included in this anthology are in boldface type.

We have retained the original texts of all the pieces, with a few minor exceptions that are marked by our insertions in brackets. Some of the works do not have a title. In those cases, we put one in brackets (for example, Walt Whitman's ["Clam-Bake at Coney Island]"). We have also provided a few brief notes, in brackets, to help clarify some references in the texts.

If we omitted material from the original source, the deletion is indicated by ellipses in brackets: [. . .]. To keep a more unified sense of chronology, the anthology is organized roughly by the dates in which the pieces are set rather than when they were actually written.

SELECTED CHRONOLOGY OF CONEY ISLAND

1609   Henry Hudson's ship *Half Moon* believed by many to have arrived at
         Gravesend Bay

1643   Lady Deborah Moody and a group of English religious dissenters settle in
         Gravesend

1823   Shell Road opens

1829   Coney Island House, the first hotel on the island, opens

1845   Coney Island Pavilion opens

1865   Railroad reaches Coney Island from Brooklyn

1869   John McKane becomes commissioner of Gravesend, going on to run
         Coney until 1894

1874   Charles Feltman "invents" the hot dog

1880   Surf Avenue, the main street in Coney Island, opens

1884   LaMarcus Thompson builds the Switchback Gravity Railroad, generally
         considered to be America's first roller coaster

1885   Elephantine Colossus (Elephant Hotel) opens

1894   George C. Tilyou's Ferris wheel opens

1895   Sea Lion Park opens

1896   Elephantine Colossus is destroyed by fire

1897   Steeplechase Park opens

1898   First direct rail line from Manhattan to Coney Island opens

1899   First indoor world championship heavyweight fight, between Tom
         Sharkey and Jim Jeffries, is held on November 3

1902   Sea Lion Park closes

1903 Topsy the elephant is electrocuted

Luna Park opens

First Mardi Gras parade is held

1904 Dreamland opens

1907 Steeplechase Park partly burns down

1910 Racetracks close

1911 Dreamland closes after a fire

Samuel Gumpertz opens Dreamland Circus Sideshow

1916 Nathan's, home of the hot dog, opens

1920 Wonder Wheel opens

Subway extension to Stillwell Avenue (Coney Island) opens

1923 Boardwalk opens

1927 Cyclone opens

Half Moon Hotel opens

1937 Robert Moses, New York City Parks Commissioner, proposes major zoning changes and regulations at Coney

1941 Parachute Jump opens

1946 Luna Park closes

1949 Public housing projects open, with support from Robert Moses

Half Moon Hotel closes

1954 Last Mardi Gras parade is held

1957 New York Aquarium opens, having moved from Battery Park

1962 Astroland opens

1964 Steeplechase Park closes

Parachute Jump closes (some sources indicate 1968)

1968 Race riot breaks out

1972 International Hot Dog–Eating Contest resumes at Nathan's

1983 First Mermaid Parade is held

1995 Half Moon Hotel, which had been converted into a home for senior citizens in the 1950s, is demolished

2001 KeySpan (now MCU) Park, home field of the minor-league Brooklyn Cyclones, opens

2008 Astroland closes

2009 Major city rezoning plan for Coney Island and its amusement area is announced

2012 Superstorm Sandy hits, causing severe damage

A CONEY ISLAND READER

INTRODUCTION

CONEY ISLAND IS AN ICONIC PLACE, the home of the Wonder Wheel, the Parachute Jump, the Cyclone, Nathan's Famous hot dogs, a world-class boardwalk, and an extraordinary beach. It has routinely attracted more than 100,000 visitors a day during its summer season, one time even topping 2.5 million in 1947. Its lights provided the first glimpse of America for many immigrants entering New York Harbor at the turn of the twentieth century. Despite its fame, however, as Coney historians Oliver Pilat and Jo Ranson observe, "Coney Island [has] stood for different things during different periods and at times meant all things to all men."[1] This is demonstrated by a stunning gallery of essays, poems, and stories by some of the world's finest authors—including Walt Whitman, José Martí, Stephen Crane, Maxim Gorky, Djuna Barnes, Federico García Lorca, Isaac Bashevis Singer, Joseph Heller, and Bernard Malamud—all of whom have been inspired by Coney. Each wrote of Coney from his or her unique vantage point, offering a panoply of perspectives on this exciting place.

(TOP) REGINALD MARSH, AMERICAN, 1898-1954, *WONDERLAND CIRCUS, SIDESHOW, CONEY ISLAND*, 1930. (TEMPERA ON CANVAS STRETCHED ON MASONITE, 48¾ × 48 INCHES. SN591 MUSEUM PURCHASE, 1976. COLLECTION OF THE JOHN AND MABLE RINGLING MUSEUM OF ART, THE STATE ART MUSEUM OF FLORIDA)

(BOTTOM) EDWARD LANING, *CONEY ISLAND BEACH SCENE*, 1938. (OIL ON CANVAS, 36 × 42 INCHES. WEATHERSPOON ART MUSEUM, THE UNIVERSITY OF NORTH CAROLINA AT GREENSBORO. GIFT OF THE FAMILY IN HONOR OF MR. BENJAMIN CONE'S 80TH BIRTHDAY, 1980)

Coney Island has long been a rich source of inspiration, a palimpsest that is open to individual analyses, lending itself to a variety of interpretations. It presents a kaleidoscopic, ever-changing landscape, providing, as Lawrence Ferlinghetti, channeling Henry Miller, claimed, "A Coney Island of the Mind." For some, it is a restful seaside resort, while for others it is a symbol of the best of America's democratic nature, a playground for the masses, welcoming all regardless of race, social class, gender, or ethnicity. It is a place that not only amuses youngsters, but brings out the child in all of us, where we can enjoy breathtaking rides, witness the spectacular, or simply relax by the ocean side. For others, however, it is a much darker place, a Sodom by the sea, a venue that elicits our flawed nature. It is a garish display of America's capitalistic excesses, a site of blighted dreams and urban decay, a place that routinely exploits its most vulnerable visitors. These views often shift, depending on the period in Coney's history, whether it was a quiet bathing resort, a great amusement park, a nickel empire, or a neighborhood in various stages of decline or regeneration. On occasion, these conflicting perspectives may even exist simultaneously, perhaps not surprising because Coney, in fact, embodies all these identities. Coney has always led us, as E. E. Cummings states, "through dizzy gates of illusion," so it is not surprising that the appearance it presents is often open to differing interpretations of reality.

Our goal is to provide a representative sample of the best of these differing interpretations of Coney. Rather than simply choosing literary works, we have offered a composite of fiction, poetry, nonfiction prose, newspaper accounts, and municipal reports. We have attempted to create a collection of literary and historical works that can provide a context to understand better the enigma that is Coney Island. The anthology is divided into four somewhat permeable chronological periods that trace Coney's history through its humble beginnings, its rapid ascent, its gradual decline, and its hopeful, albeit somewhat tenuous, future. Although Coney has traditionally been partitioned into three geographic areas (the tony Manhattan Beach, the middle-class Brighton Beach, and the plebian West Brighton), the chief (though not exclusive) focus of our work is on the last section, which is the center of Coney's amusement district. As early as 1885, Thomas L. Russell observed that "to the democratic masses [West Brighton is] the real Coney Island."[2]

THE BEGINNINGS THROUGH 1896

European colonists first began to settle the area known as Coney Island in the middle of the seventeenth century. Henry Hudson, sailing aboard the *Half Moon* for the Dutch East India Company, was believed by many historians to have anchored in Gravesend Bay, west of the island, in 1609 and encountered the Canarsie Indians, who inhabited the area.[3] Although the island and the nearby section of the mainland soon became part of the colony of New Netherland, the Dutch chose not to settle there. In 1643, Lady Deborah Moody, an English Mennonite who had fled the Puritan colony in Massachusetts, and her co-religionists were granted a patent or title to the land. They established the town of Gravesend on the mainland. Although the land grant included the island, which the Dutch apparently called Conyne Eylant (possibly after the "coneys," or rabbits, that lived there, although this derivation is disputed), the English colonists negotiated a separate agreement with the Canarsies for the island in 1654. When the English took possession of New Netherland from the Dutch in 1664, Coney Island, a sandbar about five miles in length, was being used by the colonists as common grazing land for their livestock. The island remained essentially uninhabited for the next 150 years.

THE RESORT

As sea bathing became increasingly popular in the eighteenth century, a few colonial aristocrats visited Gravesend's beach. Efforts to use Coney Island as a summer resort, however, did not begin until the nineteenth century. As Manhattan grew in population, its inhabitants needed a place where they could escape the overcrowding and heat. As architectural historian Rem Koolhaas posits, this was the beginning of a long-standing bond between Manhattan and Coney, which was "the nearest zone of virgin nature that can counteract the enervations of urban civilization."[4] John Terhune, the town supervisor of Gravesend, and his brother built a private toll-road causeway in the 1820s, spanning the creek that separates the island from the mainland and thus making Coney more accessible (and no longer truly an island). They also built an inn called the Coney Island House on the island, providing food and accommodations, and promoted the tonic value of sea bathing. Many famous people eventually stayed at the hotel, including P. T. Barnum, Washington Irving, Herman Melville, Daniel Webster, and Edgar Allan Poe. Soon regular stagecoach service from the Brooklyn mainland was instituted, and in 1844, daily ferry service to the island was initiated. The tent-covered Coney Island Pavilion—with facilities for bathing, dining, and dancing—was also soon established near the pier.[5]

Walt Whitman, the earliest writer represented in this anthology, penned ["Clam-Bake at Coney Island"] in 1847, long before the days of the great amusement parks. Then, Coney Island was regarded more as a refuge from the crowded city than as a tourist destination. Its main appeal for Whitman, however, does not seem to have been simply as a place for escape. Instead, it was the inclusiveness of the outing, befitting America's greatest poet of democracy, that stirs the author: "The members of the party were numerous and various—embracing all the professions, and nearly all the trades, besides sundry aldermen, and other officials."[6]

Getting to Whitman's idyllic outpost was a slow process, although the opening of a second toll road in 1850 and the initiation of a horse-car rail line in the 1860s made the trip somewhat easier and quicker.[7] It was not until after the Civil War, however, that Coney truly began to flourish as a popular resort. A spate of hotels, many of which included restaurants and facilities for renting bathing costumes, were constructed along the beach. Roasted clams, a local specialty, as Whitman had indicated, were consumed by the thousands at these establishments. In 1868, one guidebook listed Coney Island as the best beach on the Atlantic coast, and by 1873 it was attracting 25,000 to 30,000 visitors on weekends.

Transportation to the island blossomed in the 1870s, when four steam-railroad lines were built to bring passengers rapidly from Downtown Brooklyn to Coney. By 1878, some 250 trains a day were transporting visitors to and from the island. Two large ocean piers were also constructed in this period, as well as a major public road, Ocean Parkway, that extends from Prospect Park to the beach at Coney. The opening of the Brooklyn Bridge, in 1883, which linked the separate cities of Brooklyn and New York, further encouraged travel to Brooklyn. As a result, "on summer Sundays Coney Island's beach becomes the most densely occupied place in the world."[8] A description of Coney Island as it was in 1874 is provided in Charles Dawson Shanly's essay "Coney Island," in which he notes that

Coney was the most "unfashionable" part of the suburb of Long Island, attracting a "motley crowd" and thus, in a backhanded manner, reinforcing Whitman's claim for the resort's democratic nature.

The openness of Coney, unfortunately, also allowed for the introduction of a criminal element.[9] The ten-square-block area of the West End known as the "Gut," filled with "brothels, dance halls, peep shows, and gambling dens [that] provided plentiful helpings of sin,"[10] was a particularly notorious section. One inn, for example, in 1890 "claimed a seasonal sale of 10,000 kegs of lager beer, or 1,500,000 glasses full."[11] A sampling of numerous articles from the *New York Times* attests to the rampant vices on display at Coney and the need for reform.[12]

From about 1869 to 1894, when he was convicted on eleven felony counts, John McKane was the unofficial "boss" of Coney Island. McKane was a town supervisor of Gravesend, one of the commissioners of the common lands on Coney Island, and chief of the Coney police force, which he had established. As Coney Island historian Charles Denson explains: "He fixed elections, used his police department thugs as a private army to assault his opponents, and collected bribes and a percentage of every deal transacted in Coney Island. No business operated without his approval."[13] Along with William Stillwell, the town surveyor of Gravesend, McKane was responsible for selling off the common lands to cronies at cheap prices, with both men profiting from these transactions. As the crime boss remarked, "I don't suppose there was a wickeder place on the globe than the Gut in its palmy days."[14] McKane was eventually sentenced to six years at Sing Sing for election-rigging and other crimes, and the New York State Legislature annexed the town of Gravesend to Brooklyn (which itself became a borough of New York City in 1898 when the separate counties that make up the city were consolidated).[15]

Coney, as throughout its history, was open to conflicting visions. For example, one early traveler, William Henry Bishop, in "**To Coney Island**" (1880), describes Coney at this time as "the greatest resort for a single day's pleasure in the world." He also stresses the uniquely American qualities of Coney, a symbol of the relatively new nation's greatness. Coney has frequently been evoked in patriotic terms throughout its history. But another visitor, the well-known Cuban-born author and activist José Martí, in "**Coney Island**" (1881), looked at the amusement area as a symbol of

American capitalism, a product of a nation dominated by the "eagerness to possess wealth." No matter their views, for many visitors, as an English tourist, Henry Spencer Ashbee, notes, Coney was "a reproduction in miniature of the United States."[16]

During the McKane era, the West End (particularly the area of West Brighton) of Coney Island featured much more than just illicit activities, such as prostitution and gambling. A vast amusement zone grew up there, helping Coney receive some 100,000 daily visitors in the summer months.[17] While Coney originated as a nature resort, by the 1880s, it was "forced to mutate: [to] turn itself into the total opposite of Nature . . . to counteract the artificiality of the new metropolis with its own Super-Natural."[18] The first roller coaster built in the United States, LaMarcus Thompson's Switchback Gravity Railway, was opened at Coney Island in 1884. It was a primitive ride by today's standards. Passengers had to climb a fifty-foot-high loading platform to board a train, which was propelled along a wooden track by gravity at the breakneck speed of six miles an hour. It came to a stop at the crest of a hill at the other end of the track, where passengers then reboarded the train (after it had been switched to the opposite track) for the return ride. The popularity of the coaster encouraged the construction of other amusement rides, including the first roller coaster in the country with a mechanical conveyor to carry the cars to the top of the track.[19] Other rides included carousels, toboggan rides, and an aerial slide. Ironically, the industrial workers beginning to frequent Coney "screamed with delight at the transformation of . . . the grimly efficient 'el' [the elevated train that took them to work each day] that blocked the sun, fouled the air and cluttered the mind with the noise of the factory"[20] into an instrument of pleasure. In addition to the mechanical rides, there were dining establishments, dime museums, concert halls, dance pavilions, sideshows, circuses, boxing exhibitions, racetracks, fireworks displays, games of chance, an aquarium, and other forms of entertainment, including John Philip Sousa's marching band and Buffalo Bill's Wild West Show.[21] Many of these amusements were part of the Bowery Midway, named for the area in Manhattan that had long been "the heartland of working-class amusements."[22] The midway featured many games, shows, and attractions such as the Streets of Cairo, where one could ride an elephant or a camel or watch an erotic "couch-ee-couchee" dance by performers, including the famed Little Egypt.

A landmark in Coney was the Elephantine Colossus, or Elephant Hotel, which opened in 1885. This huge structure in the shape of an elephant housed thirty-four guest rooms and a shopping mall. Windows in the head provided panoramic views of the beach and the sea. Although visitors flocked to see this marvel, it never proved to be a financial success in part because of a reputation for seediness. In fact, the phrase "seeing the elephant" became synonymous with indulging in illicit sexual pleasure. The hotel was eventually abandoned, and in 1896, it was destroyed by fire, like so many places in Coney's history.[23] Kevin Baker provides a fictionalized setting at the Elephant Hotel in an excerpt from his novel *Dreamland* (1999).

THE VISITORS

Coney Island was essentially divided at this time into three districts. The West End, especially West Brighton, largely attracted the working class, while the other areas drew a more affluent crowd. Those individuals who did not like the noise and hubbub of West Brighton, and who did not care to rub elbows with ordinary laborers, could go instead to Brighton Beach or Manhattan Beach on the eastern end of the island. Separate rail lines delivered more upscale visitors directly to these destinations. Large and luxurious facilities—such as the Manhattan Beach, Oriental, and Brighton hotels—were designed for the more genteel classes. Brighton Beach and Manhattan Beach became communities in their own right, but our focus here, as indicated earlier, will be on West Brighton. A good contemporary overview of Coney Island's evolution into a seaside tourist resort is provided by Julian Ralph in "**Coney Island**" (1896). Ralph contrasts the more secluded Manhattan and Brighton beaches with the noisy, colorful West Brighton, with its rides, games, concert halls, and sideshow museums.

The movement to grant workers a "half-holiday" on Saturdays, beginning in the 1880s, led to increased leisure time, which benefitted Coney's entertainment industry. Coney provided a perfect day trip for New York workers seeking amusement. It became increasingly easier and cheaper to travel to Coney by rail, and the district offered a variety of inexpensive forms of entertainment. Although private interests controlled access to the beach at the time and the public had to pay admission fees of 50 cents and up to use the bathhouses, the typical ride cost only a nickel. It was also

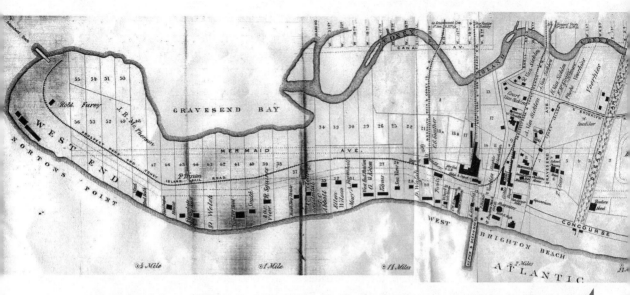

MAP OF CONEY ISLAND AND SHEEPSHEAD BAY, 1879.

possible to eat cheaply in Coney, one of the most popular meals being the "hot dog," the invention of which is often attributed to Charles Feltman, a Coney restauranteur.[24] Feltman's Ocean Pavilion could serve 8,000 people at one time.[25]

Working-class women were among the groups using Coney as an outlet from their dreary lives. Such women were left with few places where they could socialize, and they often would go to Coney to meet men. Kathy Peiss, in **"The Coney Island Excursion"** (1986), describes "the system of treating, [whereby] women could enjoy a day at Coney's resorts with their only expense being transportation." From its beginning, Coney had provided a casual and fun atmosphere that encouraged interaction between the sexes.[26] It offered forms of recreation that were less structured and regulated than those in normal social situations. This is best "expressed . . . in less restrained forms of ocean bathing, in a more casual mixing of the sexes, and in the sensory thrills provided by the mechanical rides."[27] Coney encouraged its "visitors to shed momentarily their accustomed roles and status."[28] This freedom is perhaps best reflected in the lure of the beach,

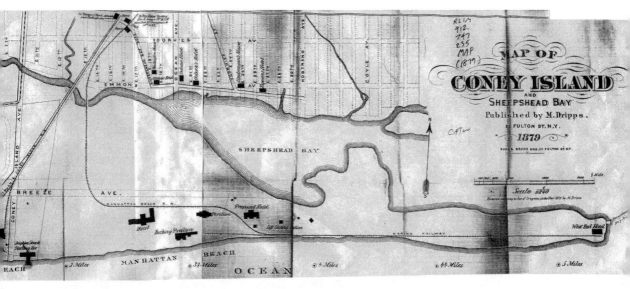

with its, for the time, scandalous attire, even though such bathing outfits were "about as comfortable as trying to swim in a suit of armor."[29]

Despite these restrictions, bathing suits, compared with normal dress, not only "expose[d] more of the wearer's body, but they also encouraged freer deportment in general."[30] This behavior was disturbing enough to cause one observer to remark that bathers were acting "precisely as if the thing to do in the water was to behave exactly contrary to the manner of behaving anywhere else."[31]

In Stephen Crane's "**Coney Island's Failing Days**" (1894), the resort, depicted toward the end of the summer season, appears "somewhat gloomy." This environment is connected with the despair that the masses feel after leaving Coney on a Sunday excursion and knowing that they have to go back to "that inevitable, overhanging, devastating Monday." Rather than seeing Coney as a temporary respite from the drudgery of work, a place of fantasy and escape, for the stranger who philosophizes through much of the sketch, it seems like a cruel reminder of the temporality of our dreams, of the fragility of our hopes and expectations.[32]

Furthermore, despite Whitman's early claims about Coney's democratic spirit, the segregation universal in American society was also prevalent there. Although Coney was often called the People's Playground, not

"VACATION SPORTS AT THE SEASIDE," CONEY ISLAND, 1897. (STEREOGRAPH PUBLISHED BY STROHMEYER & WYMAN, NEW YORK. LIBRARY OF CONGRESS, PRINTS AND PHOTOGRAPHS DIVISION)

everyone was always allowed to play in the same places. Efforts to keep out or at least segregate the new immigrants from southern and eastern Europe were implemented, not always with success: "At Coney's rides and beaches, diverse peoples swam, ate, played, and rode together, encouraging development of an interethnic—albeit white—'New York' sensibility."[33] Jews and African Americans, however, had to use segregated bathhouses and were discouraged from occupying certain sections of the beach. In the late 1870s, the owner of the Manhattan Beach Hotel, Austin Corbin, banned Jews from the hotel and its beach.[34] "Kill the Coon" games, where the public threw baseballs at the head of a black man protruding through an opening in a canvas screen, were exceedingly popular at Coney. In spite of these prejudices, however, blacks, as well as Jews, continued to visit Coney.[35] In fact, many of the vendors and racetrack workers at West Brighton were African Americans and Jews, and by 1880 "blacks made up 8.3 percent of Coney Island's year-round population."[36] African Americans "congregated on the beach near the Municipal Baths of 1911, [and] were welcomed at Steeplechase (apart from the bathing pool)."[37] The pool at Steeplechase would continue to exclude blacks until its closing in 1964. Unfortunately, prejudice against such groups as Jews, Latinos, and blacks would pervade Coney's legacy even in the heady times that lay ahead. The often roiling tensions between different ethnic groups and classes help account for Coney's continuously complicated place in New York City (and American) history.

THE ERA OF THE THREE GREAT AMUSEMENT PARKS, 1897–1911

GEORGE C. TILYOU AND STEEPLECHASE PARK

Coney entered what was likely its most famous period at the end of the nineteenth century. The short-lived Sea Lion Park, the first enclosed amusement park with an admission fee, opened in 1895. The park's founder, Captain Paul Boyton, had made a name for himself in the 1870s as a result of his having swum the English Channel wearing an inflatable rubber suit originally designed as a life-saving device for steamship passengers. The most popular ride in Sea Lion Park, Shoot-the-Chutes, featured flat-bottomed toboggan boats that slid down a steep slide into a lagoon. Although Sea Lion Park lasted only until 1902, it served as the inspiration for entrepreneur and showman George C. Tilyou's more elaborate Steeplechase Park, which opened in 1897.[38]

Tilyou and other entrepreneurs faced the challenge of changing the widespread perception of Coney as an immoral, crime-infested area.[39] Temperance advocate Carrie B. Nation lectured against the presence of alcohol on the grounds. Social reformer Jane Addams warned that "'Looping the loop' amid shrieks of stimulated terror or dancing in disorderly saloon halls" is not the best form of recreation for young people.[40] In the Progressive era (ca. 1890–1920), "reformers sought to uplift the masses by cleansing Coney and replacing its Bowery with a seaside park, creating a Central Park by the seashore."[41] They hoped that such an environment might engender a more refined community. In keeping with the Progressive reformers of the turn of the century, Tilyou and other park founders sought to appeal to the middle class by enclosing their amusement areas, banning alcohol, and hiring their own security guards. They had learned that "vice does not pay as well as decency."[42]

Tilyou, after visiting the World's Columbian Exposition, held in Chicago in 1893, saw the invention of George Ferris's enormous steel wheel. When Tilyou was unsuccessful in his effort to purchase the wheel, he ordered his own giant steel wheel to be placed at Coney Island. Although Tilyou's ride was half the size of the original Ferris wheel, he proclaimed it, as was his wont, to be "the world's largest" wheel. He also opened several other innovative rides at Coney, leading to his most spectacular project: Steeplechase Park. The signature ride was the Steeplechase, where participants rode mechanical horses along a metal track. Other attractions included a boat ride along the Grand Canals of Venice, a miniature railroad, a bathhouse, formal gardens, and a large ballroom. When half the park burned down in 1907, Tilyou rebuilt it on an even grander scale. His resilience is indicated by the sign that he posted on the site's charred ruins:

> I have troubles today that I did not have yesterday.
> I had troubles yesterday that I have not today.
> On this site will be erected shortly a better, bigger, greater Steeplechase Park.
> Admission to the Burning Ruins—10 cents.[43]

The new Steeplechase included the large enclosed Pavilion of Fun, which enabled the park to remain open on rainy days. Somewhat less of a family park than the original, a number of its "anti-alienation" attractions threw the sexes together and broke down inhibitions.[44] Tilyou, shrewd businessman that he was, learned that sex, at least if provided in fairly safe, limited doses, did in fact sell, even in the Progressive era. He realized that the appeal of Coney often came precisely from its fierce refusal to be tamed or homogenized. He somehow managed to blend "good clean fun" with the sensuous. To enter the park, for example, visitors had to walk through the Barrel of Fun, a rolling barrel that tossed them around and into one another. Popular rides that also threw people together included the

"ALL SMILES": A WORKER APPLIES A FRESH COAT OF PAINT TO THE STEEPLE-CHASE FUNNY FACE SIGN IN PREPARATION FOR THE PARK'S OPENING, 1951. (BROOKLYN PUBLIC LIBRARY, BROOKLYN COLLECTION. ORIGINALLY PUBLISHED IN THE *BROOKLYN EAGLE*)

Human Roulette Wheel, the Whirlpool, and the Human Pool Table. Even more daring for the time was the Blowhole Theater, located at the end of the Steeplechase ride. As a couple walked across a stage, jets of air blew the woman's skirt up and the man often received an electric shock from a clown, while earlier victims looked on from the audience and laughed. In a sense, the visitors to the park were part of the entertainment, laughing at one another's public embarrassment. Even the famous Funny Face logo of the park (with its oversize mouth in some illustrations containing forty-four teeth, twelve more than normal) was, in the words of historian Michael Immerso, "a leering libidinous carnival mask." As Immerso has stated, "Steeplechase's appeal can be attributed to the spirited, liberated, physical play at its core. Everything in the park revolved about the human body and no holds were barred."[45]

Tilyou was a master at understanding his audience. His successful formula was, in the words of his nephew Edo McCullogh, "a matchless mixture of sentimentality, shrewd psychology, a sound sense of civic expansion, and a suffusion of sophomoric sex."[46] Tilyou himself said, "We Americans want either to be thrilled or amused, and we are ready to pay well for either sensation."[47] Peter Lyon's "**The Master Showman of Coney Island**" (1958) provides an excellent summation of Tilyou's philosophy and career. George's oldest son, Edward F. Tilyou, who became the manager of Steeplechase Park after his father's death in 1914, reveals in "**Human Nature with the Brakes Off**" (1922) the shrewd understanding of human psychology possessed by his family and others who were successful in the amusement business. At these parks, Tilyou commented, people could act like children again and "cut-up."[48]

The "in-your-face" atmosphere that already prevailed at Coney Island by the beginning of the twentieth century, on the eve of the construction of two more spectacular amusement parks, is described by Guy Wetmore Carryl in "**Marvelous Coney Island**" (1901). According to Carryl, Coney "leaps with a shout upon the casual visitor as he steps from a five cent trolley car," leaving him or her to choose from a "horn of plenty" of amusements. "One has simply to decide in what manner he prefers to be made uncomfortable, for it is Coney Island's claim to celebrity that she is prepared to make you so in a variety of ways approaching infinity, and, if you are of the majority, you are there for that express purpose." This paradoxical desire to pay to be made to feel uncomfortable was at the center of the allure of Steeplechase Park.[49]

FREDERIC THOMPSON, ELMER DUNDY, AND LUNA PARK

A Trip to the Moon, designed by Frederic Thompson—an architect by trade—and Elmer Dundy, was one of the most popular rides at the Pan-American Exposition, held in Buffalo, New York, in 1901. The ride used motion and scenery to simulate a trip to the moon in an airship. When the ship "landed" on the "moon," the passengers disembarked to tour subterranean caverns, where they met moon maidens and midget moon men and visited the palace of the Man in the Moon. After the Pan-American Exposition closed, Thompson and Dundy reached an agreement to bring A Trip to the Moon to Steeplechase Park, where they operated it as an independent concession. Following the 1902 season, Tilyou tried to renegotiate the agreement, but Thompson and Dundy chose to strike out on their own.

Paul Boyton decided to close Sea Lion Park after the 1902 season. Thompson and Dundy leased the land and tore down essentially all of Sea Lion Park's attractions to make way for their own amusement park, which included A Trip to the Moon. Even before its opening, Luna Park gained notoriety when the owners allowed Topsy, an elephant that had killed a person who allegedly burned her with a cigarette, to be electrocuted by alternating current on the construction site of the park grounds on January 3, 1903. The killing was famously recorded on film by Thomas Edison to show how "unsafe" his rival George Westinghouse's alternating current was compared with his own direct current.[50]

The spectacular Luna Park opened on May 16, 1903. Dubbed the "Electric Eden," Luna Park was a fantasyland illuminated by some 250,000 electric lights. A contemporary visitor, Winthrop Alexander, said of Luna Park: "The general effect is a realization of what imagination might paint as a fairy city, and the visitor is bewildered by the beautiful picture presented on every hand."[51] Indeed, architecture, sculpture, and electricity were key components of Coney Island's appeal, and nowhere was this more true than at Luna Park. Thompson arranged the park "in seemingly incongruous, yet nonetheless effective, ways."[52] Despite its seeming complexity, as Thompson himself observed, the genius of his architecture was based

A Greeting from Coney Island

on straight lines and trap doors, but onto these simple ideas, he superimposed "over its skyline a network of wires and light bulbs." Thompson used electricity to create "a separate *city of night*," a city built on illusion.[53] Electricity was utilized to provide a sense of safety and illusion. As Thompson stated, "'In the glare of the thousands of electric bulbs, [Coney Island] was ashamed of its sordidness' and reformed itself where public officials and preachers had for decades failed."[54]

The park included such attractions as Thompson and Dundy's A Trip to the Moon, a new illusion called Twenty Thousand Leagues Under the Sea, Boyton's Shoot-the-Chutes and lagoon, a circus, theatrical performances, and various new rides such as the Helter-Skelter and the Dragon's Gorge. There were spectacular re-creations of several historical disasters, such as the destruction of Pompeii and the hurricane and flood that devastated Galveston, Texas, in 1900. Several rides, such as the Tickler and the Whip, were designed by master ride builder William F. Mangels.[55] There were elephant and camel rides, a two-hundred-foot tower decorated with lights that changed color, and replicas of many cultures, including Japan, Ireland, and Italy. These cultural exhibits were often stereotypical and woefully inaccurate; nevertheless, as John Kasson observes, "while the resort served as an agent of Americanization for immigrants and their children, Coney's amusements also indicated a countervailing urge to venture beyond the confines of an assimilationist culture, to rediscover the exotic, if only in the safe precincts of what amounted to cultural zoos."[56]

Luna Park was really Thompson's brain child (he was the showman, and Dundy the financial man), and he continued to add attractions, often without consideration of the costs involved, eventually leading to his bankruptcy. His idea was "to erect a park where people would laugh, enjoy themselves, and would spend money while being amused"[57] Thompson's philosophy of entertainment is reflected in "**Amusing the Million**" (1908), in which he emphasizes the necessity of an amusement park providing a carnival spirit, or spirit of gaiety, which does not occur spontaneously but must be manufactured by the entrepreneur. Unlike Tilyou, who made the

"A GREETING FROM CONEY ISLAND," 1909. (COLLECTION OF JOHN PARASCANDOLA)

spectators part of the act, Thompson relied on carefully constructed illusion and manipulation of his audience.[58] As a result, the cerebral Luna Park tended to attract a more affluent, middle-class crowd than the physically based Steeplechase Park.

DREAMLAND AND THE CORPORATE MODEL

The last of the big-three amusement parks in Coney Island was Dreamland. Unlike Steeplechase Park and Luna Park, Dreamland was owned by a corporation consisting of politicians (the principal owner was William H. Reynolds, a former senator from New York) and businesspeople, giving it a less personal feel than the other parks. The park, which opened in 1904, was designed to be a grander, even more sophisticated, version of Luna Park, as described by Charles Denson:

> While Luna was colorful and Steeplechase was silly, Dreamland was refined, orderly, and symmetrical with every classical building painted pristine white. The park enclosed a double Shoot-the-Chutes built out over the ocean. Towering over the chute's lagoon stood the park's centerpiece: the magnificent 375-foot-tall Beacon Tower, Coney's tallest structure. The impressive entrance had an immense statue of a nude angel whose wings shrouded the Creation biblical exhibit.[59]

The many attractions at Dreamland included a midget city; Frank Bostock's wild-animal show; scenic railways; a ballroom; a Japanese tea pavilion; the Hell Gate boat ride; Dr. Martin Couney's Infant Incubators, a spectacle in which many premature babies' lives were actually saved; and Fighting the Flames, which featured more than 120 firefighters battling a staged blaze at a tenement building and rescuing hundreds of tenants.[60] The last two attractions had begun at Luna Park (the latter called Fire and Flames in Luna Park), but again, Dreamland tried to outdo its rival. As magnificent as the park was, however, it was not a financial success. Perhaps the owners' efforts to provide a somewhat more high-toned, didactic amusement did not catch on with most of Coney's visitors. It became to many of them more of a moral lesson than fun, as Maxim Gorky describes in "**Boredom**" (1907).

In 1909, the park hired Samuel W. Gumpertz, who added to the park's attractions, but it was too little, too late. Dreamland soon went bankrupt and was sold at auction in 1910. Gumpertz, who stayed on as manager, repainted the white buildings in bright colors in an effort to revamp the park's image. Dreamland never had another chance to succeed, since a fire largely destroyed the park in 1911. The impact of the fire, as well as Coney's resilience, is poignantly recorded in "**Ruins Help Draw 350,000 to Coney**" (1911), an article by an unnamed *New York Times* reporter. Since the park was not insured, it was never rebuilt.

On the grounds of the vanished Dreamland, however, Gumpertz erected the Dreamland Circus Sideshow, where for years he exhibited human curiosities, including midgets, legless wonders, and Ubangi women with lips enlarged by implanted wooden disks. Building on the history of the dime museums, particularly P. T. Barnum's American Museum in New York in the 1840s and 1850s, Coney became a center of the so-called freak show. A number of the performers were featured in Tod Browning's cult film *Freaks* (1932).[61] Unlike some earlier showmen, Gumpertz tried his best to bring in "authentic" oddities, scouring the world for his human exhibits. In the process, he "steered 3,800 startling human beings past the American immigration authorities."[62]

THE BOWERY

The amusement parks were, of course, not the only attractions at Coney. The Bowery also drew large crowds. Such famous performers as Harry Houdini, Harpo Marx, Mae West, Buster Keaton, W. C. Fields, Sophie Tucker, Al Jolson, Bert Williams, Eubie Blake, Cary Grant, and Jimmy Durante at one time worked at Coney. Many began their careers in such venues as Henderson's Music Hall, Louis Stauch's eponymous restaurant and dance hall, and Solomon Perry's Glass Pavilion. Elmer Blaney Harris eloquently captures the feel of the Bowery in 1906:

> Bands, orchestras, pianos, at war with gramophones, hand-organs, calliopes; overhead, a roar of wheels in a deathlock with shrieks and screams; whistles, gongs, rifles all busy, the smell of candy, popcorn, meats, beer, tobacco,

blended with the odor of the crowd redolent now and then of patchouli; a streaming river of people arched over by electric signs—this is the Bowery at Coney Island.[63]

Still, the Bowery was the site of much of Coney's underside and was the center of attempts at reform. Many felt little regret when the Bowery fell prey to Coney's eternal adversary, fire, on November 1, 1903, devastating the area. It would never be rebuilt to this scale, resulting in a new Coney Island.[64]

REPRESENTATIONS OF CONEY ISLAND IN THE ERA OF THE THREE GREAT PARKS

As usual throughout Coney's history, it was viewed very differently, depending on the visitor. To Maxim Gorky, the "city of fire" had enthralled the masses with its gaudy delight, its "ugly variety." For those in the working class who made up the bulk of its clientele, it ensnared them in "a brilliant cobweb of translucent buildings." In reality, to Gorky, Coney epitomized the people's boring existence, the hypocrisy of their lives, "the insatiable power of their greed." Conversely, Marietta Holley, a popular humorist often compared with Mark Twain in the late nineteenth and early twentieth centuries, whimsically wrote of the park in *Samantha at Coney Island and a Thousand Other Islands* (1911). Her heroine, Samantha Smith Allen, is a commonsensical small-town woman searching for her dim-witted husband, Josiah, who has absconded to Coney with a friend. Samantha dutifully decides that she must save him from the perceived dangers of Coney: "Spozein' the elephants should tread on him? Or the boyconstructors or tigers git after him? Or he should go to the moon and git lost there and be obleeged to stay?"[65] The narrator of O. Henry's short story **"The Greater Coney"** (1911) was already lamenting changes taking place at Coney, particularly after the opening of Dreamland in 1904, resulting in its "moral reconstruction." It was now a more crowded, more commercial, and more glittery place. Still, in the end, the narrator of the story concludes, "The old Coney is gone[.] . . . 'Tis a greater Coney we have here." Sara Teasdale's poem **"Coney Island"** (1911) presents lovers who will not be reunited as happily as O. Henry's. Their visit to the beach in the winter symbolizes the death of their relationship.

Delmore Schwartz, Robert Olen Butler, and Kevin Baker are three more recent authors who present historical glimpses of Coney in their fiction. All of them depict it as a place that allows escape from the everyday world, but also as a place where danger, even death, is lurking. In Schwartz's "**In Dreams Begin Responsibilities**" (1937), the narrator recalls a day in 1909 when his parents, while courting, visited Coney Island. Despite the frivolity of the scene, the narrator looks at it as an ominous augury of what lay ahead for him and his family as a consequence of the disastrous union.[66] Butler's story "**Sunday**" (2004), set in 1910, deals with a middle-aged man who looks forward to a lazy day at the beach, spent reading his newspaper, but who ends up "amidst the revelry" that is typical of Coney, quietly meeting his death. In part, his death is due to his beloved "red hots" (hot dogs), which secretly clog his chest, leading to a heart attack. Kevin Baker's kaleidoscopic historical novel ***Dreamland*** (1999) weaves together both fact and fiction (Sigmund Freud and Carl Jung, both of whom actually did visit Coney in 1909, are among the cast of characters) in reflecting Coney Island during its glory days in the early years of the twentieth century.[67] It was a brutally violent, desperately poor place as well as a source of solace for those who could not find comfort elsewhere (including such diverse groups as sideshow performers, criminals, and working-class women) in the outside world. Together, these fictional works depict some of the conflicting sides of Coney during its most famous period.

THE THREE PARKS IN RETROSPECT

Coney was at its peak during the years 1897 to 1911, when the three major amusement parks dominated the scene. It was the premier tourist destination in the United States. Crowds routinely topped 100,000 per day during Coney's four-month summer season: "200,000 [post]cards were mailed from Coney on a single day in early September of 1906."[68] Coney became a symbol of Americans' increasing pride in their country just as the nation was coming of age on the world stage. Reginald Wright Kauffman's article **"Why Is Coney?"** (1909) eloquently sums up this view: "It is blatant, it is cheap, it is the apotheosis of the ridiculous. But it is something more: it is like Niagara Falls, or the Grand Canyon, or Yellowstone Park; it is a national playground; and not to have seen it is not to have seen your own country."

As John Kasson has argued, Coney in this period also reflected major changes in American society, with the emergence of a new mass culture, one in opposition to the more genteel standards in taste and comportment of the Victorian era.[69] The activities available at Coney—such as ocean bathing, dancing, vaudeville shows and circus attractions, mechanical rides, and exotic exhibits—catered to this new cultural mood. However, dancing, in particular, disturbed many from the Progressive era, who were concerned about its possibly immoral effect on young women.[70] Reformer Belle Lindner Israels, in "**The Way of the Girl**" (1909), vividly describes Coney and other venues' dance halls as outlets for young working women. Coming from another perspective, Djuna Barnes laments the attempts to censor Coney's Bohemianism in "**The Tingling, Tangling Tango as 'Tis Tripped at Coney Isle**" (1913). She fears that Coney was becoming too proper and its dance halls too respectable.

Coney Island, in the early years of the twentieth century, reflected the tensions between the ending of the reformist Progressive era and the beginning of the freer, more liberated decade of the Roaring Twenties. Coney was challenging prevailing notions of public conduct and social order, of wholesome amusement, of democratic art—of all the institutions and values of proper behavior.[71] Coney "was a battleground of American thought and intentions . . . a synthesis of American hopes and fears."[72] In "**Human Need of Coney Island**" (1905), Richard Le Gallienne discusses this dilemma and ultimately speaks in favor of Coney's freer, more decadent side, claiming that every nation "has its needs of orgiastic escape from respectability," and Coney Island satisfies these needs. It is, he states while somewhat in awe of its conflicting tendencies, "the most human thing that God ever made, or permitted the devil to make."

THE NICKEL EMPIRE: CONEY IN TRANSITION, 1912–1948

A number of important changes were introduced to Coney Island between 1912 and 1927. One milestone was the establishment of Nathan's, the iconic hot dog eatery, by Nathan Handwerker in 1916. Handwerker, who had once been employed by Charles Feltman, undercut his former boss, who priced his hot dog at a dime, charging a nickel (including a glass of root beer and a pickle for free). Nathan's, in a textbook example of capitalism, soon was outselling its venerable predecessor.[73] Plans for a boardwalk and a public beach also finally moved ahead, although construction did not begin until 1920. The boardwalk, eighty feet wide and almost two miles long and designed by Edward Riegelmann, was opened in 1923. Coney's beach thus became much more accessible to the masses.[74] With the completion of the subway extension to the Stillwell Avenue station in Coney Island in 1920, crowds increased to as many as 1 million people in a single day. Many of the visitors to Coney came from the vast number of immigrants who had arrived in the United States between 1880 and 1920.[75] As Italian immigrant author Giuseppe Cautela wrote in **"Coney Island"** (1925): "Nowhere else in the United States will you see so many races mingle in a common purpose for a common good." Michael Immerso describes the ethnic diversity of Coney:

> During the summer months, the masses from the city's teeming ethnic enclaves poured into Coney Island, and visitors to the resort marveled at what they saw. Whereas four decades earlier visitors from abroad such as José Martí had marveled at the diversity of the *classes* of people that mingled at Coney Island, they now marveled at the diversity of *nationalities* and *cultures* spread out before them.[76]

While some, such as Cautela, praised Coney's egalitarian spirit, others felt that "civilization faced a new situation that seemed to threaten vaunted traditions of self-control and edification that an educated elite was supposed to perpetuate."[77] The increasing arrival of immigrants from eastern and southern Europe heightened racial and ethnic tensions. Cultural critic James Huneker, in his book ***New Cosmopolis*** (1915), lamented the presence of Jewish and Italian immigrants who, he felt, were turning Coney into a "vicious open-air slumming spot" and "a disgrace to our civilisation." By 1921, reporter Bruce Bliven noted "that the hair on most [heads along Coney Island's beach] is black" and that "Coney is one more place from which the native Yankee stock has retreated before the fierce tide of the south European and Oriental."[78] The influx of immigrants and ethnic minorities to Coney Island, and the criticism of them, although their places of origin would change, has continued unabated.

Coney Island's traditional audience, largely of northern European origin, increasingly grew fearful of the amusement area's cultural diversity. Coney's proprietors, however, tried to keep both its old and its new clienteles satisfied by offering such gimmicks as beauty pageants and new rides in the 1920s. For example, the 150-foot-tall Wonder Wheel, capable of carrying 169 passengers, opened in 1920. Five new roller coasters also were erected during this decade, including the Thunderbolt and the Tornado. Coney's most famous coaster, and the only one still standing, is the Cyclone, which opened for business in 1927. The Cyclone boasts 3,000 feet of wooden track, with the cars attaining speeds of more than sixty miles per hour.[79]

Even a large luxury hotel, the Half Moon (named after Henry Hudson's ship), was built in 1927. Unfortunately, its most famous connection is with the death of the gangster Abe Reles, who allegedly was pushed out a window in 1941 after becoming a government witness and turning over some of his former mob cronies. One wise guy remarked of Kid Twist: "He could sing [to the authorities], but he couldn't fly."[80] The linkage of Coney's finest hotel with a criminal element reflected the increase in crime in the area, particularly in the years of Prohibition (1920–1933). During part of this time, such gangsters as Francisco Uale (Ioele; Frankie Yale) resided in Coney and Brooklyn native Al Capone bartended at Coney's Harvard Inn.[81]

E. E. Cummings's essay "**Coney Island**" (1926) vividly captures the frenetic spirit of Coney in the 1920s: "The incredible temple of pity and terror, mirth and amazement, which is popularly known as Coney Island, really constitutes a perfectly unprecedented fusion of the circus and the theatre." Although Cummings may be able to characterize Coney, he is at a loss when trying to define it: "[T]he IS or Verb of Coney Island escapes any portraiture." Unfortunately, what Cummings so colorfully depicts is a final lush image of Coney Island, one last high, before it would feel the stifling effects of the impending Great Depression, which began in 1929.

THE IMPACT OF THE DEPRESSION AND THE THREAT OF ROBERT MOSES

Although crowds continued to visit the amusement area during the 1930s, the Depression dampened Coney's economy. Most people spent less money than they would have done in better economic times. More expensive restaurants such as Feltman's Ocean Pavilion suffered, while fast-food vendors of hot dogs and other take-away items, such as Nathan's, rose to further prominence. Even the bathing pavilions such as Ravenhall were affected, as many of the new visitors, called "drippers," wore their bathing suits under their clothes to avoid having to pay to use a changing station.

The effects of the downturn in the economy are felt in Spanish poet Federico García Lorca's "**Landscape of a Vomiting Multitude**" (1929). In the poem, Lorca provides a nightmarish vision of Coney Island as a symbol of the United States at the beginning of the Great Depression. In this work, Coney's, and America's, promise of hope had faded. Fittingly set at dusk and written at the end of the year, the poem is dominated by images of illness, death, and decay while the narrator is left helpless, "without arms, lost / in the vomiting multitude."[82]

Unlike Lorca, who was a visitor to Coney, residents Joseph Heller and Nobel Prize winner Isaac Bashevis Singer give us insider perspectives, particularly through a Jewish lens, into Coney Island in the 1930s.[83] Although Coney was in a period of decline, a sense of vitality still dominates their writings. Heller, who was born in Coney Island in 1923, recalls his youth in sharp detail in *Now and Then: From Coney Island to Here* (1988), speaking of what it was like to grow up not just in an amusement area, but in an actual neighborhood. He remarks that people were always stunned to realize that he grew up in Coney, "that families lived there, and still do, and that children were brought up there, and still are." To him, Coney Island was simply home.

Singer's autobiographical story "**A Day in Coney Island**" (1982) provides an immigrant's take on life in Sea Gate, a somewhat exclusive neighborhood away from the commercial strip of Coney Island. He writes of his financial and cultural struggles in adjusting to America. What predominates in the story, though, is the support and strong sense of community that Singer felt in the émigré Jewish area. It was this support that enabled him to survive tough times and to spur his initial success as a writer.

Perhaps the more serious threat to Coney's economy and continued existence as an amusement area came not from the economic downturn of the Depression, but from the actions of Robert Moses, New York City Parks Commissioner, who had long expressed a distaste for Coney Island, saying that "there is no reason to perpetuate out-of-doors the overcrowding of our tenements."[84] In 1937, he gained control of Coney Island when jurisdiction over its beaches and boardwalk was transferred from the Brooklyn borough president to the Department of Parks. Moses soon wrote an **Attachment to Letter to Mayor Fiorello LaGuardia** (1937) that accompanied a planning report for what he regarded as the improvement of Coney Island. If the goal of George Tilyou, Elmer Dundy, Frederic Thompson, and William Reynolds had been to make Coney into a more urban area, Moses desired to restore it to its original natural state. By the time he was finished, he had "turned 50 percent of Coney's surface into parks."[85]

Moses wanted to build a new resort, focused on bathing and outdoor recreation, with much less in the way of mechanical rides and amusements. He quickly took steps to try to impose his vision. Moses attempted to close the sideshows through an ordinance that prohibited free outside exhibitions by barkers, the main method of attracting customers into the shows. He enacted regulations to govern behavior on the beach, including imposing fines for such activities as tumbling, playing phonographs, and using newspapers as beach blankets. He ordered stricter enforcement of laws that banned the sale of food on the beach and even instituted fines for not disposing of peanut shells properly. Moses's goal was to reinvent Coney along the lines of another of his creations, Jones Beach, in suburban Long Island. In his design, Moses did not appear to appreciate or understand Coney's nature. As Marshall Berman points out, "All the density and intensity, the anarchic noise and motion, the seedy vitality that is expressed in Weegee's photographs and Reginald Marsh's etchings, and celebrated symbolically in Lawrence Ferlinghetti's 'A Coney Island of the Mind,' is wiped off the map in the visionary landscape of Jones Beach."[86] Although most of Coney's amusements survived Moses's efforts, at least for the time being, his efforts dealt a serious blow to the area's overall health.[87]

The state of Coney Island in the late 1930s, at the time of Moses's planned implementations, is described in **"To Heaven by Subway"** (1938), an article published in *Fortune* that cautions readers, despite its decline, not to sell Coney short. The optimism displayed in *Fortune*, however, is undercut by Henry Miller's **"Into the Night Life"** (1936), which provides an impressionistic, grotesque glimpse into a hellish world, symbolized by Coney, in which "everything is a lie, a fake. Pasteboard. A Coney Island of the Mind." Although most people believe that the phrase "a Coney Island of the Mind" was coined by Lawrence Ferlinghetti, it actually comes from Miller's unsettling portrait of the amusement area.[88]

Amram Ducovny's *Coney* (2000) and Sarah Hall's *The Electric Michelangelo* (2004) also depict Coney Island at this period. The writers do not romanticize its history but graphically depict scenes of crime, poverty, violence, and all varieties of eccentric, even bizarre, behavior. Still there is a sense that Coney is a community, a sometimes magical place where seeming misfits can establish an, albeit troubled, home.

WORLD WAR II AND BEYOND

The outbreak of World War II and its immediate aftermath provided a temporary boost to Coney's economy, fueled by the many men and women in uniform who visited Coney Island while on leave and the rationing of gasoline, which forced New Yorkers to vacation closer to home. An exciting new ride, the Parachute Jump, was added to Coney in 1941, when it was moved from its original site at the New York World's Fair (1939–1940).[89] A record 46 million visitors descended on Coney in 1943.[90] More than 2.5 million people enjoyed an air show and fireworks display on July 3, 1947.[91]

Other events during and just after the war, however, contributed to the gradual decline in Coney's fortunes. In August 1944, Luna Park, which had been experiencing financial problems for years, lost half of its attractions to a fire, and it never reopened, closing officially in 1946. Only Steeplechase remained of Coney's big-three amusement parks. Luna's real demise, however, had come years before the fire. Its death was symbolized by the introduction of such "entertainment" as cockroach racing and "a White Mouse Hotel—a doll's house inhabited by mice."[92] And instead of elephants going down a slide, as it once featured, the park was reduced to using pigs. One can only wonder what pioneers such as Tilyou and Thompson would have thought of such amusements.

Kenneth Fearing's poem **"Stranger at Coney Island"** (1948) in some ways epitomizes the hopes and fears of America and, in turn, the views of Coney Island, in the postwar years. The frightening journey of recent years, likened to a trip to an amusement park, is now ended. In language similar to that of William Butler Yeats's poem "The Second Coming," we await, with some trepidation, the coming era. However, it is suggested in Fearing's poem that the possible savior is not headed toward Bethlehem, but is already at Coney, "perhaps sprawled beneath a striped umbrella, asleep in the sand, or tossing a rubber ball to a child, / Or even now awaiting us, aware of our needs, knowing the very day and the hour."

THE YEARS OF DECLINE AND THE HOPE OF REBIRTH, 1949 TO THE PRESENT

Lawrence Ferlinghetti's *A Coney Island of the Mind* (1958) is one of the best-known volumes of American poetry to be published in the second half of the twentieth century. Although Ferlinghetti's collection never actually references Coney other than in the title, the amusement area's spirit of freedom and imagination, yet lurking danger, is omnipresent. Poem **20**, for example, perfectly captures this sense of fantasy when the narrator remembers the loss of his childhood:

> The pennycandystore beyond the El
> is where I first
>> fell in love
>>> with unreality

The bittersweet memories of a long-gone youth colliding with the harsh realities of the present in the poem reflect what was happening to Coney Island in the 1940s. Unfortunately, the grim path toward decline on which Coney had slowly been lurching was soon to arrive at its terrible destination.

Against the protests of the business community, Robert Moses moved the boardwalk inland in 1941, reducing the size of the amusement area and demolishing a number of buildings. His ability to reshape Coney was strengthened by the passage of the Housing Act of 1949. Title I of the act gave local governments the power to seize land not for its own use, but for reassignment to another individual, such as a private developer. An aide to Moses made clear the park commissioner's plans for Coney at a public hearing, as reported by the *New York Times*: "[I]t is proposed to shift an area encompassing nearly all of the resort from its present unrestricted and business classification to a mixture of business, retail, local retail and residential designations. The change is expected to enable Coney Island to fit into the pattern envisioned for it as a largely residential seaside area."[93]

Moses managed to get his first housing project built at Coney in 1949, and his efforts intensified in the 1950s. The New York City Housing Authority, largely controlled by Moses, built five high-rise apartment buildings, which opened in 1956. Coney's year-long residents had been steadily increasing in number since the turn of the century, but this sudden influx of so many people, many of them poor, was too much to add so quickly to an amusement area. The city had made no plans to help these newcomers adjust to their environment. In 1950, a company that proposed to build an entertainment complex, with amusements and a drive-in theater, purchased the Luna Park property, but Moses opposed the project and it eventually died. Fred Trump, a real-estate speculator and the father of Donald Trump, purchased the Luna Park site with the blessing of Moses. He intended to make a profit by building government-subsidized apartment housing on the lot. Before Trump could carry out his plan, however, he was called before a Senate investigative committee and accused of rent gouging, overbidding on construction projects and pocketing the difference, and related actions. Barred from participating in the Federal Housing Administration program, Trump decided to sell the Luna Park property, at a handsome profit.

Moses acquired and demolished other blocks in the Coney Island area. Some of the land found its way into the hands of Trump, who was able to use state rather than federal funds to help construct his housing projects, including Trump Village. Some properties remained vacant for years. Coney's landlords, fearful that Moses would seize more buildings, were reluctant to make major improvements and repairs.[94]

Strangely enough, Moses was responsible for bringing one of the new attractions to Coney. As early as 1941, he announced a plan to move the New York Aquarium from Clinton Castle in Battery Park to the Bronx Zoo. However, Mayor Fiorello LaGuardia believed that the Bronx Zoo was too inaccessible and vetoed the proposal. Moses, not used to being thwarted, was angered by the mayor's decision. So he decided to move the aquarium to Coney, not to reward the amusement area, but to banish the aquarium to what he regarded as an undesirable location. The new aquarium was built on the site of the fire-razed Dreamland. Its presence, however, did not really benefit Coney Island for many years. It took sixteen years to build, and it further shrank the amusement area. Moses also set the entrance fees very high, which discouraged attendance. As Charles Denson states:

> [F]or nearly a decade after it was built in 1957, the Aquarium was a financial disaster and sparsely attended. It did not even advertise the fact that it was located in Coney Island because of the neighborhood's poor reputation. The condemnation and destruction of amusement frontage on Surf Avenue to make room for the Aquarium's parking lot were another serious blow to the area. It took decades for the new facility to catch on and become popular.[95]

As Denson indicates, by the late 1950s and the 1960s Coney had begun to develop a "poor reputation." John Berman, in his history of Coney Island published in conjunction with the Museum of the City of New York, describes the decline of Coney in this period:

> By the early 1960s, the development of low-income housing complexes led to an escalation in gang violence among the youth in the neighborhood. The old fun zone on the Bowery became a place full of crime, which instilled fear in would-be patrons. . . . The 1964 race riots in Harlem and Bedford-Stuyvesant clearly also had an impact on the level of fear—residents and visitors were concerned that Coney Island [where the minority population and racial tensions had increased] might be next.[96]

THE CLOSING OF STEEPLECHASE AND ITS AFTERMATH

A critical blow to Coney Island was the death of the last of the big-three parks, Steeplechase, on September 20, 1964. As Denson reports, "Thousands of lights were switched off slowly, row after row, on each toll of the bell. As it turned out, the park went dark for the last time."[97] Despite frantic attempts to save the park, eventually it was sold to Trump on July 1, 1965, for $2.2 million. Two months later, Trump invited guests to a party to complete the destruction of Steeplechase Park, offering "bricks to guests to throw through the funny face painted on the windows" of the Pavilion of Fun.[98]

Steeplechase's official closing may have come in 1964, but its decline, like that of Coney Island itself, had been in process for at least thirty-five years. The reasons for Steeplechase's falling fortunes were numerous, including the gang violence suggested by Berman. For one, the growth of automobile ownership after World War II allowed for the development of many competitors, including "recreational beaches like Jones Beach and Riis Park, combination beach–amusement parks like Rockaway and [Rye] Playland in Westchester County and amusement parks like New Jersey's Palisades Park."[99] And although Coney Island was never, because of geographic differences, in competition with the new highly sanitized mega-amusement parks such as Disneyland (which opened on July 17, 1955, well after the Brooklyn "fun zone" had slipped into decline), it did pale in comparison, further tarnishing its image.[100] In addition, Coney's aging rides were no longer perceived as the technological achievements they once were. The amusement area, in fact, came to be regarded as antiquated and seedy rather than cutting-edge entertainment, and the rides were not the only thing that was aging; New York City's population was getting older as well, and Coney Island had lost much of its younger target audience.[101] Finally, other inexpensive attractions—including radio, television, and movie theaters—drew from Coney's base.[102]

The impact of the closing of Steeplechase Park was sorely felt in the area. Whereas once Coney Island had been seen as an exciting destination, a place filled with fun and entertainment, now it "became a symbol of urban decay and decline."[103] Newspaper articles spoke about the decrease in business, increase in crime, and "long, lonely, fearful" subway ride to and from Coney.[104] Street crime intensified, and a local gang, the Homicides, became famous along the Bowery.[105] Racial tensions that had been simmering for decades finally erupted on Easter Sunday, April 14, 1968, when some 5,000 black youths allegedly rampaged, more than a dozen people were hurt, and 36 were arrested, as reported by George Todd in "**Mayor Blasts TA Brass on Coney Island Debacle**" (1968). Much of the West End of Coney—declared a "poverty zone" in 1967 and home to a large African American and Hispanic population—was subsequently razed, and block busting drove out many of the remaining white residents while the building of projects expanded.[106]

Despite all this turmoil, it is important to remember that this was a neighborhood where the vast majority of people lived their lives peacefully, working and struggling every day just as in any other neighborhood. Coney Island for them, just as it had been for Joseph Heller a generation earlier, was simply home. It remained, even in its darkest days, a unique location in which to reside, as Narciso Urquiola, who lived there in the 1960s and 1970s, records: "I grew up in a place where the terms *bored* and *boredom* were virtually nonexistent. . . . Despite the fact that most families in Coney Island—in the sections alongside the amusement grounds—had lived in relative poverty, there was always somewhere to go, something to do, something to watch, or something to talk about with others."[107] It was the strength of these residents and this community that would finally begin to turn Coney Island around from its darkest period.

Sol Yurick's novel ***The Warriors*** (1965), perhaps even more famous when adapted as a film replete with crumbling and burned-out buildings,[108] helped perpetuate the predominant view of Coney Island at this time: a gang-filled, crime-ridden wasteland. In actuality, the plot comes not from the blight of Coney Island but from classical antiquity: the Persian expedition recorded in Xenophon's *Anabasis* (fourth century B.C.E.). As Yurick himself has said, gangs are "a universal phenomenon," and *The Warriors* is simply his updating of an ancient story.[109] That he chose Coney Island, however, as the site for this apocalyptic vision is telling. For the Warriors, believed to be modeled on the Homicides, though, Coney is not a violent place. Rather, it is the one area of safety in an otherwise dangerous world. And the members of the gang, instead of being portrayed as villains, are heroes in their quest to return to their home base, with its "comforting familiarity" by the ocean.

The novel and film version of *The Warriors* undoubtedly remains the indelible image of Coney in the 1960s and 1970s, but countervailing narratives exist. In Edwin Torres's poem "**Coney Island 1969**," for example, the narrator's father is a manager at Nathan's. Although the speaker claims, "My father was never Coney Island to me," his bittersweet memories of his dead parent are inexorably intertwined with his reflections on the city of fire.

Three stories written in the 1960s depict the troubled times at Coney Island and in the United States in general. In Josephine W. Johnson's "**Coney Island in November**" (1963), the desolate landscape of the off-season allows for an introspective reflection on the narrator's distant relationship with her deceased father. Bernard Malamud's "**My Son the Murderer**" (1968) is a dark tale about a lonely young man, just graduated from college, who has been drafted to serve during the height of the Vietnam War. Desperate and confused, he goes to Coney Island, where he walks into the water. As critic Paul Kareem Tayyar states, in Malamud's story the water is "a terrifying emblem of nature's eternal indifference to man's suffering."[110] Edward Hoagland's "**Kwan's Coney Island**" (1969) is somewhat more optimistic than Johnson's and Malamud's tales. Kwan, a middle-aged immigrant from Hong Kong, is struck by the diversity of ethnicities around him at Coney. Despite the tensions among the groups, a measure of racial and ethnic bonding is achieved in the story through distinctly Coney Island ways: a steam bath, a freak who inserts pins into his body, and a young black prostitute.

THE 1970S AND BEYOND

Conditions at Coney Island continued to deteriorate in the 1970s. More property was abandoned or destroyed, drugs and crime ravaged the area, and the New York's bleak financial situation did not provide a means for relief. Plans were considered for casino gambling in the late 1970s, and in the mid-1980s, developer Horace Bullard hoped to create a theme park at Coney. But all these attempts failed.[111] Not everything in Coney Island, of course, was dying. Even in its darkest moments, Coney continued to have moments of revival. Despite the closing of Steeplechase Park, Coney's amusement area hung on in the form of Astroland, which opened in 1962. Astroland, the creation of Dewey Albert and Jerome Albert, extended Coney Island's great amusement history, operating the Cyclone and even introducing such "space age" novelties as an observation tower and a sky ride that traversed the grounds. The three-acre amusement park was built on the property once occupied by Charles Feltman's Ocean Pavilion. Despite a game effort, however, Astroland was no match for the memory of the parks that had ceased to operate at Coney. It was simply not enough of an attraction to draw large throngs. When the park's lease was not renewed in 2008, Jerome's widow, Carol Albert, was forced to close at the end of the season. Although Astroland became another Coney Island casualty, it should be credited with helping to preserve the amusement area for almost half a century, and its presence augured the slow turnaround of Coney's fortunes.[112]

There were other hopeful signs of improvement beginning in the 1980s. For one, large crowds continued to visit the beach on summer weekends. In addition, Coney began to become a center for the arts. A major figure in developing this burgeoning arts movement was Dick Zigun, often called the "Mayor of Coney Island." In 1980, Zigun was the principal founder of a non-profit organization called Coney Island USA, whose purpose is "to defend the honor of American popular culture through innovative exhibitions and performances."[113] The group continues to document, preserve, and further the "honky-tonk subculture" of Coney Island and its unique arts. In 1983, Zigun launched the first of what was to become the annual Mermaid Parade, which has become a major event. The celebration is "part Mardi Gras, part art parade" and attracts up to 750,000 people, many of them young.[114] Soon Zigun was expanding the activities of Coney Island USA, producing plays, poetry readings, musical events, and other types of entertainment. He opened the Coney Island Museum and a traditional ten-act sideshow (now called "Sideshows by the Seashore"), with snake charmers, fire-eaters, sword swallowers, and other acts. The autobiographical piece by Donald Thomas (Donny Vomit), **"Confessions of a Coney Island Sideshow Performer,"** gives a vivid account of what it is like to perform in a Coney Island sideshow. In time, Coney Island USA initiated film festivals, burlesque shows, and various other events. All these activities helped to enliven the atmosphere at Coney.[115]

While much of Coney Island has been destroyed over the years, many reminders of its storied past remain. Although the Thunderbolt (a popular roller coaster that opened in 1925 and is immortalized in Woody Allen's film *Annie Hall* [1977]) was closed in 1983 (and razed in 2000), its famous cousin, the Cyclone (although threatened with closure in 1975), continues to rumble along on its wooden tracks and is landmarked, preserving it from demolition.[116] The Wonder Wheel (opened in 1920 and also landmarked) still revolves (under the ownership of the Vouderis family since 1993; the family has also operated a small amusement area since 1976). The B&B Carousell (opened in 1919) has been restored and recently reopened.[117] The Parachute Jump, although it ceased operation in 1964, has been stabilized and is landmarked, serving as a kind of Statue of Liberty for Coney, dominating the landscape around it. The New York Aquarium no longer is a stepchild. It has been improved and expanded, and welcomes about 800,000 visitors a year.[118] The members of the Coney Island Polar Bear

Club, founded in 1903 by Bernarr Macfadden, still take their annual dip in the Atlantic Ocean every New Year's Day.[119]

Many of the famous Coney Island eateries continue to feed hungry visitors. Nathan's, despite some talk of being forced to relocate, still occupies its familiar location on Surf Avenue, serving hot dogs and other edibles day and night. The annual Fourth of July International Hot Dog–Eating Contest, begun in 1916 and resumed in 1972 after a long hiatus, continues with much fanfare. Totonno's (opened in 1924) also provides a glimpse of the old Coney Island. It is said to be "the oldest continuously operating pizzeria in the U.S. run by the same family."[120] For those who want a more formal dining experience, Gargiulo's (opened in 1907) serves its patrons Italian cuisine.

An important addition to Coney Island has been the Brooklyn Cyclones minor-league baseball team, an affiliate of the New York Mets, who play in a field built on the grounds once occupied by Steeplechase Park. There was controversy in the community about the use of the space for a ballpark. For example, Brooklyn Borough President Howard Golden wanted the city to build an indoor sports arena on the site. Through the efforts of Mayor Rudolf Giuliani and others, however, a new stadium was built. Opening day was June 25, 2001, and the team immediately became a success.[121]

The Coney Island History Project was founded in 2004, with Charles Denson as its executive director. The project "aims to increase awareness of Coney Island's legendary and colorful past and to encourage appreciation of the Coney Island neighborhood of today."[122] Denson and his nonprofit organization have been at the forefront, along with Zigun, of the attempts to preserve Coney Island's legacy and enhance its future.

Although all these developments helped to lift Coney Island from its lowest point, it was clear that more drastic rebuilding efforts would be needed to revitalize the amusement area. In 2003, Mayor Michael Bloomberg and the City Council, along with Brooklyn Borough President Marty Markowitz, formed the Coney Island Development Corporation (CIDC) "to spearhead and implement a comprehensive planning process for Coney Island and to create a coordinated economic development strategy for the area."[123] A strategic plan was released in 2005 that provides a roadmap for the renewal of Coney Island. It envisioned three goals for

Coney: to make it a year-round entertainment destination, to enhance the amusements and seaside attractions, and to develop a vibrant neighborhood. Building on these recommendations, the New York Department of City Planning proposed a comprehensive but controversial rezoning plan that was approved by the City Council in 2009. The department's press release "**City Planning Begins Public Review on Rezoning of Coney Island**" (2009) highlights the proposed changes.

The rezoning plan covers nineteen blocks and provides for a variety of uses for the land. The centerpiece is a twenty-seven-acre amusement and entertainment district, including a twelve-acre amusement park. In February 2010, the city signed an agreement with Central Amusement International to manage the amusement area, which is called Luna Park, a reminder of Coney's heyday. An Italian company, the Zamperla Group, is the majority stockholder in Central Amusement International and is designing the rides. The park opened for the 2010 season with twenty-two rides, with significant expansion set for the future. The rezoning plan also calls for new housing, retail shops, restaurants, and hotels in Coney Island.[124]

Not everyone was pleased with the plan, as is reflected in "**Comments on the Revised Draft Scope of Analysis for Coney Island Rezoning Project**" (2008), from the Municipal Art Society, arguing that the proposal provides too little space for outdoor amusements and that even within the twenty-seven-acre zone, high-rise hotels and shops could be built. The organization also charges that historical buildings would be destroyed. In addition, the Municipal Art Society objects to the fact that Thor Equities, which still holds some prime land, can build thirty-story towers, which would effectively block out the view of the beach from the newly renovated Stillwell Avenue subway station. Save Coney Island, a volunteer nonprofit, has been established to fight aspects of the rezoning plan. Legal challenges have also been raised. How this latest iteration of Coney plays out remains to be seen. Given its history, it is not surprising that there continue to be varied and conflicting visions of what "America's playground" should be.[125] And the challenges that Coney Island faces continue. Superstorm Sandy,

NATHAN'S, CONEY ISLAND, 2007. (PHOTOGRAPH BY WILLYUMDELIRIOUS; REPRODUCED UNDER THE GNU FREE DOCUMENTATION LICENSE)

"HEARTBREAKERS ALONG THE SEASHORE," CONEY ISLAND, 1897. (STEREOGRAPH PUBLISHED BY STROHMEYER & WYMAN, NEW YORK. LIBRARY OF CONGRESS, PRINTS AND PHOTOGRAPHS DIVISION)

which inflicted much damage on October 29, 2012, reminded us that despite all its incarnations, Coney is still a seaside resort, as it always has been, and thus is at the mercy of the elements.[126]

Coney, of course, is a source of inspiration for a new generation of writers as well. They continue to interpret it according to their own perspective. Colson Whitehead's sketch **"Coney Island"** (2003) is an impressionistic ode to Coney. It is a place where thousands of New Yorkers are thrown together and where the city and nature come into sometimes contentious contact with each other.[127] Katie Roiphe, in **"A Coney Island of the Mind"** (2008), provides a humorous (if slightly ominous) recollection of her first date with her future husband, on the Cyclone. Maureen McHugh's short story, also called **"A Coney Island of the Mind"** (1993), fittingly offers a glimpse of Coney's future. Here, a virtual Coney Island is constructed that one can visit online from anywhere. It is possible to invent one's own persona and one's own Coney landscape—the ultimate opportunity to create one's own Coney Island of the mind.

As the numerous writers in this anthology have demonstrated, Coney Island has long been a fecund source to kindle the imagination. Its richness has made it iconic, whether in good or bad times and throughout its various incarnations. Why has it had such an enduring appeal? Perhaps it is for the reason that Richard Le Gallienne proposed in 1905. Its existence, both good and bad, embodies the inherent contradictions that make up humanity. No matter the era in Coney's history, one always feels, as Katie Roiphe suggests, its duality, "the seediness and greatness of the place, the vague feeling of menace, of leisure and unemployment mixing, along with the elation of a day at the beach." As such, it is timeless and will exist not only in memory as a museum piece but as it continues to be reborn in all its future reinterpretations.

NOTES

1   Oliver Pilat and Jo Ranson, *Sodom by the Sea: An Affectionate History of Coney Island* (Garden City, N.Y.: Doubleday, Doran, 1941), 5.

2   Thomas L. Russell, ed., *Thompson's Coney Island Guide* (New York: Tracy, 1885), 21.

3   Charles Denson, *Coney Island: Lost and Found* (Berkeley, Calif.: Ten Speed Press, 2002), 62.

4   Rem Koolhaas, *Delirious New York: A Retrospective Manifesto for Manhattan* (New York: Monacelli Press, 1994), 30.

5   Denson, *Coney Island*, 2–7; Michael Immerso, *Coney Island: The People's Playground* (New Brunswick, N.J.: Rutgers University Press, 2002), 12–14; Charles Denson, "Coney Island: A History of Pavilions," in *Coney Island: The Parachute Pavilion Competition*, ed. Zoë Ryan and Jonathan Cohen-Litant (New York: Princeton Architectural Press, 2007), 14.

6   For more on Whitman's experiences at Coney and his cultural views in general, see Justin Kaplan, *Walt Whitman: A Life* (New York: Harper, 2003); and David Reynolds, *Walt Whitman's America: A Cultural Biography* (New York: Vintage, 1996).

7   Brian J. Cudahy, *How We Got to Coney Island: The Development of Mass Transportation in Brooklyn and Kings County* (New York: Fordham University Press, 2002).

8   Koolhaas, *Delirious New York*, 33.

9   Immerso, *Coney Island*, 15–19.

10 Edwin G. Burrows and Mike Wallace, *Gotham: A History of New York City to 1898* (New York: Oxford University Press, 1999), 1134.

11 Lucy Gillman, "Coney Island," *New York History*, July 1955, 268.

12 See, for example, "The Coney Island Gamblers," *New York Times*, September 9, 1883; "Robbed at Coney Island," *New York Times*, August 26, 1883; "Coney Island Park Urged," *New York Times*, June 12, 1899; and "The Pests of Coney Island," *New York Times*, July 13, 1885. Ironically, John McKane is praised in the last article for attempting to rein in crime.

13 Denson, *Coney Island*, 15–16.

14 Quoted in Pilat and Ranson, *Sodom by the Sea*, 99.

15 For more on John McKane, see Immerso, *Coney Island*, 46–51; and Denson, *Coney Island*, 8–25.

16 [Henry Spencer Ashbee], "A Sunday at Coney Island," *Temple Bar*, May–August 1882, 266.

17 Callahan Pauline Seltzer, "Coney Island: The Limits and Possibilities of Leisure in Turn of the Century American Culture" (master's thesis, Georgetown University, 2011), 22.

18 Koolhaas, *Delirious New York*, 33.

19 For more on roller coasters, see Robert Cartmell, *The Incredible Scream Machine: A History of the Roller Coaster* (Fairview Park, Ohio: Amusement Park Books, 1987).

20 Stephen F. Weinstein, "The Nickel Empire: Coney Island and the Creation of Urban Seaside Resorts in the United States" (Ph.D. diss., Columbia University, 1984), 175.

21 Immerso, *Coney Island*, 38–44; Jon Sterngass, *First Resorts: Pursuing Pleasure at Saratoga Springs, Newport, and Coney Island* (Baltimore: Johns Hopkins University Press, 2001), 94–98.

22 Burrows and Wallace, *Gotham*, 1138.

23 Immerso, *Coney Island*, 38–39; "The Colossal Elephant of Coney Island," *Scientific American*, July 11, 1885, 15, 21; "Coney Island's Big Elephant," *New York Times*, May 30, 1885, 8.

24 Immerso, *Coney Island*, 42; John S. Berman, *Coney Island* (New York: Barnes & Noble, 2003), 18–19.

25 Jeffrey Stanton, "Coney–Food and Dining," 1997, Coney Island History Site, www.west land.net/coneyisland/articles/food.htm (accessed March 1, 2014). Stanton's Web site, although now somewhat dated, is an excellent source of information about most areas of Coney Island history.

26 For more on women and Coney at this time, see Christine Frieman, "Redefining Respectability: Women and Coney Island at the Turn of the Century" (master's thesis, Sarah Lawrence College, 2010).

27 Immerso, *Coney Island*, 41.

28 John F. Kasson, *Amusing the Million: Coney Island at the Turn of the Century* (New York: Hill & Wang, 1978), 41.

29 Gillman, "Coney Island," 267.

30 Kasson, *Amusing the Million*, 45.

31 Quoted in Burrows and Wallace, *Gotham*, 1136.

32 John Fagg, "Stephen Crane and the Literary Sketch: Genre and History in 'Sailing Day Scenes' and 'Coney Island's Failing Days,'" *American Literary Realism* 38, no. 1 (2005): 1–17.

33 Burrows and Wallace, *Gotham*, 1136.

34 *Coney Island and the Jews: A History of the Development and Success of This Famous Seaside Resort Together with a Full Account of the Recent Jewish Controversy* (New York: Carleton, 1879), 21–48.

35 Sterngass, *First Resorts*, 105–108; Gary Cross and John Walton, *The Playful Crowd: Pleasure Places in the Twentieth Century* (New York: Columbia University Press, 2005), 22, 54.

36 Weinstein, "Nickel Empire," 114.

37 Cross and Walton, *Playful Crowd*, 61.

38 Berman, *Coney Island*, 31; Immerso, *Coney Island*, 53–56.

39 See for example, "An Effort to Improve Coney Island," *New York Times*, March 14, 1878. A dissenting view is offered by Albert Bigelow Paine, who claimed that visitors to Coney were "'well-mannered,' 'even cultivated . . . a crowd as handsome and charming to gaze upon as any to be found at Newport or Long Branch'" (quoted in Edo McCullough, *Good Old Coney Island: A Sentimental Journey into the Past*, 2nd ed. [1957; New York: Fordham University Press, 2000], 186). For more on these reformers, see Seltzer, "Coney Island."

40 Quoted in Kasson, *Amusing the Million*, 100.

41 Immerso, *Coney Island*, 5.

42 Edwin Slosson, quoted in Kasson, *Amusing the Million*, 34–35.

43 Quoted in McCullough, *Good Old Coney Island*, 202.

44 Koolhaas, *Delirious New York*, 35–37.

45 Immerso, *Coney Island*, 78.

46 McCullough, *Good Old Coney Island*, 285.

47 Quoted in Kasson, *Amusing the Million*, 58.

48 On Edward Tilyou and Steeplechase Park, see Denson, *Coney Island*, 53–55.

49 P. G. Wodehouse makes a similar claim in "The Pleasure of Coney Island," *Atlanta Constitution*, July 13, 1930, sec. 1, 20.

50 Edison's film, *Electrocuting an Elephant*, is available on many Internet sites. It has also been written about in numerous literary works, including Kevin Baker's *Dreamland* (this volume), Sarah Hall's *Electric Michelangelo* (this volume), Nick Arvin's *In the Electric Eden* (New York: Penguin, 2003), and Christopher Bram's *The Notorious Dr. August: His Real Life and Crimes* (New York: Morrow, 2000). In addition, Topsy appears in Paul Muldoon's poem "Plan B" and W. S. Merwin's poem, "The Chain to Her Leg." A memorial was erected for Topsy at the Coney Island Museum on July 20, 2003. For more, see Michael Daly, *Topsy: The Startling Story of the Crooked-Tailed Elephant, P. T. Barnum, and the American Wizard, Thomas Edison* (New York: Atlantic Monthly Press, 2013).

51 Winthrop Alexander, "Coney Island's New Wonder-World," in *From Traveling Show to Vaudeville: Theatrical Spectacle in America, 1830–1910*, ed. Robert M. Lewis (Baltimore: Johns Hopkins University Press, 2003), 287.

52 Michele H. Bogart, "Barking Architecture: The Sculpture of Coney Island," *Smithsonian Studies in American Art* 2, no. 1 (1988): 11.

53 Koolhass, *Delirious New York*, 41. For more on Coney's architecture, see Koolhaas, *Delirious New York*, 29–79; Bogart, "Barking Architecture"; Frederic Thompson, "Amusing

the Million" (this volume); Barr Ferree, "The New Popular Resort Architecture: Dreamland, Coney Island," *Architects' and Builders' Magazine*, August 1904, 490–513; Ryan and Cohen-Litant, eds., *Coney Island*; and "Coney Island: Its Architecture Is the Stuff That People's Dreams Are Made Of," *Architectural Forum*, August 1947, 83–87. For information on art influenced by Coney, see Richard Cox, "Coney Island: Urban Symbol in American Art," *New-York Historical Society Quarterly* 64, no. 1 (1980): 35–52.

54 Woody Register, *The Kid of Coney Island: Fred Thompson and the Rise of American Amusements* (New York: Oxford University Press, 2001), 132.

55 William F. Mangels, *The Outdoor Amusement Industry: From Earliest Times to the Present* (New York: Vintage Press, 1952).

56 Kasson, *Amusing the Million*, 70.

57 Quoted in Register, *Kid of Coney Island*, 124.

58 Weinstein, "Nickel Empire," 245. Thompson also wrote about Coney and amusement areas in "The Summer Show," *Independent*, June 20, 1907; "Fooling the Public: The Growth of the Big Show, as Described by a Master Showman," *Delineator*, February 1907; and "Amusing People," *Metropolitan Magazine*, August 1910. For more on him, see Register, *Kid of Coney Island*.

59 Denson, *Coney Island*, 38. For a contemporary view on Dreamland, see Ferree, "New Popular Resort Architecture."

60 For more on Martin Couney, see the Coney Island History Project (www.coneyisland history.org), which includes interviews with people who, as infants, had been part of the exhibition. See also Richard F. Snow, "Martin Couney," *American Heritage*, June–July 1981. Couney was a pioneer in using incubators, and more than 8,000 babies (many of whose lives had been saved) were part of the exhibit between 1903 and 1943. For more on the incubator babies, see "To Heaven by Subway" (this volume). Hall writes of the incubator exhibit in *The Electric Michelangelo*. See also Steven Popke, "Doctor Couney's Island," in *Coney Island Wonder Stories*, ed. Robert J. Howe and John Ordover (Rockville, Md.: Wildside Press, 2005), 22–37. For more on Fighting the Flames, see Lynn Kathleen Sally, *Fighting the Flames: The Spectacular Performance of Fire at Coney Island* (New York: Routledge, 2006).

61 James Lilliefors, *America's Boardwalks: From Coney Island to California* (New Brunswick, N.J.: Rutgers University Press, 2006), 36.

62 Pilat and Ranson, *Sodom by the Sea*, 179. For more on Dreamland, see Immerso, *Coney Island*, 68–74, 82–86, 134–136; Berman, *Coney Island*, 34–36; and Koolhaas, *Delirious New York*, 47–62. For more on Samuel Gumpertz, see Robert Bogdan, *Freak Show: Presenting Human Oddities for Amusement and Profit* (Chicago: University of Chicago Press, 1990), 55–58; Ava Johnston, "Boss of the Circus," *New Yorker*, May 6 and May 13, 1933; and Joseph Gustaitis, "The Character of Coney Island: Stalking the Strange with Sam Gumpertz," *American History Illustrated*, February 1981.

63 Elmer Blaney Harris, "The Day of Rest at Coney Island," *Everybody's Magazine*, July 1908, 33.

64 Seltzer, "Coney Island," 96–102; "Coney Island Swept by Fire," *New York Times*, November 2, 1903; "A New Coney Island Rises from the Ashes of the Old," *New York Times*, May 8, 1904; "New Coney Dazzles Its Record Multitude," *New York Times*, May 15, 1904.

65 Josiah Allen's Wife [Marietta Holley], *Samantha at Coney Island and a Thousand Other Islands* (New York: Christian Herald, 1911), 214. In recent years, Samantha has come to be regarded as an important early female comic protagonist, and several of Holley's novels have been brought back into print and begun to be written about by scholars such as Kate Winter, *Marietta Holley: Life with Josiah Allen's Wife* (Syracuse, N.Y.: Syracuse University Press, 1984); and Jane Curry, *Marietta Holley* (New York: Twayne, 1996).

66 A posthumous collection of Schwartz's short stories, *In Dreams Begin Responsibilities and Other Stories* (New York: New Directions, 1978), was edited by James Atlas, who also wrote *Delmore Schwartz: The Life of an American Poet* (New York: Farrar, Straus and Giroux, 1976).

67 In one of the many positive reviews of *Dreamland*, J. Kingston Pierce stated that Baker "has done as fine a job as any author I know of in capturing [Coney Island's] garish excesses in print and superimposing upon them a comparably compelling and complex tale" ("Over the Big Top," *January Magazine*, May 1999). A quasi-fictional account of Freud and Jung's visit may be found in Norman M. Klein, *Freud in Coney Island and Other Tales* (Los Angeles: Otis Books, 2006).

68 Richard Snow, *Coney Island: A Postcard Journey to the City of Fire* (New York: Brightwaters Press, 1984), 20.

69 Kasson, *Amusing the Million*, 41–49.

70 For more on the dance halls, see Kathy Peiss, "The Coney Island Excursion" (this volume); Elizabeth I. Perry, "'The General Motherhood of the Commonwealth': Dance Hall Reform in the Progressive Era," *American Quarterly* 37, no. 5 (1985): 719–733; and Immerso, *Coney Island*, 106–113. For brief accounts of the dance halls by immigrant women, see Hamilton Holt, *The Life Stories of Undistinguished Americans as Told by Themselves*, in Lewis, *From Traveling Show to Vaudeville*, 304–305.

71 Kasson, *Amusing the Million*, 49–50.

72 Seltzer, "Coney Island," 126.

73 Immerso, *Coney Island*, 131. For more on Nathan's, see McCullough, *Good Old Coney Island*, 244–249.

74 On the battle for land and the building of the boardwalk, see Denson, *Coney Island*, 40–52; and Immerso, *Coney Island*, 125.

75 Immerso, *Coney Island*, 125–129; Berman, *Coney Island*, 72.

76 Immerso, *Coney Island*, 127.

77 Cross and Walton, *Playful Crowd*, 99.

78 Bruce Blivin, "Coney Island for Battered Souls," *New Republic*, November 23, 1921, 374.

79 Immerso, *Coney Island*, 130, 137–141.

80 Quoted in Immerso, *Coney Island*, 160. The fate of the Half Moon is reflective of Coney's decline. It was converted into a seniors' home in the 1950s and finally demolished in 1995.

81 Pilat and Ranson, *Sodom by the Sea*, 272–296. For more on crime in Coney Island at this time, see John Osnato Jr., *Coney Island Diary, 1935* (New York: Vantage Press, 1991). Osnato had been a detective in Coney.

82 Lorca wrote elsewhere about the amusement area:

> Coney is a great fair where every Sunday in the summer more than a million creatures come. They drink, they shout, they eat, they writhe about leaving a sea of newspapers and the streets littered with tin cans, cigarette butts, bites of food and shoes with broken heels. No one can imagine the loneliness a Spaniard feels there; because if you fall you will be trampled and if you slide into the water, they will throw lunch wrappers on you. (quoted in Sandra Forman and Allen Josephs, *Only Mystery: Federico García Lorca's Poetry in Word and Image* [Gainesville: University Press of Florida, 1992], 89)

83 For more on Jewish Coney Island and literature, see David G. Roskies, "Coney Island, USA: America in the Yiddish Literary Imagination," in *The Cambridge Companion to Jewish American Literature*, ed. Hana Wirth-Nesher and Michael Kramer (Cambridge: Cambridge University Press, 2003), 70–91. For biographical information on Heller and Coney Island, see Tracy Daugherty, *Just One Catch: A Biography of Joseph Heller* (New York: St. Martin's Press, 2011).

84 Quoted in Pilat and Ranson, *Sodom by the Sea*, 333.

85 Koolhaas, *Delirious New York*, 79. For more on Moses and Coney, see Hillary Ballon, *Robert Moses and the Modern City: The Transformation of New York* (New York: Norton, 2007).

86 Marshall Berman, *All That Is Solid Melts into Air: The Experience of Modernity* (1982; New York: Penguin, 1988), 297. Weegee (Arthur Fellig) took a number of photographs of Coney Island, perhaps most notably "Coney Island Beach" (1940). See David Corey, "Weegee's Unstaged Coney Island Drama," *American Art* 5, nos. 1–2 (1981): 16–21. Other well-known Coney photographers include Harold Feinstein and Harvey Stein. For a sampling of Reginald Marsh's Coney Island artwork—one of which, *Wonderland Circus, Sideshow, Coney Island* (1930), appears in this anthology—see *Reginald Marsh: Coney Island* (Fort Wayne, Ind.: Fort Wayne Museum of Art, 1991).

87 Berman, *Coney Island*, 75; Denson, *Coney Island*, 65–67; Immerso, *Coney Island*, 158–160.

88 In a biographical pamphlet, George Wickes declares that "Into the Night Life" is "the scenario of a nightmare" (*Henry Miller* [Minneapolis: University of Minnesota, 1966], 25). He adds that this "Coney Island of the mind" is like a "surrealistic film" in which scenes shift constantly and "memories are jumbled together with Gothic visions in a world of crazy symbols that make sense."

89 Denson, *Coney Island*, 67–71.

90 Immerso, *Coney Island*, 8.

91 McCullough, *Good Old Coney Island*, 328.

92 Pilat and Ranson, *Sodom by the Sea*, 159.

93 "Moses Asks Coney Island Rezoning to 'Upgrade' It as Residential Area," *New York Times*, April 2, 1953, 1.

94 On Robert Moses, Fred Trump, and urban renewal in Coney Island, see Charles Denson, *Wild Ride! A Coney Island Roller Coaster Family* (Berkeley, Calif.: Dreamland Press, 2007), 69–83; Immerso, *Coney Island*, 169–171; Denson, *Coney Island*, 72–76, 82–90; and Robert A. Caro, *The Power Broker: Robert Moses and the Fall of New York* (New York: Vintage, 1975).

95 Denson, *Coney Island*, 67, 73; Immerso, *Coney Island*, 171.

96 Berman, *Coney Island*, 107.

97 Denson, *Coney Island*, 136.

98 Denson, *Coney Island*, 140. For more on the demise of Steeplechase Park, see Michael Paul Onorato, *Another Time, Another World: Coney Island Memories* (Fullerton: California State University Oral History Program, 2000).

99 Weinstein, "Nickel Empire," 288.

100 For a comparison of the two amusement parks, see Raymond Weinstein, "Disneyland and Coney Island: Reflections on the Evolution of the Modern Amusement Park," *Journal of Popular Culture* 26, no. 1 (1992): 113–164.

101 Judith A. Adams, *The American Amusement Park Industry: A History of Technology and Thrills* (Boston: Twayne, 1991), 53–55.

102 Kasson, *Amusing the Million*, 112.

103 Berman, *Coney Island*, 108.

104 See, for example, Martin Tolchin, "Coney Island Slump Grows Worse: Decline in Business Since the War Years Has Been Steady," *New York Times*, July 2, 1964, 33; Martin Arnold, "Subway Ride from Coney Island Can Be Long, Lonely, Fearful," *New York Times*, June 8, 1964, 32; Paul Hofmann, "Coney Island's Slums and Tidy Homes Reflect Big-City Problems," *New York Times*, July 24, 1967, 28, 36; and "4,000 Teen-Agers Brawl at Coney," *New York Times*, May 31, 1966, 28.

105 Denson, *Coney Island*, 151. See also Narciso Urquiola, *Coney Island: Unforeseen Times* (Catawba, 2008), 200–203.

106 For more on the riot and its aftermath, see "Youths Loot Coney Island Shops and Fight Police," *New York Times*, April 15, 1968, 23; Denson, *Coney Island*, 142–144, 152–160; Victoria W. Walcott, *Race, Riots and Roller Coasters: The Struggle over Segregated Recreation in America* (Philadelphia: University of Pennsylvania Press, 2012), 206–208; "Nazi War Camp Laid to TA," *New York Amsterdam News*, April 27, 1968, 25; and Bernard Collier, "Coney Islanders Anticipate Flare-Ups," *New York Times*, April 22, 1968, 36.

107 Urquiola, *Coney Island*, 5.

108 The film version of *The Warriors* was released in 1979. Hubert Selby Jr.'s novel *Requiem for a Dream* (New York: Playboy Press, 1978) has also been seen as a symbol of Coney at this time. However, unlike the movie based on it, produced in 2000, Coney is not prominently featured in Selby's book.

109 Sol Yurick, "How I Came to Write *The Warriors* and What Happened After," in *The Warriors* (1965; New York: Grove Press, 2003), 201.

110 Paul Kareem Tayyar, "'Because We Could Not Walk on Water': Bernard Malamud's 'My Son the Murderer' and the Limits of Magical Realism," July 2008, Americana: An Insti-

    tute for American Studies and Creative Writing, http://www.americanpopularculture
.com/archive/politics/malamud.htm (accessed March 1, 2014).

111 Cross and Walton, *Playful Crowd*, 152.

112 For more on Astroland, see Charles Denson, *Coney Island and Astroland* (Charleston, S.C.: Arcadia, 2011); and J. L. Aronson, *Last Summer at Coney Island*, produced and directed by J. L. Aronson (Astoria, N.Y.: Indiepix and Films Creative Arson Productions, 2010), DVD.

113 "About Coney Island USA," Coney Island USA: Defending the Honor of American Popular Culture!, http://www.coneyisland.com/about-coney-island-usa (accessed March 1, 2014).

114 Immerso, *Coney Island*, 184–185.

115 On Dick Zigun and Coney Island USA, see Denson, *Coney Island*, 233–239; and http://www.coneyisland.com. See also Rachel Adams, *Sideshow U.S.A.: Freaks and the American Cultural Imagination* (Chicago: University of Chicago Press, 2001), 212–217.

116 A new Thunderbolt is in the planning stages, as reported in Lisa W. Foderaro, "Thunderbolt Promises a Return of Thrills," *New York Times*, March 11, 2014, A17.

117 For more on the Ferris wheel, see Norman D. Anderson, *Ferris Wheels: An Illustrated History* (Bowling Green, Ohio: Bowling Green State University Popular Press, 1992). For more on Coney and carousels, see Immerso, *Coney Island*, 88–95. For the reopening of the B&B Carousell, see Lisa W. Foderaro, "Summer's Steeds, Back Home," *New York Times*, May 26, 2013, L6.

118 New York Aquarium, http://www.nyaquarium.com (accessed March 14, 2014).

119 The Polar Bears are mentioned in Josephine W. Johnson's "Coney Island in November" (this volume). For more, see Coney Island Polar Bear Club USA, www.polarbearclub.org (accessed March 1, 2014). For more on Bernarr Macfadden, see Robert Ernst, *Weakness Is a Crime: The Life of Bernarr Macfadden* (Syracuse, N.Y.: Syracuse University Press, 1991); and Mark Adams, *Mr. America: How Muscular Millionaire Bernarr Macfadden Transformed the Nation Through Sex, Salad, and the Ultimate Starvation Diet* (New York: HarperCollins, 2009).

120 "Totonno's," Coney Island Fun Guide: The One and Only Coney, www.coneyislandfunguide.com/EatAndShop/Totonnos.htm (accessed March 1, 2014).

121 Ben Osborne, *The Brooklyn Cyclones: Hardball Dreams and the New Coney Island* (New York: New York University Press, 2004); Ed Shakespeare, *When Baseball Returned to Brooklyn: The Inaugural Season of the New York-Penn League Cyclones* (Jefferson, N.C.: McFarland, 2003). See also Brooklyn Cyclones, www.brooklyncyclones.com (accessed March 14, 2014).

122 "About the Coney Island History Project," Coney Island History Project, http://www.coneyislandhistory.org/index.php?g=about (accessed March 1, 2014).

123 "Strategic Plan," Coney Island Development Corporation, http://www.thecidc.org/Planning/StrategicPlan.html (accessed March 1, 2014).

124 On Coney Island's redevelopment, see Coney Island Development Corporation, http://www.thecidc.org (accessed March 1, 2014); New York City Department of Planning,

"Coney Island Comprehensive Rezoning Plan, NYC Planning, http://www.nyc.gov/html/dcp/html/coney_island/index.shtml (accessed March 10, 2014); and Elisabetta Povoledo, "Coney Island Getting a $30 Million Italian Makeover," *New York Times*, April 24, 2010, B1.

125 Save Coney Island!, http://www.saveconeyisland.net (accessed March 1, 2014).

126 For more on Superstorm Sandy, see W. M. Akers, "A Cold Winter in Coney," February 6, 2013, *Narratively*, http://narrative.ly/100-days-later/a-cold-winter-in-coney/ (accessed March 1, 2014).

127 In a review of *The Colossus of New York: A City in Thirteen Parts*, the work from which this sketch is taken, Luc Sante wrote: "The book is a tour de force of voice, restlessly hopscotching from first to second to third person, from observation to speculation to reminiscence to indirect citation, in a staccato rhythm that effectively mimes the noise of the city" ("Eight Million Reasons," *New York Times*, October 19, 2003). For more on the book, see Robert Butler, "The Postmodern City in Colson Whitehead's *The Colossus of New York* and Jeffery Renard Allen's *Rails Under My Back*," *CLA Journal* 48, no. 1 (2004): 71–87.

THE BEGINNINGS THROUGH 1896

[CLAM-BAKE AT CONEY ISLAND]

Walt Whitman

Walt Whitman (1819–1892), a native of Long Island, is one of America's best-known poets and journalists. *Leaves of Grass* (1855) is a landmark volume of poetry. Whitman was editor of the *Brooklyn Eagle* from 1846 to 1848 when he wrote several reflections on Coney Island, including ["Clam-Bake at Coney Island,"] published in the newspaper on July 15, 1847. Although often thought of as a poet of the city, Whitman enjoyed Coney's bucolic, relaxed setting. Along the way there, visitors would pass fields of corn and wheat. Upon arrival, they could engage in convivial conversation, a leisurely swim, and a feast of roasted clams. For Whitman, a journey to Coney was like going on "an excursion from city to country, or from pavement to the sea-shore!" Whitman visited Coney numerous times, bathing naked in its soothing waters and reading Shakespeare on its shores.

RIDE TO CONEY ISLAND, and clam-bake there. Never was there a time better fitted than yesterday, for an excursion from city to country, or from pavement to the sea-shore! The rain of the previous evening had cooled the air, and moistened the earth; there was no dust, and no unpleasant heat. It may well be imagined, then, that a jolly party of about sixty people, who, at 1 o'clock, p.m., met at the house of Mr. King, on the corner of Fulton and Orange streets, (where they laid a good *foundation* for after pleasures,) had every reason to bless their stars at the treat surely before them. Yes: there was to be a clam-bake—and, of all places in the world, a clam-bake at Coney-Island! Could moral ambition go higher, or mortal wishes delve deeper? . . . At a little before 2, the most superb stages, four of them, from Husted & Kendall's establishment, were just nicely filled, (no crowding, and no vacant places, either,) and the teams of four and six horses dashed off with us all at a merry rate.— The ride was a most inspiriting one. After crossing the railroad track, the signs of country life, the green fields, the thrifty corn, the orchards, the wheat lying in swathes, and the hay-cocks here and there, with the farming-men at work all along, made such a spectacle as we dearly like to look upon. And then the clatter of human tongues, inside the carriages—the peals upon peals of laughter! the jovial witticisms, the anecdotes, stories, and so forth!— Why there were enough to fill ten octavo volumes! The members of the party were numerous and various—embracing all the professions, and nearly all the trades, besides sundry aldermen, and other officials.

Arrived at Coney Island, the first thing was to "take a dance," at which sundry distinguished personages shook care out of their heads and dust from their heels, at a great rate. Then a bathe in the salt water; ah, that was good indeed! Divers marvellous feats were performed in the water, in the way of splashing, ducking and sousing, and one gentleman had serious thoughts of a sortie out upon some porpoises who were lazily rolling a short distance off. The beautiful, pure, sparkling, sea-water! one yearns for you (at least we do,) with an affection as grasping as your own waves!

Half-past five o'clock had now arrived, and the booming of the dinner bell produced a sensible effect upon 'the party,' who ranged themselves at table without the necessity of a second invitation. As the expectation had been only for a 'clam-bake' there was some surprise evinced at seeing a regularly laid dinner, in handsome style, too, with all the et-ceteras. But as an adjunct—by some, made the principal thing—in due time, on came the roasted clams, well-roasted indeed! in the old Indian style, in beds, covered with brush and chips, and thus cooked in their own broth. When hunger was appeased with these savory and wholesome viands, the champagne, (good stuff it was!) began to circulate—and divers gentlemen made speeches, introductory to, and responsive at, toasts. A great many happy hits were made, and, in especial, one of the aldermen, at the head of one of the tables, conceived a remarkable toast, at which the people seemed tickled hugely. The healths of Messrs. Masterton, Smith, and King, of Mr. Murphy, and of the corporation of Brooklyn, etc., were drank [*sic*]. Nor were the artisans and workingmen forgotten; nor were the ladies, nor the Brooklyn press, which the member of congress from this district spoke in the most handsome manner of, and turned off a very neat toast upon.

The return to Brooklyn, in the evening, was a fit conclusion to a day of enjoyment. The cool air, the smell of the new mown hay, the general quiet around, (there was any thing but quiet, however, inside our vehicles,) made it pleasant indeed. We ascended to the tower-like seat, by Mr. Carnfield, the driver of the six-horse stage, and had one of the pleasantest sort of eight-mile rides back to Brooklyn, at which place our party arrived a little after 9 o'clock. All thanks, and long and happy lives, to the contractors on the new city hall! to whose generous spirit we were indebted for yesterday's pleasure.

CONEY ISLAND

Charles Dawson Shanly

Charles Dawson Shanly (1811–1875) was born in Ireland and earned a bachelor's degree at Trinity College, Dublin. He emigrated with his family to Canada in 1836 and then moved to New York in 1857 to pursue a full-time career as a writer and journalist. He wrote for various publications and was one of the founders and editors of *Vanity Fair*. His article "Coney Island," published in the *Atlantic Monthly* in September 1874, describes Coney at an early stage of its development as a resort. Shanly emphasizes that because Coney had, in recent years, become more accessible by steamboat and horsecar, it was less exclusive than it had been, "since its advantages are attainable by all." Fashionable families of New York would be shocked, Shanly contends, if they were asked whether they intended to go to Coney Island for the season, although occasionally a "heavy swell" visits with his friends "by way of a lark."

THE FACT THAT IT [CONEY ISLAND] is within one hour's journey from New York by steamboat, and but little more than that by the horse-cars from Brooklyn, renders Coney Island unfashionable, since its advantages are attainable by all. Twelve years ago the facilities for reaching it were fewer than at present, as were the accommodations on the beach, and it is only within seven or eight years past that it has assumed the appearance of a great bathing-place now presented by it. Stretching out into the sea at the southwestern end of Long Island, this desolate strip of barren sand-hills and shingly beach offers no attraction beyond that of the surging of the great Atlantic upon its shore. It is separated from Long Island only by a narrow, marshy creek, thus being so indistinctly an island that, whether approaching it by land or by water, a stranger visiting it would hardly take it to be one. The origin of its name appears to be a matter of surmise rather than of tradition or record. Some guess that it is called Coney Island on account of the rabbits by which its sparse patches of brushwood are inhabited; but this can hardly be accepted as the origin of the name, seeing that the only rabbits to be found upon the island, which are of the domesticated kind, were introduced long after it was known to mariners and explorers by the name. A better reason is afforded by the topographical features of the island itself, which, a low delta about a mile and a half a mile wide, and without shelter of any kind, has been blown by the winds into a series of truncated cones of fine sand. Thus the word "coney," allowable as an adjective, fitly characterizes the appearance of the place. [...]

During the three summer months vast numbers of people are daily to be seen bathing all along the stretches of this beach. Out from the bathing-houses come tumbling, indiscriminately, men, women, and children, all of them disguised beyond any possibility of recognition in their "wild attire." The scene enables one to realize the notion of a lunatic asylum let loose, its inmates chasing each other with mad gesticulations about the shore and into the lapping surf. The women flap about in the water and scream like the fowls to which that element is natural; and some of them are strong swimmers, too, striking out boldly to a good distance from the beach. Numbers of the men lie wallowing for hours in the sand, in which they roll like wild beasts, rubbing it madly into their hair, and plastering themselves all over with it. Some of the bathers wear fancy dresses which they have brought with them. Here comes one in a striped black and white shirt with scanty drawers to match, and he is immediately hailed as a "zebray" by one of the grovelers in the sand. The word spreads from mouth to mouth along the shore, until the striped gentleman is fain to seek an asylum beneath the friendly waves. The scene upon the beach and in the water alike is a very rough one, having nothing about it of the reserve that regulates manners at the more aristocratic summer resorts. [...]

Until after darkness has well set in, there is some show of life along the beach, but only towards the head of the island, in the hotels clustered at which many persons take up their residence for a part of the summer. The evening is the favorite time for bathing at this point, but, lower down, the beach is very quiet and deserted, as the last boat has taken its departure for the city long since, carrying away the last installment of the boisterous throng of bathers and wallowers in the sand, by whom the beach had been made lively throughout the afternoon. Desolation broods awfully dark and still over Coney Island at night, when all the lodgers in the beach houses have retired to rest after the fatigues of the day. It is then that the city man realizes the utter emptiness of life without gas and other modern conveniences. [...]

It will be seen from this brief account of a peculiar place, that Coney Island is more conspicuous for a rough side than for a smooth one. Its natural advantages as a sea-bathing place for New York city are numerous, but they are counterbalanced by many circumstances at present inseparable from it. Few things could be more shocking to the sensibilities of a fashionable New York family than to inquire whether they intended going to Coney Island for the season. Occasionally, indeed, a "heavy swell" of the fashionable avenue will take a turn down there with his team, "by way of a lark," but he does this in the confidence that he is not likely to be brought face to face with any of his set, and his account of things when he returns to the city includes nothing of Coney Island with its vulgar associations and motley crowd.

TO CONEY ISLAND

William Henry Bishop

William Henry Bishop (1847–1928) was born in Hartford, Connecticut, and educated at Yale University. He held various positions—including critic, editor, and teacher—before serving as an American consul in Italy. He also found time for writing throughout most of his life and was the author of novels, short stories, and articles. Although the essay "To Coney Island," published in *Scribner's* in July 1880, does not list an author, it is attributed to Bishop. The author mentions the four "subdivisions" into which Coney was divided at the time—Manhattan Beach, Brighton Beach, West Brighton, and Norton's—explaining that "there is something of a descending scale of fashion in them, in the order named." Coney Island, he remarks, "is a Centennial of pleasure, pure and simple," whose "essential character is bound up with the crowd." He concludes by proclaiming that Americans should take patriotic pride in contemplating Coney: "It is quite original, distinctly American, and charming."

WE EMERGE FROM THE TRAIN in a station forming part of the hotel itself. A Coney Island hotel of consequence has its railway station, and two or three special lines of land and water transportation, as another might have elevators or steam-heating. We pass through a wide corridor, wainscoted and ceiled up (as are all the interiors that meet the eye in the neighborhood) with cheerful, varnished pine, and out upon the enormous piazza. A multitude of people are dining at little tables on it, set with linen, glass and silver, and others are moving up and down in close procession. [. . .]

Turn and look back at the hotel. It is of wood, as the American hotel in the open country will probably be while our forests hold out, and is painted a pleasant shade of ocher, with "trimmings." It bristles with towers, turrets, dormers, "offsets,"—irregularities of every kind. As a dwelling, and this is true of those of the island generally, it is as uneasy as the crowds trooping through it, or the surf in front; something more restful here and there, some moderate space of untroubled surface, would be a relief from the universal movement. It is nearly an eighth of a mile in length, and its vast piazzas, running the entire length of the building, are rather to be regarded as great open pavilions. The fantastic island is not a spectacle to be reduced to tape-line and level, and I shall not do the guide-books the injury of vying with them in statistics, but here in a lump are a few of the most considerable. There are some sixty hotels, and five thousand separate bathing-rooms. The great tubular iron pier runs out a thousand feet into the sea, the tubular iron observatory three hundred feet into the air, and the captive balloon a thousand feet, carrying up fifteen persons at a time. The Brighton Beach hotel, the second in size, is five hundred and twenty feet long, and seats two thousand persons at dinner. The Manhattan Beach bathing-pavilion is five hundred feet long, has twenty-seven hundred separate rooms, and a capacity of sending away two thousand wet bathing-costumes an hour along an endless belt, to be washed in the laundry. The figures, in fact, however detailed, are quite idle. The coming season, if the rumors of the piazzas be true, our acquaintance must be formed all over again, and our wonder excited anew. The size of the two principal hotels is to be doubled, the pavilion at the eastern end is to be erected into a great new hotel, and still another of the first magnitude is to be built on the long vacant stretch between. As it is, the face of things is altered at each successive visit. [. . .]

Along the beach establishments of many sorts and a regiment of charlatans detain you, one after another. The *Hotel de Clam* sets forth its tempting bill of fare; the minor bathing establishments vie with one another in advertisements of the newness of their bathing-suits; children ride on donkeys; the pail-and-shovel tree springs numerously from the sand; the tin-type man is driven to distraction with business; the Punch-and-Judy shows give Americanized exhibitions, of which the ethnologist should take note, with negroes and so on in the companies; and I buy, for a dime, of two glass demons, worked by hydraulic pressure, called by the merry German-American, their proprietor, Solomon and Columbia, an envelope containing my fortune and a picture of the girl I shall marry. Pray heaven the decree of fate be not immutable, upon this showing! [. . .]

Coney Island is curiously like the Centennial; that is the only description that does it justice. It is a Centennial of pleasure, pure and simple, without any tiresome ulterior commercial purposes, held amid refreshing breezes, by the sea. There is the same gay architecture, the same waving flags, the same delightful, distracting whirl, the same enormous masses of staring, good-natured, perpetually marching and counter-marching human beings. Its essential character is bound up with the crowd. Its virtues are those of a crowd, and so are its faults. Waiters and landlords in such circumstances are apt, like some philanthropists, to lose their interest in the individual in their devotion to the race. There are numerous minor failings which are no doubt to be looked after as things settle quietly into place. [. . .]

A touch of patriotic pride really ought to mingle with our contemplation of Coney Island. It is quite original, distinctively American, and charming. There is nothing like it abroad, and its proximity and extraordinary ease of access seem to insure it against rivalry at home. Trouville is six hours by express from Paris; and Brighton and Margate and Ramsgate (all of which it is the habit to mention as in the season mere suburbs of their parent city) are fifty or sixty miles from London. Even were they nearer, and had they white sand and blue ocean for shingle beach and muddy Channel waves, there are not, in either metropolis, the fierce heats of a New York summer to drive the populace forth to seek their refreshment in anything like an equal degree. It is difficult to see why the strange new island which has all at once taken so considerable a place in the chart, should not permanently remain what it seems now to be—the greatest resort for a single day's pleasure in the world.

"HEALTH AND PLEASURE BY THE SEA," CONEY ISLAND, 1885. (STEREOGRAPH PUBLISHED BY KIL-BURN BROTHERS, LITTLETON, N.H. LIBRARY OF CONGRESS, PRINTS AND PHOTOGRAPHS DIVISION)

CONEY ISLAND

José Martí

Translated by Esther Allen

....

Cuban-born poet, essayist, and political activist José Martí (1853–1895) is one of the best-known figures in Latin American literature and politics. His political activities on behalf of Cuban independence led to his imprisonment, exile, and eventual death. From 1881 to 1895, while spending much of his time in New York City, he compiled a large collection of essays. These writings skillfully combine journalism, fiction, and poetic language. In "Coney Island," published in the newspaper *La Pluma* (Bogotá, Colombia) on December 3, 1881, and later included in *Letters from New York* (1883), Martí captures the beauty, the excesses, the splendor, the size, the energy, and the fears (what he felt was America's imperialistic tendencies) that Coney, and the new American empire—with the enormous wealth and resources that it personified—represented to many people. His depictions of the freak show and the train transporting people portray "the United States as monstrous other" (Susan Antebi, *Carnal Inscriptions: Spanish American Narratives of Corporeal Difference and Disability* [New York: Palgrave-Macmillan, 2009], 35). Still, Coney Island was a place where the masses of Americans went to find a temporary, if artificial, escape from their ordinary lives.

FROM THE FARTHEST REACHES of the American Union, legions of intrepid ladies and gallant rustics arrive to admire the splendid landscapes, the unrivaled wealth, the bedazzling variety, the Herculean effort, the astonishing sight of the now world-famous Coney Island. Four years ago it was a barren heap of dirt, but today it is a spacious place of relaxation, shelter, and amusement for the hundred thousand or so New Yorkers who repair to its glad beaches each day.

There are four little towns, joined by carriage roads, tramways, and stream trains. One of them—which has a hotel with a dining room that can comfortably seat four thousand—is called Manhattan Beach. Another, which has sprung up like Minerva with her helmet and spear, armed with ferries, plazas, boardwalks, softly crooning orchestras, and hotels that are not like towns but like nations, is called Rockaway; another, the smallest of them, which takes its name from a hotel of extraordinary capacity and ponderous construction, is called Brighton. But the main attraction of the island is not far-off Rockaway or monotonous Brighton or grave and aristocratic Manhattan Beach: it is Gable [West Brighton], laughing Gable, with its elevator that goes higher than the spire of Trinity Church in New York—twice as high as the spire of our cathedral—and allows travelers to rise to the dizzying heights of its summit, suspended in a tiny, fragile cage. Gable, with its two iron piers that advance on elegant pillars for three blocks out over the sea, and its Sea Beach Palace, which is only a hotel now but was the famous Agricultural Building at the Philadelphia Centennial Exposition, transported to New York as if by magic and rebuilt in its original form down to the last shingle on the coast of Coney Island. Gable, with its fifty-cent museums exhibiting human freaks, preposterous fish, bearded ladies, melancholy dwarves, and stunted elephants grandiloquently advertised as the largest on earth; Gable, with its hundred orchestras, its mirthful dances, its battalions of baby carriages, its gigantic cow, perpetually milked and perpetually giving milk, its twenty-five-cent glasses of fresh cider, its innumerable pairs of amorous wanderers who bring the tender lines of [Antonio] García Gutiérrez to the lips:

> Two by two they go
> over the hills
> the crested larks
> and the turtledoves.

Gable, where families gather to seek respite from the rank, unwholesome New York air in the healthy and invigorating seaside breeze; where impoverished mothers—as they empty the enormous box containing the family's lunch onto one of the tables provided without cost in vast pavilions—clasp to their hearts their unlucky little ones, who appear to have been gnawed, devoured, consumed by infantile cholera, the terrible disease that cuts children down as the scythe cuts wheat.

Ferries come and go; trains blow their whistles, belch smoke, depart, and arrive, their serpentine bosoms swollen with families they disgorge onto the beach. The women rent blue flannel bathing costumes and rough straw hats that they tie under their chins; the men, in less complicated garments, hold the women's hands and go into the sea, while barefoot children wait along the shore for the roaring wave to drench them, and flee as it reaches them, hiding their terror behind gales of laughter, then return in bands—the better to defy the enemy—to this game of which these innocents, prostrate an hour earlier from the terrible heat, never tire. Like marine butterflies, they flit in and out of the cool surf. Each one has his little pail and shovel, and they play at filling their pails with the beach's burning sand—in imitation of more serious persons of both sexes, who are indifferent to the reproachful astonishment of those who think as we do in our lands—and let themselves be covered, pounded, kneaded, and buried beneath the blazing hot sand, for this is considered a healthy exercise and provides, as well, an unparalleled occasion for that superficial, vulgar, and boisterous intimacy of which these prosperous folk seem so fond.

But the amazing thing here is not this manner of having a sea-bath, or the cadaverous faces of the little children, or the capricious headgear and incomprehensible garments of the demoiselles, who are notable for their prodigality, their outlandish behavior, and their exaggerated gaiety; nor is it the colloquies of lovers, or the bathhouses, or the operas sung over café tables by waiters dressed as Edgar and Romeo, Lucía and Juliet, or the grins and shrieks of the black minstrels who cannot, alas, much resemble the minstrels of Scotland, or the majestic beach, or the serene, gentle sunlight. The amazing thing here is the size, the quantity, this sudden result of human activity, this immense valve of pleasure opened to an immense people, these dining rooms that, seen from afar, look like the encampments of armies, these roads that from two miles away are not roads at all but long carpets of heads, the daily surge of a prodigious people onto a prodigious beach, this mobility, this faculty for progress, this enterprise, this altered form, this fevered rivalry in wealth, the monumentality of the whole, which makes this seaside resort comparable in majesty to the earth that bears it, the sea that caresses it, and the sky that crowns it, this rising tide, this overwhelming and invincible, constant and frenetic drive to expand, and the taking for granted of these very wonders—that is the amazing thing here.

Other peoples—ourselves among them—live in prey to a sublime inner demon that drives us to relentless pursuit of an ideal of love or glory. And when, with the joy of grasping an eagle, we seize the degree of ideal we were pursuing, a new zeal inflames us, a new ambition spurs us on, a new aspiration catapults us into a new and vehement longing, and from the captured eagle goes a free, rebellious butterfly, as if defying us to follow it and chaining us to its restless flight.

Not so these tranquil spirits, disturbed only by their eagerness to possess wealth. The eyes travel across these reverberating beaches; the traveler goes in and out of these dining rooms, vast as the pampas, and climbs to the tops of these colossal buildings, high as mountains; seated in a comfortable chair by the sea, the passerby fills his lungs with that powerful and salubrious air, and yet it is well known that a sad melancholy steals over the men of our Hispanoamerican peoples who live here. They seek each other in vain, and however much the first impressions may have gratified their senses, enamored their eyes, and dazzled and befuddled their minds, the anguish of solitude possesses them in the end. Nostalgia for a superior spiritual world invades and afflicts them; they feel like lambs with no mother or shepherd, lost from the flock, and though their eyes may be dry, the frightened spirit breaks into a torrent of the bitterest tears because this great land is devoid of spirit.

But what comings and goings! What spendings of money! What opportunities for every pleasure! What absolute absence of any visible sadness or poverty! Everything is out in the open: the noisy groups, the vast dining rooms, the peculiar courtship of the North Americans—almost wholly devoid of the elements that comprise the bashful, tender, and elevated courtship of our lands—the theater, the photographer, the bathhouse—all of it out in the open. Some weigh themselves, because for the North Americans it is a matter of positive joy or real grief to weigh a pound more or less; others, for fifty cents, receive from the hands of a robust German girl an envelope containing their fortune; others, with incomprehensible delight, drink unpalatable mineral waters from glasses as long and narrow as artillery shells.

Some ride in spacious carriages that take them at twilight's tender hour from Manhattan to Brighton; one man, who has been out rowing with a laughing lady friend, beaches his boat, and she, resting a determined hand on his shoulder, leaps, happy as a little girl, onto the lively beach. A group watches in open-mouthed admiration as an artist cuts from black paper, which he then pastes onto white cardboard, the silhouette of anyone who wants to have so singular a portrait of himself made; another group celebrates the skill of a lady who, in a little stall no more than three-quarters of a yard wide, creates curious flowers out of fish skins. With great bursts of laughter others applaud the skill of someone who has succeeded in bouncing a ball off the nose of an unfortunate man of color, who, in exchange for a paltry day's wage, stands day and night with his head poking out through a piece of cloth, dodging the pitches with ridiculous movements and extravagant grimaces. Others, even some who are bearded and venerable, sit gravely atop a wooden tiger, a hippogriff, a boa constrictor, all ranged in a circle like horses, which revolve for a few minutes around a central mast while a handful of self-styled musicians play off-key sonatas. Those with less money eat crabs and oysters on the beach, or cakes and meats at the free tables some of the large hotels provide for such meals; those with money throw away enormous sums on the purplish infusions that pass for wine, and on strange, leaden dishes that our palates, preferring lighter and more artistic fare, would surely reject.

These people eat quantity; we, class.

And this squandering, this uproar, these crowds, this astonishing swarm of people, lasts from June to October, from morning until late night, without pause, without any change whatsoever.

And by night, such beauty! It is true that a thinking man is startled to see so many married women without their husbands, so many mothers who stroll along the damp seashore, their little ones on their shoulders, concerned only with their own pleasure and never fearing that the biting air will harm the child's natural delicacy, so many ladies who abandon their babies in hotel rooms to the arms of some harsh Irishwoman and who, on returning from their long walks, do not take their children in their arms, or kiss their lips, or sate their hunger.

But no city in the world offers a more splendid panorama than that of the beach of Gable by night. Were there heads by day? Well, by night there are even more lights. Seen from the water, the four towns are radiant against the darkness; it looks as if the stars that populate the sky had gathered together in four colossal clusters and fallen suddenly to the sea.

With its magical, caressing clarity, electric light floods the hotels' little plazas, the English gardens, the bandstands, and even the beach itself, where in its bright glow every grain of sand can be counted. From afar, the electric lights look like blithely superior spirits, laughing and diabolical, cavorting among the sickly gaslights, and the rows of red streetlights, Chinese lanterns, and Venetian lamps. Everywhere, newspapers, programs, advertisements, and letters are being read as if it were broad daylight. It is a town of stars—and of orchestras, dances, chatter, surf sounds, human sounds, choruses of laughter and praise for the air, hawkers' loud cries, swift trains and speedy carriages, until it is time to go home. Then, like a monster emptying out its entrails into the ravenous jaws of another monster, this immense crush of humanity squeezes onto trains that seem to groan under its weight in their packed trajectory across the barren stretches to cede their turbulent cargo to gigantic ferries, enlivened by the sound of harps and violins, which carry the weary day-trippers back to the piers and pour them out into the thousand trams and thousand tracks that crisscross the slumbering city of New York like iron veins.

"SHADOWS ON BEACH": AFRICAN-AMERICAN BATHERS ARE REFLECTED IN THE WET SAND AT
CONEY ISLAND, 1896. (STEREOGRAPH PUBLISHED BY ALFRED S. CAMPBELL, ELIZABETH, N.J.
LIBRARY OF CONGRESS, PRINTS AND PHOTOGRAPHS DIVISION)

CONEY ISLAND'S FAILING DAYS

Stephen Crane

....

Stephen Crane (1871–1900) was born in Newark, New Jersey. He is the author of such literary classics as *Maggie: A Girl of the Streets* (1893) and *The Red Badge of Courage* (1895). Crane was a journalist and poet as well as a fiction writer. He wrote many literary sketches, including "Coney Island's Failing Days," in which he reported on scenes that he had observed. This sketch, published in the *New York Press* on October 14, 1894 (and reprinted in *Prose and Poetry* [1984]), reflects the melancholy of Coney as it approaches its off-season. The narrator, probably Crane, is speaking to a stranger who feels "sad" about "the mammoth empty buildings" that contrast with the optimism of those who built them. The stranger's disappointment is linked to his own disillusionment over the failure of his "youthful dreams," of which Coney, in its "failing days," is a symbol.

["]DOWN HERE AT YOUR CONEY ISLAND, toward the end of the season, I am made to feel very sad," said the stranger to me. "The great mournfulness that settles upon a summer resort at this time always depresses me exceedingly. The mammoth empty buildings, planned by extraordinarily optimistic architects, remind me in an unpleasant manner of my youthful dreams. In those days of visions I erected huge castles for the reception of my friends and admirers, and discovered later that I could have entertained them more comfortably in a small two story frame structure. There is a mighty pathos in these gaunt and hollow buildings, impassively and stolidly suffering from an enormous hunger for the public. And the unchangeable, ever imperturbable sea pursues its quaint devices blithely at the feet of these mournful wooden animals, gabbling and frolicking, with no thought for absent man nor maid!"

As the stranger spoke, he gazed with considerable scorn at the emotions of the sea; and the breeze from the far Navesink hills gently stirred the tangled, philosophic hair upon his forehead. Presently he went on: "The buildings are in effect more sad than the men, but I assure you that some of the men look very sad. I watched a talented and persuasive individual who was operating in front of a tintype gallery, and he had only the most marvelously infrequent opportunities to display his oratory and finesse. The occasional stragglers always managed to free themselves before he could drag them into the gallery and take their pictures. In the long intervals he gazed about him with a bewildered air, as if he felt his world dropping from under his feet. Once I saw him spy a promising youth afar off. He lurked with muscles at a tension, and then at the proper moment he swooped. 'Look-a-here,' he said, with tears of enthusiasm in his eyes, 'the best picture in the world! An' on'y four fer a quarter. On'y jest try it, an' you'll go away perfectly satisfied!'

"'I'll go away perfectly satisfied without trying it,' replied the promising youth, and he did. The tintype man wanted to dash his samples to the ground and whip the promising youth. He controlled himself, however, and went to watch the approach of two women and a little boy who were nothing more than three dots, away down the board walk.

"At one place I heard the voice of a popcorn man raised in a dreadful note, as if he were chanting a death hymn. It made me shiver as I felt all the tragedy of the collapsed popcorn market. I began to see that it was an insult to the pain and suffering of these men to go near to them without buying anything. I took new and devious routes sometimes.

"As for the railroad guards and station men, they were so tolerant of the presence of passengers that I felt it to be an indication of their sense of relief from the summer's battle. They did not seem so greatly irritated by patrons of the railroad as I have seen them at other times. And in all the beer gardens the waiters had opportunity to indulge that delight in each other's society and conversation which forms so important a part in a waiter's idea of happiness. Sometimes the people in a sparsely occupied place will fare more strange than those in a crowded one. At one time I waited twenty minutes for a bottle of the worst beer in Christendom while my waiter told a charmingly naive story to a group of his compatriots. I protested sotto voce at the time that such beer might at least have the merit of being brought quickly.

"The restaurants, however, I think to be quite delicious, being in a large part thoroughly disreputable and always provided with huge piles of red boiled crabs. These huge piles of provision around on the floor and on the oyster counters always give me the opinion that I am dining on the freshest food in the world, and I appreciate the sensation. If need be, it also allows a man to revel in dreams of unlimited quantity.

"I found countless restaurants where I could get things almost to my taste, and, as I ate, watch the grand, eternal motion of the sea and have the waiter come up and put the pepper castor on the menu card to keep the salt breeze from interfering with my order for dinner.

"And yet I have an occasional objection to the sea when dining in sight of it; for a man with a really artistic dining sense always feels important as a duke when he is indulging in his favorite pastime, and, as the sea always makes me feel that I am a trivial object, I cannot dine with absolute comfort in its presence. The conflict of the two perceptions disturbs me. This is why I have grown to prefer the restaurants down among the narrow board streets. I tell you this because I think an explanation is due to you."

As we walked away from the beach and around one of those huge buildings whose pathos had so aroused the stranger's interest, we came into view of two acres of merry-go-rounds, circular swings, roller coasters, observation wheels and the like. The stranger paused and regarded them.

"Do you know," he said, "I am deeply fascinated by all these toys. For, of course, you perceive that they are really enlarged toys. They reinforce me in my old opinion that humanity only needs to be provided for ten minutes with a few whirligigs and things of the sort, and it can forget at least four centuries of misery. I rejoice in these whirligigs," continued the stranger, eloquently, "and as I watch here and there a person going around and around or up and down, or over and over, I say to myself that whirligigs must be made in heaven.

"It is a mystery to me why some man does not provide a large number of wooden rocking horses and let the people sit and dreamfully rock themselves into temporary forgetfulness. There could be intense quiet enforced by special policemen, who, however, should allow subdued conversation on the part of the patrons of the establishment. Deaf mutes should patrol to and fro selling slumberous drinks. These things are none of them insane. They are particularly rational. A man needs a little nerve quiver, and he gets it by being flopped around in the air like a tailless kite. He needs the introduction of a reposeful element, and he procures it upon a swing that makes him feel like thirty-five emotional actresses all trying to swoon upon one rug. There are some people who stand apart and deride these machines. If you could procure a dark night for them and the total absence of their friends they would smile, many of them. I assure you that I myself would indulge in these forms of intoxication if I were not a very great philosopher."

We strolled to the music hall district, where the sky lines of the rows of buildings are wondrously near to each other, and the crowded little thoroughfares resemble the eternal "Street Scene in Cairo." There was an endless strumming and tooting and shrill piping in clamor and chaos, while at all times there were interspersed the sharp cracking sounds from the shooting galleries and the coaxing calls of innumerable fakirs. At the stand where one can throw at wooden cats and negro heads and be in danger of winning cigars, a self reliant youth bought a whole armful of base balls, and missed with each one. Everybody grinned. A heavily built man openly jeered. "You couldn't hit a church!" "Couldn't I?" retorted the young man, bitterly. Near them three bad men were engaged in an intense conversation. The fragment of a sentence suddenly dominated the noises. "He's got money to burn." The sun, meanwhile, was muffled in the clouds back of Staten Island and the Narrows. Softened tones of sapphire and carmine touched slantingly the sides of the buildings. A view of the sea, to be caught between two of the houses, showed it to be of a pale, shimmering green. The lamps began to be lighted, and shed a strong orange radiance. In one restaurant the only occupants were a little music hall singer and a youth. She was laughing and chatting in a light hearted way not peculiar to music hall girls. The youth looked as if he desired to be at some other place. He was singularly wretched and uncomfortable. The stranger said he judged from appearances that the little music hall girl must think a great deal of that one youth. His sympathies seemed to be for the music hall girl. Finally there was a sea of salt meadow, with a black train shooting across it.

"I have made a discovery in one of these concert halls," said the stranger, as we retraced our way. "It is an old gray haired woman, who occupies proudly the position of chief pianiste. I like to go and sit and wonder by what mighty process of fighting and drinking she achieved her position. To see her, you would think she was leading an orchestra of seventy pieces, although she alone composes it. It is great reflection to watch that gray head. At those moments I am willing to concede that I must be relatively happy, and that is a great admission from a philosopher of my attainments.

"How seriously all these men out in front of the dens take their vocations. They regard people with a voracious air, as if they contemplated any moment making a rush and a grab and mercilessly compelling a great expenditure. This scant and feeble crowd must madden them. When I first came to this part of the town I was astonished and delighted, for it was the nearest approach to a den of wolves that I had encountered since leaving the West. Oh, no, of course the Coney Island of to-day is not the Coney Island of the ancient days. I believe you were about to impale me upon that sentence, were you not?"

We walked along for some time in silence until the stranger went to buy a frankfurter. As he returned, he said: "When a man is respectable he is fettered to certain wheels, and when the chariot of fashion moves, he is dragged along at the rear. For his agony, he can console himself with the law that if a certain thing has not yet been respectable, he need only wait a sufficient time and it will eventually be so. The only disadvantage is that he is obliged to wait until other people wish to do it, and he is likely to lose his own craving. Now I have a great passion for eating frankfurters on the street, and if I were respectable I would be obliged to wait until the year 3365, when men will be able to hold their positions in society only by consuming immense quantities of frankfurters on the street. And by that time I would have undoubtedly developed some new pastime. But I am not respectable. I am a philosopher. I eat frankfurters on the street with the same equanimity that you might employ toward a cigarette.

"See those three young men enjoying themselves. With what rakish, daredevil airs they smoke those cigars. Do you know, the spectacle of three modern young men enjoying themselves is something that I find vastly interesting and instructive. I see revealed more clearly the purposes of the inexorable universe which plans to amuse us occasionally to keep us from the rebellion of suicide. And I see how simply and drolly it accomplishes its end. The insertion of a mild quantity of the egotism of sin into the minds of these young men causes them to wildly enjoy themselves. It is necessary to encourage them, you see, at this early day. After all, it is only great philosophers who have the wisdom to be utterly miserable."

As we walked toward the station the stranger stopped often to observe types which interested him. He did it with an unconscious calm insolence as if the people were bugs. Once a bug threatened to beat him. "What 'cher lookin' at?" he asked of him. "My friend," said the stranger, "if any one displays real interest in you in this world, you should take it as an occasion for serious study and reflection. You should be supremely amazed to find that a man can be interested in anybody but himself!" The belligerent seemed quite abashed. He explained to a friend: "He ain't right! What? I dunno. Something 'bout 'study' er something! He's got wheels in his head!"

On the train the cold night wind blew transversely across the reeling cars, and in the dim light of the lamps one could see the close rows of heads swaying and jolting with the motion. From directly in front of us peanut shells fell to the floor amid a regular and interminable crackling. A stout man, who slept with his head forward upon his breast, crunched them often beneath his uneasy feet. From some unknown place a drunken voice was raised in song.

"This return of the people to their battles always has a stupendous effect upon me," said the stranger. "The gayety which arises upon these Sunday night occasions is different from all other gayeties. There is an unspeakable air of recklessness and bravado and grief about it. This train load is going toward that inevitable, overhanging, devastating Monday. That singer there to-morrow will be a truckman, perhaps, and swearing ingeniously at his horses and other truckmen. He feels the approach of this implacable Monday. Two hours ago he was engulfed in whirligigs and beer and had forgotten that there were Mondays. Now he is confronting it, and as he can't battle it, he scorns it. You can hear the undercurrent of it in that song, which is really as grievous as the cry of a child. If he had no vanity—well, it is fortunate for the world that we are not all great thinkers."

We sat on the lower deck of the Bay Ridge boat and watched the marvelous lights of New York looming through the purple mist. The little Italian band situated up one stairway, through two doors and around three corners from us, sounded in beautiful, faint and slumberous rhythm. The breeze fluttered again in the stranger's locks. We could hear the splash of the waves against the bow. The sleepy lights looked at us with hue [*sic*] of red and green and orange. Overhead some dust colored clouds scudded across the deep indigo sky. "Thunderation," said the stranger, "if I did not know of so many yesterdays and have such full knowledge of to-morrows, I should be perfectly happy at this moment, and that would create a sensation among philosophers all over the world."

CONEY ISLAND

Julian Ralph

Journalist and author Julian Ralph (1853–1903) was born in New York City and is best known for his work as a reporter for the *New York Sun* from 1875 to 1895. In 1893, Ralph covered the trial of the infamous Lizzie Borden, writing a series of articles that provided a compassionate portrayal of the defendant as an isolated and dispossessed woman. In "Coney Island," published in *Scribner's* in July 1896, he compares Coney Island to a great comedian who cheers and lightens the hearts of many. Ralph emphasizes that Coney is different from "the great watering-places" of Europe because it is not primarily a place where visitors come from afar to spend days or weeks at a time, but is "purely and wholly an excursion resort." Coney attracts the great majority of its customers from New York City, and most visit just for the day. Ralph considers it a blessing that people can travel to Coney "in an hour at the cost of a quarter of a dollar" and return "home at a reasonable time."

NOW AND THEN, upon the death of a great comedian, we are reminded of the thousands of lives he has cheered and hearts he has lightened. Suppose, when Coney Island was absorbed by the city of Brooklyn, a year or two ago, that its future as a pleasure resort had been threatened. What sermons the chroniclers of the press and of history might have preached upon the good it had wrought—not to mere thousands, and not in the simple, unplanned ways in which other resorts have scattered their benefits, but in unique ways, by means better and more varied than the masses knew of or enjoyed anywhere else on the continent. For Coney Island was not only the pioneer with modern improvements for giving the crowds a good time: it still remains *sui generis*, enthroned, the king of all the popular resorts of America.

The drama which it daily provides for the delight of its patrons, is declared to freshen the souls of so many millions annually that in order to comprehend the bulk of the multitude we must fancy gathered together all the inhabitants of London, all the people of New York, every soul in Chicago, and every man, woman, and child in Brooklyn. And even then, we would be assuming that the largest boasts of those cities were truths, for one year's crowd on Coney Island was composed of eight million souls!

No painter has perpetuated its bewildering scenes, and no poet has sought to immortalize its wonders. It is doubtful whether the foreign world—the "other barbarians" as the Chinese call the others—has heard of the place; certainly the Atlantic Garden, in the Bowery, is tenfold farther and better known. And yet eight millions of fares were paid by travellers to it in a year—by travellers who journeyed only the time that a cigar lasts. It no more wants or depends upon better fame than grass needs painting, or fresh air needs a rhymer. It is New York's resort almost exclusively; our homoeopathic sanitarium, our sun-bath and ice-box combined, our extra lung, our private, gigantic fan. All our cities, except Chicago, have such places, and we are content that they should. Boston may keep little Nantasket; Philadelphia may continue to reach across New Jersey for her beaches; New Orleans is welcome to all of Lake Pontchartrain, and San Francisco may monopolize her opera-glass spectacle of the Seal Rocks, if she pleases. We do not want their resorts or need their patronage. In this we are as narrow and provincial as every stranger delights in saying that New Yorkers are in all things. Certainly, New York and Coney Island are sufficient to each other—whether they are sufficient in themselves or not. [...]

This glance at Coney Island shows us that while it has some of the main features of the great watering-places of Europe, it is yet different from all of them in being purely and wholly an excursion resort. It is true that the Oriental Hotel at Manhattan Beach is the summer home of hundreds, but the secret of that hotel's success and the charm of it is, that it is not at Coney Island at all, nor even at Manhattan Beach, as its proprietors say, but is, of and by itself, cut off from all the neighborhood, with its own beach and, I was going to say, its own ocean. Its tenants see the tip-ends of the fireworks and they hear the tooting of the railway locomotives, but these things are to them, like seeing Saturn and hearing the distant guns of a man-of-war in New York Harbor. What is peculiar to Coney Island is that no one lives there. It embraces practically no cottage settlement—none at all, except a few homes of those who are in business there—and from one point of view, all its tenements, halls, hotels, and houses are temporary, like its delights, all being wooden, however costly some may be. Other resorts offer change and rest, but Coney Island offers only change. A reporter having to announce the formal opening of one of the beaches there, put the case of Coney Island in a verbal nutshell in this brief sentence, one day: "Manhattan Beach has opened, and now New Yorkers have a place by the seaside where they may go for dinner, spend an evening enjoyably, and get home at a reasonable time."

That is true, and since that is all Coney Island is for, we understand why it is peculiar among the really crowded resorts in the absence of summer costumes among its votaries. What we call the typical "summer girl" is seen there, now and then, in sailor hat and thin white gown, but her champion in white flannels, yachting cap, and tennis shoes never, perhaps, set foot on this glistening strand. In his place we see the costumes of Broadway and the Stock Exchange, of Tompkins Square and Central Park. On summer Saturdays the clerks and merchants and the professional men who are kept in town, take an early luncheon in the city and catch the Bay Ridge boat for the races at Sheepshead Bay, across the creek from the island. Such a crowd, dressed as this is, would look out of place in Saratoga or Narragansett Pier, but on the boat it looks like a tatter torn out of Broadway and when, after the races, it bursts upon the verandas of Brighton and Manhattan Beaches, it fits into the multitude there precisely as if it was of the same web and woof.

Another bit of evidence that Coney Island's crowds are made up most largely of those who are town-stayed all summer, lies in the color of the crowd's hands and faces. From the waxen whiteness of the women and girls whose waking hours are spent amid gaslight, to the pinker hue of the men who have leisure to walk to and from luncheon—if not to business— every morning the color of all is the same and only the shades of it differ. How much more admirable, how almost blessed, Coney Island seems in the light of these facts! How grand an acquisition it is for us to possess a beach to which we can go in an hour at the cost of a quarter of a dollar, to get a new environment and have old ocean's pure tonic breath blow the cobwebs out of our brain—and then, as the chronicler saith, "get home at a reasonable time."

THE ERA OF THE THREE GREAT AMUSEMENT PARKS, 1897–1911

"SOUTH END OF THE BOWERY," CONEY ISLAND, 1903. (PHOTOGRAPH PUBLISHED BY DETROIT PUBLISHING COMPANY. LIBRARY OF CONGRESS, PRINTS AND PHOTOGRAPHS DIVISION)

MARVELOUS CONEY ISLAND

Guy Wetmore Carryl

Guy Wetmore Carryl (1873–1904), born in New York City, was a writer and an editor for several publications, including *Munsey's Magazine* and *Harper's*. In this brief excerpt from "Marvelous Coney Island," published in *Munsey's* in September 1901, Carryl describes how Coney provides "tumultuous recreation." Coney's claim to fame, he argues, is "to toss, tumble, flop, jerk, jounce, jolt, and jostle you." If a similar thing occurred to you on a trolley car, he adds, you would most likely sue the company, "but that is where human inconsistency comes in." Of course, it is important to remember that the essay was written when only Steeplechase, the amusement park that was the most dependent of the big three on physical interaction with its audience, was in existence.

CONEY ISLAND IS NOT A RESORT of the kind which is said to grow upon the visitor. Rather she plunges at him, and, before he has time for reflection, proceeds to engulf him in a veritable maelstrom of tumultuous recreation. Hers are not the soothing methods of the nerve cure specialist, but the heroic measures of the life saver who administers a knock out blow between the eyes of a drowning man, and either rescues him thereby or puts a finishing touch to the mischief Father Ocean has begun. [...]

Coney Island [...] leaps with a shout upon the casual visitor as he steps from a five cent trolley car direct into the seething heart of her ten cent chaos, and pours out, as it were, the whole contents of her horn of plenty in a trice before his astounded eyes. Immediately recreation becomes less a question of search than of selection. One has simply to decide in what manner he prefers to be made uncomfortable, for it is Coney Island's claim to celebrity that she is prepared to make you so in a variety of ways approaching infinity, and, if you are of the majority, you are there for that express purpose. If you are not of the majority, your wisest course is to return without delay by the way you came, and leave to more appreciative mortals your place on the Scenic Railway, and the Sliding Staircase, and the Loops, and the Chutes, and the Camel. [...]

That, above all, is Coney Island's specialty; to toss, tumble, flop, jerk, jounce, jolt, and jostle you by means of a variety of mechanical contrivances, until your digestion is where your reason ought to be, and your reason has gone none knows whither. For the privilege you pay the appreciable sum of ten cents. If the same thing happened to you the next day on a trolley car, you would in all probability sue the company for a thousand dollars. But that is where human inconsistency comes in, and where human inconsistency is the issue none of us can afford to be hypercritical, because here, as in love, money making, and the desire to get ahead of our neighbors, we are all in the same class. [...]

It is time to go, before the breath of the awakening dragons falls foul across the memory of the cheap but cheerful gaiety of day. Better yet could we have gone earlier, before that last impression, the breath in our nostrils, and the voice in our ears, of the musing ocean, prying with curious fingers around the foundations of Vanity Fair! For, after all, here is no place for reflection. We have been fools with the best of them, and as for Coney Island, if we are tired of the jade and disposed to sneer, that is less her fault than ours. It was a frank bargain, my leisure for your laughter, and we had no right to lift masks and look behind the scenes. And in whatever coin this amazon of the cap and bells chooses to repay you, take it at its face value, and ask no questions!

HUMAN NEED OF CONEY ISLAND

Richard Le Gallienne

Richard Le Gallienne (1866–1947), the father of actress Eva Le Gallienne, was an English writer and poet who was an original member of the Rhymers' Club and a contributor to the *Yellow Book*, a literary journal. He settled in the United States in 1903. He spent more than twenty-five years in New York, where he struggled to earn a living as a journalist, publisher, and lecturer, before moving to Paris in the late 1920s. In "Human Need of Coney Island," published in *Cosmopolitan* in July 1905, Le Gallienne attributes Coney's popularity to the human "tragic need of coarse excitement, a craving to be taken in by some illusion however palpable." Coney's charm is that it is a fake, knows that it is a fake, and "makes so little bones about the matter." It expects the visitor to pretend to be taken in. Humans have "been made with an appetite for eccentricities of diversion," which Coney offers in abundance. America has built "a Palace of Illusion . . . and she has called it Coney Island."

TO CALL CONEY ISLAND one of the wonders of the world is not for me. I think it has been already said [. . .]. One of the wonders of the world! One! Why, surely, Coney is all the wonders of the world in one pyrotechnic masterpiece of coruscating concentration. I write—or try to write—in this style on purpose—for am I not writing of Coney Island?—and it was not till I went down to Coney Island, on a brief duck-shooting expedition, that I realized why the word "pyrotechnic" had been invented. I had often fondled the word in dictionaries, or on those circus-posters which, to my mind, are the masterpieces of a certain kind of literary style, but I had never hoped to meet with anything equal to the word. One so seldom meets with anything equal to a word. A word like "pyrotechnic" is like the name of some beautiful woman whom we never expect to meet except in dreams. But at last I have met my beautiful lady-love Pyrotechnic—in Coney Island. Her sister, too—whose name is "Coruscating." Arm in arm with Pyrotechnic and Coruscating, you and I, if you have a mind, may see all the wonders of the world in this million-faceted false diamond known as Coney Island.

All the wonders, I say, and I use the plural advisedly; for, have you noticed how men and women flock to wonders—but how little they know, or care, of Wonder? That, of all things, most struck me in Coney Island— man's voracity for wonders, and his ignorance of Wonder.

Mankind will not give a second look at the rising moon, but present it with some disagreeable monstrosity, something that nature ought never to have allowed, something also essentially uninteresting, such as, say, the Human Pin-Cushion, the Balloon-Headed Baby, or the Six-Tailed Bull-Terrier, and there is no limit to its gaping astonishment. Forlorn horrors of abortion, animals tortured into talent, or feats of fantastic daring, these win the respect and thrill the exorbitant imagination of man. Nothing pleases him better than to see some skilled human being, with ghastly courage, risking a horrible death for the sake of his entertainment. Death, or at least the fear of it, as always, still holds a foremost place in popular amusements; though we are, I suppose, a little less cruel than they were in ancient Rome.

But I must not write as though I felt superior to Coney Island. Indeed not. The human appetite for fairs has been implanted in my bosom also, and Coney, of course, is just the village fair in excelsis, catering to the undying demand for green spectacles and gilded gingerbread and quaint absurdities of amusement, and, generally speaking, man's desperate need of entertainment, and his pathetic incapacity for entertaining himself. Really, it is strange, when you think of it, that in a world with so many interesting things to do, so many, so to say, ready-made fascinations and marvels— that man should find it necessary to loop-the-loop for distraction, or ride wooden horses to the sound of savage music, or ascend a circle in the air in lighted carriages slung on a revolving wheel, or hurl itself with splashing laughter down chutes into the sea. When one might be reading Plato—ever so much more amusing.

And yet so man has been made, and there come moments when it is necessary for him to shy sticks at a mark in the hope of winning a cigar or a coconut, or divert himself with the antics of cynical mountebanks, or look at animals in cages, menagerie marvels which are interesting chiefly from being caged, or gaze upon gymnasts and athletes performing feats of skill and strength which would be really astonishing if they were not the tricks of so old a trade, professional astonishments handed down, like the craft of shoemaking, from immemorial time. There is nothing especially marvelous about snake-charming. It is a business, like any other; and to swallow knives, or "eat-'em-alive," for a living is, no doubt, hard work, yet what modes of working for a living are not? Sword-swallowing is scarcely so arduous as bricklaying, and, though one is as essentially interesting as the other, the humble bricklayer draws but small audiences for his exhibitions of skill.

But, as I said, man has been made with an appetite for eccentricities of diversion rather than the love of more normal pleasures. Personally, I am the last to blame him, and he who can look upon a merry-go-round without longing to ride the wooden horse once more before he dies, for all the maturity of his middle age, can hardly be a human being.

I said that I went down to Coney on a duck-shooting expedition. I should, of course, have explained that it was a tin-duck-shooting expedition, and even when I say that, you will hardly understand if you have not fallen under the strange spell of that perpetual progression of tin ducks which invites the tin sportsman hard by the Dreamland gates of Coney Island. If you haven't shot at those ducks, or if you disdain to shoot at them, you may as well not visit Coney Island. The Congressional Library you might find congenial, or you might go on a pious pilgrimage to Grant's Tomb, but I fear you will never understand Coney Island. Besides, Coney Island might misunderstand you, and to be misunderstood in Coney Island is no laughing matter—for to misunderstand you is one of the many serious interests of that "happy isle set in the silver sea."

Tin ducks remind me of tin-types. If you are not a friend of the Gipsy photographer, the Daguerre of the highways and byways, in the little tents pitched by the roadside, the only photographer that never calls himself an artist, but, nine times out of ten, gives you the best picture you ever had—again, don't go to Coney Island. My friend Pyrotechnic and I, being simple souls, bathing in all the pristine hallucinations of the place, sat together hand in hand with a heavenly expression under a very real electric light, and a moment after saw our faces fried over a little stove, another moment we were in gilt frames, another moment we were out again on the Broadway, with our eyes on Dreamland—but just as we were about to enter, a stout old crone of the American-Italian species beckoned us into her enchanted cave, and proposed to tell our fortunes.

Again, if you are too superior to have your fortune told by some peasant woman who knows nothing about it, and knows that you know that she doesn't—don't go to Coney Island.

The great charm of Coney is just there. It not only knows itself a fake, but, so to speak, it makes so little bones about the matter. It knows that you know, and it expects you to pretend to be taken in, as it pretends to think that it is taking you in. [...] I wonder if, perhaps, Coney Island, like all similar institutions in all times and in all lands, does not regard the public as a big baby in need of a noisy, electric-lighted rattle.

Or, on the other hand, do the magicians of "Dreamland" and "Luna Park" persuade themselves that their domes and minarets of fairy fire are really anything more than, so to speak, shareholders lit by electric light, the capitalistic torches of modern Neroism? Do they really think that "Dreamland" is dreamland, or that any one but a lunatic would look for the moon in "Luna Park"?

Yet, after all, whatever the mind and meaning of this strange congregation of showmen may be, whether they merely cater in cynical fashion to the paying needs of a contemptible uncomprehended multitude, or whether they gratify their own pyrotechnic and coruscating tastes, this much is true: that Coney Island, more than any other showman in the world, has heard and answered man's cry for the Furies of Light and Noise. Whatever else the speculators back of Coney Island don't know, they understand the—Zulu. Coney Island is the Tom-Tom of America. Every nation has, and needs—and loves—its Tom-Tom. It has its needs of orgiastic escape from respectability—that is, from the world of What-we-have-to-do into the world of What-we-would-like-to-do, from the world of duty that endureth forever into the world of joy that is graciously permitted for a moment. Some escape by one way and some by another—some by the ivory gate, and some by the gate of horn—or gold. The thing is to escape.

It is of no use to criticize humanity. Like all creations, it—survives its critics. The only interesting thing is to try to understand it, or, at least, appreciate. Perhaps Coney Island is the most human thing that God ever made, or permitted the devil to make.

Of course, the real reason of its existence in our day has nothing to do with its modern appliances, electric and otherwise. The real reason is that it is as old as the hills. Nothing younger than the hills is alive to-day. The flowers look younger—on account of their complexions—but perhaps they are even older than the hills. Coney Island is so alive with light and noise every night because it is so old-established an institution. Man needs Coney Island to-day, because he has always needed Coney Island. [. . .]

Coney Island exists, and will go on existing, because into all men, gentle and simple, poor and rich—including women—by some mysterious corybantic instinct in their blood, has been born a tragic need of coarse excitement, a craving to be taken in by some illusion however palpable.

So, following the example of those old nations, whose place she has so vigorously taken, America has builded [*sic*] for herself a Palace of Illusion, and filled it with every species of talented attractive monster, every misbegotten fancy of the frenzied nerves, every fantastic marvel of the moonstruck brain—and she has called it Coney Island. Ironic name—a place lonely with rabbits, a spit of sandy beach so near to the simple life of the sea, and watched over by the summer night; strange Isle of Monsters, Preposterous Palace of Illusion, gigantic Parody of Pleasure—Coney Island.

BOREDOM

Maxim Gorky

Russian author and political activist Aleksey Maksimovich Peshkov (1868–1936) is better known by his pseud-onym, Maxim Gorky. One of the founders of the Socialist Realism movement, Gorky is a major figure in Rus-sian literature, perhaps most famous for his play *The Lower Depths* (1902). Fearing arrest in Russia because of his political activism, Gorky traveled to the United States in 1906 at the invitation of such supporters as Theodore Roosevelt and Mark Twain. Gorky demonstrated an appreciation for the splendor of Coney Island, but ultimately—as shown in "Boredom," published in the *Independent* on August 8, 1907—he condemned it for its stultifying sense of boredom, which overpowers the observer. Coney seems to remind its visitors of the soulless horror of their lives, which is vented through wanton acts of jealousy, greed, and cruelty.

THIS IS CONEY ISLAND.

On Monday the metropolitan newspapers triumphantly announce:

"Three Hundred Thousand People in Coney Island Yesterday. Twen-ty-three Children Lost."

"There's something doing there[,]" the reader thinks.

First a long ride by trolley thru Brooklyn and Long Island amid the dust and noise of the streets. Then the gaze is met by the sight of dazzling, mag-nificent Coney Island. From the very first moment of arrival at this city of fire, the eye is blinded. It is assailed by thousands of cold, white sparks, and for a long time can distinguish nothing in the scintillating dust round about. Everything whirls and dazzles, and blends into a tempestuous fer-ment of fiery foam. The visitor is stunned: his consciousness is withered by the intense gleam; his thoughts are routed from his mind; he becomes a particle in the crowd. People wander about in the flashing, blinding fire intoxicated and devoid of will. A dull-white mist penetrates their brains, greedy expectation envelopes their souls. Dazed by the brilliancy the throngs wind about like dark bands in the surging sea of light, pressed upon all sides by the black bournes of night.

Everywhere electric bulbs shed their cold, garish gleam. They shine on posts and walls, on window casings and cornices; they stretch in an even line along the high tubes of the power-house; they burn on all the roofs and prick the eye with the sharp needles of their dead, indifferent sparkle. The people screw up their eyes, and smiling disconcertedly crawl along the ground like the heavy line of a tangled chain.

A man must make a great effort not to lose himself in the crowd, not to be overwhelmed by his amazement—an amazement in which there is neither transport nor joy. But if he succeeds in individualizing himself, he finds that these millions of fires produce a dismal, all-revealing light. Tho they hint at the possibility of beauty, they everywhere discover a dull, gloomy ugliness. The city, magic and fantastic from afar, now appears an absurd jumble of straight lines of wood, a cheap, hastily constructed toy-house for the amusement of children. Dozens of white buildings, monstrously diverse, not one with even the suggestion of beauty. They are built of wood, and smeared over with peeling white paint, which gives them the appearance of suffering with the same skin disease. The high turrets and low colonnades extend in two dead-even lines insipidly pressing upon each other. Everything is stripped naked by the dispassionate glare. The glare is everywhere, and nowhere a shadow. Each building stands there like a dumbfounded fool with wide-open mouth, and sends forth the glare of brass trumpets and the whining rumble of orchestrions. Inside is a cloud of smoke and the dark figures of the people. The people eat, drink and smoke.

But no human voice is heard. The monotonous hissing of the arc lights fills the air, the sounds of music, the cheap notes of the orchestrions, and the thin, continuous sputtering of the sausage-frying counters. All these sounds mingle in an importunate hum, as of some thick, taut chord. And if the human voice breaks into this ceaseless resonance, it is like a frightened whisper. Everything 'round about glitters insolently and reveals its own dismal ugliness.

The soul is seized with a desire for a living, beautiful fire, a sublime fire, which should free the people from the slavery of a varied boredom. For this boredom deafens their ears and blinds their eyes. The soul would burn away all this allurement, all this mad frenzy, this dead magnificence and spiritual penury. It would have a merry dancing and shouting and singing; it would see a passionate play of the motley tongues of fire; it would have joyousness and life. [...]

Inside the buildings the people are also seeking pleasure, and here, too, all look serious. The amusement offered is educational. The people are shown hell, with all its terrors and punishments that await those who have transgressed the sacred laws created for them.

Hell is constructed of papier maché and painted dark red. Everything in it is on fire—paper fire—and it is filled with the thick, dirty odor of grease. Hell is very badly done. It would arouse disgust in a man of even modest demands. It is represented by a cave with stones thrown together in chaotic masses. The cave is penetrated by a reddish darkness. On one of the stones sits Satan, clothed in red. Grimaces distort his lean, brown face. He rubs his hands contentedly, as a man who is doing a good business. He must be very uncomfortable on his perch, a paper stone, which cracks and rocks. But he pretends not to notice his discomfort, and looks down at the evil demons busying themselves with the sinners.

A girl is there who has just bought a new hat. She is trying it on before a mirror, happy and contented. But a pair of little fiends, apparently very greedy, steal up behind her and seize her under the armpits. She screams, but it is too late. The demons put her into a long, smooth trough, which descends tightly into a pit in the middle of the cave. From the pit issue a gray vapor and tongues of fire made of red paper. The girl, with her mirror and her new hat, goes down into the pit, lying on her back in the trough.

A young man has drunk a glass of whisky. Instantly the devils clutch him, and down he goes thru that same hole in the floor of the platform.

The atmosphere in hell is stifling. The demons are insignificant looking and feeble. Apparently they are greatly exhausted by their work and irritated by its sameness and evident futility. When they fling the sinners unceremoniously into the trough like logs of wood, you feel like crying out:

"Enough, enough nonsense, boys!"

A girl extracts some coins from her companion's purse. Forthwith the spies, the demons, attack her, to the great satisfaction of Satan, who sits there snickering and dangling his crooked legs joyfully. The demons frown angrily up at the idle fellow, and spitefully hurl into the jaws of the burning pit everybody who enters hell by chance, on business or out of curiosity.

The audience looks on these horrors in silence with serious faces. The hall is dark. Some sturdy fellow with curly hair holds forth in a lugubrious voice while he points to the stage.

He says that if the people do not want to be the victims of Satan with the red garments and the crooked legs, they should not kiss girls to whom they are not married, because then the girls might become bad women. Women outcasts ought not to steal money from the pockets of their companions, and people should not drink whisky or beer or other liquors that arouse the passions; they should not visit saloons, but the churches, for churches are not only more beneficial to the soul, but they are also cheaper.

He talks monotonously, wearily. He himself does not seem to believe in what he was told to preach.

You involuntarily apostrophize the owners of this corrective amusement for sinners:

"Gentlemen, if you wish morality to work on men's souls with the force of castor oil, you ought to pay your preachers more."

At the conclusion of the terrible story a nauseatingly beautiful angel appears from a corner of the cavern. He hangs on a wire, and moves across the entire cave, holding a wooden trumpet, pasted over with gilt paper, between his teeth. On catching sight of him, Satan dives like a fish into the pit after the sinners. A crash is heard, the paper stones are hurled down, and the devils run off cheerfully to rest from their labor. The curtain drops. The public rises and leaves. Some venture to laugh. The majority, however, seem absorbed in reflection. Perhaps they think:

"If hell is so nasty, it isn't worth sinning." [...]

Thus, when night comes, a fantastic magic city, all of fire, suddenly blazes up from the ocean. Without consuming, it burns long against the dark background of the sky, its beauty mirrored in the broad, gleaming bosom of the sea.

In the glittering gossamer of its fantastic buildings, tens of thousands of gray people, like patches on the ragged clothes of a beggar, creep along with weary faces and colorless eyes.

Mean panderers to debased tastes unfold the disgusting nakedness of their falsehood, the *naïveté* of their shrewdness, the hypocrisy and insatiable force of their greed. The cold gleam of the dead fire bares the stupidity of it all. Its pompous glitter rests upon everything 'round about the people.

But the precaution has been taken to blind the people, and they drink in the vile poison with silent rapture. The poison contaminates their souls. Boredom whirls about in an idle dance, expiring in the agony of its inanition.

One thing alone is good in the garish city: You can drink in hatred to your soul's content, hatred sufficient to last thruout [*sic*] life, hatred of the power of stupidity!

THE MASTER SHOWMAN OF CONEY ISLAND

Peter Lyon

Peter Lyon (1915–1996), born in Madison, Wisconsin, was a New York–based freelance writer of articles and radio scripts. He was the author of several historical works, including a biography of his grandfather, newspaper and magazine publisher Samuel Sidney McClure: *Success Story: The Life and Times of S. S. McClure* (1963), which won the George Polk Memorial Award. The source of much of "The Master Showman of Coney Island," a sketch about George C. Tilyou published in *American Heritage* in June 1958, is Edo McCullough, *Good Old Coney Island: A Sentimental Journey into the Past* (1957; New York: Fordham University Press, 2000).

ON EVERY WARM SUMMER WEEK END on Coney Island a great swarm of people may be found heading for a slow-moving line that leads always to the same entertainment device. Typically, they will wait nearly an hour to enjoy a ride that lasts for perhaps one mildly exhilarating minute. Judged as a thrill, the ride packs about as much punch as a cup of cambric tea. Yet it is a safe bet that at any given moment there are youngsters standing in this line whose fathers and mothers stood here a generation ago, and the odds would not be too high that there are even some whose grandfathers and grandmothers pressed patiently forward toward the same admission gate.

Nevertheless, this ride is, year in and year out, the most popular attraction in any amusement park in the world. On Broadway, smash hits have opened and had their laughably brief runs of four or five years and closed, but still this ride unceasingly packs them in. Something like one hundred million admissions have been checked through its turnstiles, and the end of its success is nowhere in sight. Most perplexing of all, perhaps four out of five of those who wait patiently in line nearly an hour for their brief, tepid ride know that when it is over they will be obliged to pass through a tunnel only to emerge blinking onto a small stage where they will be teased, tripped up, tickled, prodded, and submitted to various adolescent indignities at the hands of frolicsome strangers, such as having their hats whisked off or their skirts blown up about their faces, while all the time an audience of four or five hundred persons rocks in helpless laughter at their confusion and dismay.

This abiding phenomenon is called the Steeplechase Horses; it is the premier entertainment offered at Steeplechase Park, the last and only enduring amusement park at Coney Island. The Steeplechase Horses are, additionally, a lasting monument to Coney's greatest showman, the man who in 1897 installed them as the principal attraction of his prototypal carnival grounds. This was George Cornelius Tilyou, whose formula, to lapse into the alliterations of the side-show spiel, was a matchless mixture of sentimentality, shrewd psychology, a sound sense of civic expansion, and a suffusion of sophomoric sex. [...]

George C. Tilyou was born in New York City in 1862. When he was three years old his parents leased one of the huge 300-foot ocean-front lots then available on Coney for $35 a year, and on it they built the Surf House. The elder Tilyou's father had been a recorder in New York; thanks to this political background the Surf House over the years became a favorite resort for New York and Brooklyn city officials and their families. By the time young George was fourteen he had already displayed a precocious insight into the psychology of the holiday pleasure-seeker.

Coney, in the summer of 1876, was crowded with tourists from the Midwest who, drawn east by the Philadelphia Centennial Exhibition, had wandered down for their first glimpse of a real, live ocean. George showed the true Coney Island instinct. Correctly guessing that these simple folk would believe that an article had value only if it had a price upon it, he filled medicine bottles with salt water and cigar boxes with sand and sold them by the score at a quarter apiece.

In 1879, when he was seventeen, the real-estate business beckoned. At that time land on Coney could not be sold; title was firmly held by the township. But there was a brisk and piratical traffic in leases and subleases. What happened to one lot on Ocean Boulevard was common gossip. One of the more venal of the town's commissioners had leased the lot for $41 a year; one-eighth of it he subleased for $1,000 a year to a woman who in turn leased a modest fraction of her one-eighth for $4,000 a year. Where pyramids like these were a-building, there was room for a man of seventeen with vision. Presently young Tilyou was netting $250 a month, operating out of an office he had constructed by cleating two bathhouses together.

But this was just money, and it bored him. He thirsted to be a showman. Here were all these people down from New York and Brooklyn for the sun and the sea breezes; was it enough that they had a splendid beach and an ocean? Didn't they want entertainment as well? Tilyou bet that they did. When he was twenty, he and his father put up the Island's first theater: Tilyou's Surf Theatre. [...]

A successful real-estate operator, the manager of a profitable theater, Tilyou in his twenties was already a man of substance. But he had, nevertheless, his problems. The difficulty was with [John] McKane, who held Coney Island in his firm fist, extracting from every businessman a tithe that masqueraded as a license fee, encouraging the most disreputable elements to open saloons or hotels on Coney, and, although chief of police, conniving at the fracture of every statute against gambling or prostitution. Indeed, affairs had been building to a climax for some time between the Tilyous and the Pooh-Bah of Coney Island. McKane, to their way of thinking, jeopardized grosses. By appointing ruffians and rascals as his justices of the peace, by winking at prostitution, by plundering the community, he was making Coney a stench in the nostrils of decent folk everywhere; and the Tilyous wanted these decent folk as their customers.

And so when, as was inevitable, McKane's misrule of Coney Island became the subject of a legislative investigation, George Tilyou did a brave thing. He singled out for the investigators the most corrupt of McKane's henchmen. He stood alone. He was the only resident of Coney Island who dared, flatly and without qualification, to blow the whistle on the Chief. He named the houses of prostitution and placed them; he told how a doctor who was McKane's assistant police sergeant and health officer got a weekly fee of two dollars for each prostitute he examined. He had seen McKane's justices of the peace in gambling places and named names and dates. He had seen McKane's captain of police in regular attendance at one bagnio; the same man had tried to rent land from him to run a gambling joint.

In short, Tilyou reported what was common knowledge, giving chapter and verse. But while the legislative committee could stigmatize McKane as "an enemy, and not a friend, of the administration of justice," his friends in the State Assembly were too powerful; his grip on Coney, for a time, stayed secure. Young George Tilyou found it necessary to retire from the real-estate business. His capital dwindled. His father was stripped of his property and forced off the Island. It never occurred to George, however, to move away from Coney; he had sand in his shoes, and there is a saying on Coney that you never shake it loose.

In 1893 he married Mary O'Donnell and took off on his honeymoon to see the Chicago World's Columbian Exposition. There, on the Midway Plaisance, he was captivated by the wondrous invention of G. W. G. Ferris. He looked about, noting how jaws dropped and eyes popped as people looked on this first Ferris Wheel, and he coveted it. The time was propitious; back on Coney, he knew, McKane was in trouble, perhaps at last on the skids. He was too late to buy the monstrous toy; it was already promised to the St. Louis Fair for delivery in 1904. But he could have a more modest wheel built.

The Ferris Wheel was 250 feet in diameter; each of its 36 cars accommodated 60 passengers. Tilyou borrowed money and ordered for delivery in the spring of 1894 a wheel 125 feet in diameter, with 12 cars carrying 18 passengers apiece. He rented some land between Surf Avenue and the ocean and put up a sign that unblushingly announced: ON THIS SITE WILL BE ERECTED THE WORLD'S LARGEST FERRIS WHEEL. On the strength of this whopper he sold enough concession space to make payment on delivery. He studded his plaything with hundreds of incandescent lamps; it was the Island's first big, glittering attraction, and its owner was making money before it had been in operation half-a-hundred days.

By that time his old enemy McKane was in Sing Sing, Coney Island was part of Brooklyn, and decent folk were once again flocking to the beach by the scores of thousands on every summer week end. Tilyou decided to branch out. He had his Aerial Slide; he had his Ferris Wheel; he imported a something called the Intramural Bicycle Railway; he built another ride called the Double Dip Chutes. But these were scattered all over Coney. It might never have occurred to Tilyou to group them all in one place and assist them to multiply had it not been for the arrival on Coney of Captain Paul Boyton, the first frogman and an international celebrity who had swum across the English Channel in an inflated rubber suit. At Coney Boyton had opened Sea Lion Park—the first outdoor amusement park in the world—in time for the Fourth of July week end in 1895. Here his stellar attraction was the Shoot-the-Chutes, an aquatic toboggan slide in flatbottomed boats; but it was the idea of a park enclosed by a fence, with admission charged at the gate, that impressed George Tilyou.

Tilyou cast about for the one sure-fire device that would do for him what the Shoot-the-Chutes had done for Boyton. The most popular sport of the time was, by all odds, horse racing: for six months a year Coney was crowded with people who had spent the afternoon at the races at Gravesend Bay or Sheepshead Bay or Brighton Beach. When Tilyou heard of a British invention—a mechanical racecourse—he knew he had found what he needed.

He was obliged to tinker with it, to develop and improve it for his own purposes, but in time for the season of 1897 he opened Steeplechase Park on a plot slightly larger than fifteen acres. (Tilyou never said fifteen acres; he preferred to say 655,000 square feet. His sons, or their press agents, have gradually increased the size of the park. In 1922 his oldest son, the late Edward Tilyou, admitted that the claim of twenty-one acres was an exaggeration. "But who," he asked reasonably, "would ever think that the number twenty-one had been made up?" Today the same plot measures twenty-five acres, at least in the park's promotion material. As Milton Berger, the park's current press agent, says: "I inherited the figure, and I never did learn how to count acres.")

The premier attraction at the park, then as now, was the Steeplechase Horses: an undulant, curving metal track over which wooden (they are now metal) horses ran on wheels, coursing down by gravity and soaring up by momentum, in tolerable imitation of a real horse race. [. . .]

By 1905 a child who went to Coney Island could, thanks to Luna and Dreamland and the other spectacular exhibits, arrive at a fairly approximate idea of the universe around him and, in the bargain, be magnificently entertained. He could visit an Indian durbar, the streets of Cairo, an Eskimo village, an island in the Philippines complete with 51 allegedly headhunting

Igorots, a garden in Japan, the Alps of Switzerland, or the canals of Venice; he could watch Mount Pelée erupt, killing 40,000, or sit enthralled while in front of him the dam burst and the rivers engulfed Johnstown; he could be taken through the Great Deep Rift Coal Mine of Pennsylvania; he could see the huge tidal wave destroy Galveston; he could go under the sea in a submarine or whirl giddily aloft in an airplane; he could crawl into a tepee or an igloo or a Lilliputian village; he could see a petrified whale or a performing flea; he could ride on a camel or feed an elephant. It would take him a week to absorb all the marvels proffered and a lifetime to remember them.

But all these delights had by no means crowded Steeplechase into the ocean. George Tilyou enthusiastically welcomed the competition: the more attractions, the bigger the crowds, the greater the gaiety, the higher the profits. Nor did he fret over the fact that at Luna and Dreamland the diversions were more expensive and spectacular. His intuition had equipped him with a different formula. There is only one creation, this formula insisted, endowed with infinite variety—this is the amusement devised by the Peerless Showman—it is people. All that Tilyou needed to do was to contrive the most appropriate backgrounds for his star performers. [. . .]

Remarkable as it may seem, each of these simple entertainments was notably popular in the early years of the century; around each of them thronged scores of people eager to see their fellows make fools of themselves; summer after summer they drew the same throngs back. In 1905 Steeplechase boasted 25 attractions, "every one of them original, up-to-date, and snappy," and since most of them were owned and controlled by Tilyou they could all be sampled by buying a combination ticket for 25 cents. [. . .]

With the coming of the subway Coney gained millions of patrons and lost some of its old effervescence. But neither these changes nor Tilyou's death in 1914 have made any difference to the Steeplechase formula. Whether Coney is glittering or dowdy, cheap or expensive, raffish or respectable, secure or facing a questionable future, Steeplechase packs them in. Season after season the crowds flock into the park, as many as fifteen thousand at a time. Once within, if they are not too distracted by the sophomoric horseplay, they may notice, set in the middle of the Pavilion of Fun, what is surely the most magnificent carrousel in the world. Bedecked with handsomely carved horses, pigs, ducks, cupids, and gondolas, this splendid toy was originally built for William II, emperor of Germany; his imperial seal still adorns one of the chariots.

But whatever attracts the patrons to Steeplechase, sooner or later they end up standing in line to ride on the Steeplechase Horses, as people have done now for two generations. [...]

It is the founder's formula, unchanged. It is the abiding proof that George C. Tilyou was a master showman.

AMUSING THE MILLION

Frederic Thompson

Frederic Thompson (1872–1919), born in Irontown, Ohio, was one of the master showmen of his time and a co-founder of Luna Park in 1903 and the Hippodrome Theater in 1905. He teamed up with Elmer Dundy in 1900 to create the highly successful Trip to the Moon concession at the Pan-American Exposition, held in 1901 in Buffalo, New York. They moved the attraction to Steeplechase Park in Coney Island in 1902 and, the following year, made it a signature feature of their Luna Park. In "Amusing the Million," published in *Everybody's Magazine* in September 1908, Thompson outlines his philosophy of the amusement business. People are just children "grown tall," and "what they want on a holiday" is "elaborated child's play." An amusement park must provide a variety of shows and rides, but the rides must be speedy and the shows must be short to keep people on the go and maintain the "carnival spirit," and it is the showman's job to manufacture this spirit.

THE DIFFERENCE BETWEEN THE THEATRE and the big amusement park is the difference between the Sunday-school and the Sunday-school picnic. The people are the same; the spirit and the environment are wholly different. It is harder to make the picnic successful than successfully to conduct a session of the school; and it is harder to make a success of a big amusement park than of a theatre. There isn't any irreverence in this comparison with the Sunday-school, for if the amusement park doesn't attract people who are interested in the Sunday-school, it isn't going to succeed.

For I want to say at the beginning that ninety-five per cent of the American public is pure and good, and it is this public that it pays to serve. This isn't just a general statement. I always believed it. I have proved it by studying the twenty-five million people that have visited Luna Park in the past five years. I haven't any use for the bad five per cent. As a showman I don't want them to come near my enterprises.

In the theatre and in the Sunday-school conventional standards of behavior are accepted as a matter of course. The picnic and the open-air park are designed to give the natural, bubbling animal spirits of the human being full play, to give people something fresh and new and unusual, to afford them respite from the dull routine of their daily lives.

The one thing that makes a picnic or an amusement park a success—it doesn't make any difference whether the picnic is made up of ten people or ten thousand, whether the park is a little one or a great international exposition—the one thing absolutely necessary is the carnival spirit. Without that no show in the open, nothing that has to do with people in the mass, can hope to succeed. Whenever any enterprise that is intended to appeal to the million fails, the failure can always be traced to the lack of carnival enthusiasm.

This spirit of gaiety, the carnival spirit, is not spontaneous, except on extraordinary occasions, and usually its cause can be easily traced. Almost always it is manufactured. Take a big political meeting, for instance. Ninety-nine times out of a hundred the steps that culminate in a great outburst are carefully planned. There are men who make it a business to insure the success of great mass meetings. When you get right down to it, the fundamentals are the same, whether the application is to a church picnic, a political meeting, a circus, or a big exposition. The first step, as far as the public is concerned, is to create an impression that there will be things doing, to get emotional excitement into the very air. In the Sunday-school picnic they talk about the picnic for weeks in advance, telling the children and grown-ups what a fine time they are going to have. The circus does the same thing with its flaming bill-boards and its parade. The political managers talk about the famous speakers who will address the meetings, about the band. You see, it's all the same, fundamentally.

In big amusement enterprises that appeal to the masses the spirit of gaiety is manufactured just as scenery, lights, buildings, and the shows generally are manufactured. That's the business of the showman—to create the spirit of gaiety, frolic, carnival; and the capacity to do this is the measure of his mastery of the craft. Nearly all the big national expositions fail financially because, while in essence they are really nothing but shows, almost never is one run by a showman. When people go to a park or an exposition and admire the buildings, the exhibits, and the lights without having laughed about half the time until their sides ached, you can be absolutely sure that the enterprise will fail.

I have been giving generalities. The only way I know of driving home these points is to tell some of my own experiences. [. . .]

When I was studying architecture [. . .] I began designing, not after classical models, but with a sense of their proportions. I stuck to no style. I adopted what I thought was best in Free Renaissance, but reserved the right to use all the license in the world and to inject into everything I did the graceful, romantic curves of the Oriental.

One result is Luna Park, the sky-line of which is utterly unlike anything else of its kind in the two Americas. The architecture of Luna Park helps rather than hinders the spirit of carnival. Luna Park has been, and is, tremendously successful. There are other amusement parks in its vicinity that are chastely beautiful from an artistic standpoint, but that so far as dollars and cents are concerned are utter failures. Visitors admire the buildings—and don't go near the shows. I have built their sort of buildings, too, but not for a Luna Park. They don't pay. An exposition is a form of festivity, and serious architecture should not enter into it if it will interfere with the carnival spirit.

In amusing the million there are other essential elements besides gaiety. One is decency – the absolutely necessary quality in every line of the world's business. There is nothing that pays so well. When Coney Island used to have a pretty bad reputation, there were good shows there, and clean shows, but the influence of evil dives was dominant. The police couldn't, or at least didn't, check them. The hooligan was everywhere. It's different now. The clean, decent shows have driven the dives out of business. They can't pay the rents the good places easily afford.

The ground that Luna Park occupies is one-third of a tract that was offered to us for less than $600,000. We didn't buy it because we couldn't. I remember that just about that time I had occasion to go to New York on important business. I had to meet men high in the financial world. My best pair of trousers had holes worn through the patches. I went to [Elmer] Dundy and told him I wanted some money.

"How much?" he asked.

"Five or six dollars."

"What for?"

"I must have a new pair of trousers," I explained, and showed him the convincing proofs.

"Five dollars?" said Dundy, in a tone that made me feel like a criminal. "Five dollars for pants! Do you know how many nails that would buy?"

I didn't, and I didn't have the courage to ask. I didn't get the trousers. The money went for the nails. So you see there were reasons why we didn't buy the land at that time. The other day the property on which Luna Park stands sold for a million dollars, so that the value of the whole tract would be about three millions. Making Coney Island a decent, respectable place has increased the value of the property about five times in as many years.

The problem of handling the roughs promised to be serious at first, but it was solved very quickly and easily. The first rowdy I caught in Luna Park was soundly thrashed, and before he was thrown out of the grounds I told him the place was not run for him, but for his mother and sister. I think that did him more good than the punishment. For several seasons I advertised the park as "the place for your mother, your sister, and your sweetheart." If I hadn't believed it was that I wouldn't have spent upward of a hundred thousand dollars in impressing the fact upon the public.

Courtesy on the part of the employee is as necessary as decency on the part of the visitor. If I hear of one of my employees resenting an insult offered by a visitor, I dismiss him. I tell him that so long as he wears my uniform he is representing me, and that I am the only person who can be insulted inside the gates.

An amusement park is a condensed Broadway, if that is understood to represent metropolitan theatreland. In a park the best things of a theatrical nature must be presented in capsule form. The shows must be diversified because the appeal must be universal. The whole gamut of the theatre must be run, and no show can last more than twenty minutes. If you have a two-hour show, it should be boiled down to a quarter of an hour. It is foolish to make people serious or to point a moral, for you are dealing with a moral people. Nor is it worth while to try to educate the amusement-seeking public. It is better to take it for granted that they are educated, and if you start out to amuse them, to stick to that.

People are just boys and girls grown tall. Elaborated child's play is what they want on a holiday. Sliding down cellar doors and the make-believes of youngsters are the most effective amusements for grown-ups. An appreciation of that fact made "The Trip to the Moon" possible, and "The Trip to the Moon" made for me and my partner, Dundy, half a million dollars. "The Tickler," "Bump the Bumps," and "The Virginia Reel" are nothing more than improved cellar doors. "The Trip to the Moon," "Night and Morning," "The Witching Waves," and "The Lost Girl" are only elaborations of the doll-house stunts of childhood, and they are successful largely for that reason. But they must be short and decisive. I would rather have a good show that lasts three minutes than a better one that runs an hour. And I prefer one that is over in a minute but enables the spectator to become a part of it to one that runs three minutes and never permits him to become more than an onlooker.

Speed is almost as important a factor in amusing the millions as is the carnival spirit, decency, or a correct recollection of school days. Speed has become an inborn American trait. We as a nation are always moving, we are always in a hurry, we are never without momentum. "Helter Skelters," "Scenic Railways," "Shoot the Chutes," "The Dragon's Gorge," the thousand and one varieties of roller-coasters are popular for the same reason that we like best the fastest trains, the speediest horses, the highest powered motor-cars, and the swiftest sprinters.

Not only must some rides be speedy and all shows be short, but the employees must work fast visibly, thereby promoting by suggestion speed in the mind, heart, and steps of the most laggard visitors. Throughout Luna Park and all exposition grounds there are benches for the weary. I want the benches there, but I don't want people to sit on them. Whenever, on my frequent tours of the grounds, I find men and women seated watching the lights or the crowds or the free shows, I order out a band, make the musicians march about playing the liveliest tunes, and inject into the very atmosphere such excitement, gaiety, and speed that the resters get up and again take an interest in things. I have never seen this ruse fail.

To keep up the carnival spirit everybody and everything must be on the "go." There can be no carnival without speed. The moment a crowd of folk who are slowly meandering around catch this spirit they walk faster, they laugh, they spend money, they have a good time. I instruct my "talkers" to be always on the alert and to interest people while they are approaching.

"Mills won't grind with water that's past," is an old motto, but a good one. It applies to the business of amusing the millions perhaps more than to any other kind of human activity. [...]

It costs a lot of money to build and operate an amusement park on a large scale.

I suppose that more than twenty-five million dollars are invested in these parks in this country. Dreamland on Coney Island cost about $2,500,000; Riverview Park and the White City in Chicago cost about a million each.

Luna Park cost $2,400,000. The total annual expenses, including the cost of rebuilding, of putting in new shows, and the operating expenses, average about a million dollars, and the season lasts four months. I spent $240,000 on one show alone, of which $68,000 was for animals, mostly elephants and camels—it was the representation of the Indian Durbar—and I lost $100,000 on it. I charged the loss up to education, and it was worth it. It costs $5,600 a week to light Luna Park, and $4,500 for the music. The salaries of the free performers this season are $2,300 a week. And all of these expenditures, as well as a good many others, go simply to manufacture the carnival spirit.

THE WAY OF THE GIRL

Belle Lindner Israels

....

Belle Lindner Israels (1877–1933) was born in New York City. Israels was a social activist at the Educational Alliance and took a particular interest in the conditions of dance halls, often the most accessible source of recreation for poor young women on New York's Lower East Side, as discussed in "The Way of the Girl," published in *Survey* on July 3, 1909. After her first husband, Charles Henry Israels, died, she met her second husband, Henry Moscowitz, while working on a commission that was investigating the infamous fire that broke out at the Triangle Shirtwaist Factory on March 25, 1911. She was a strong supporter of Al Smith, serving as his campaign adviser when he was the Democratic Party's presidential nominee in 1928.

IT IS AN INDUSTRIAL FACT that the summer months find thousands of working girls either in the position of compulsory idleness through slack season in the trades with which they are familiar, or attempting "to kill time" through one or two weeks of a vacation, unwelcome because it bears no definite recreative fruit. The general aspects of the amusement problem of the working girl bear certain undetermined relation to the undercurrents besetting society in a large city, in proportion as opportunities for healthful outlet for social desire are adequate or inadequate. Industrial activity demands diversion. Industrial idleness cries out for rational recreation. As these are provided wisely and freely, the population of the underworld decreases. As they are neglected, the tide rises. Like Janus, the problem looks two ways—towards an escape from enforced idleness and relaxation from necessary labor. Active participation in athletics gives a natural outlet for the boy. The recreative desire of the young girl leads not to Sunday baseball—except as "he" may be playing—nor is it able to content itself with a comparatively expensive and therefore infrequent visit to the theater. Her aspirations demand attention from the other sex. No amusement is complete in which "he" is not a factor. The distinction between the working woman and her more carefully guarded sister of the less driven class is one of standards, opportunities, and a chaperon. Three rooms in a tenement, overcrowded with the younger children, make the street a private apartment. The public resort similarly overcrowded, but with those who are not inquisitive, answers as her reception room. [. . .]

The range of summer amusements around New York city covers first, beach resorts; second, amusement parks; third, the picnic park utilized for the outing, the chowder and the summernight's festival; fourth, the excursion boat; fifth, the vacation home or camp provided by settlements, churches, and girls' clubs.

Of the beach resorts, Coney Island and Rockaway are naturally in the van of public thought. Rockaway is expensive to reach. Its *clientèle* is of the upper class of saleswomen and office workers. They enjoy the ocean bath and spend a comparatively simple day at the beach; and, being better provided with the world's goods than the average girl whom we wish to consider, are not seeking the same kinds of excitement.

Coney Island—the people's playground—where each year "everything is new but the ocean" is the most gigantic of the efforts to amuse.

A dancing master said: "If you haven't got the girls, you can't do business! Keep attracting 'em. The fellows will come if the girls are there."

Coney Island does attract them. It only costs fare down and back, and for the rest of it the boys you "pick up," "treat."

When the girl is both lucky and clever, she frees herself from her self-selected escort before home-going time, and finds a feminine companion in his place for the midnight ride in the trolley. When she is not clever, some one of her partners of the evening may exact tribute for "standing treat." Then the day's outing costs more than carfare. With due recognition of the simpler amusement places on the island—such as Steeplechase Park, where no liquor is sold, and also of the innocent pleasure along the beach front, not even belittling the fact that "nice" people dance in the Dreamland ball room, the fact remains that the average girl has small powers of discrimination. So many hundred places abound on the island to counterbalance the few safe ones, that "careers" without number find their initial stage in a Raines law hotel at this resort.

The danger is not in the big places on the island, where orderly shows and dance halls are run, and where young persons may go unattended. But the greatest number of music halls and dance resorts are along the side streets of the Bowery, and, with the exception of one or two semi-respectable places, are thoroughly disreputable. On Saturday and Sunday nights many young working girls are attracted to these places. They know the bad reputation of some of them, but the dancing floor is good, there are always plenty of men, and there are laughter and liberty galore.

WHY IS CONEY?

Reginald Wright Kauffman

Reginald Wright Kauffman (1877–1959) was a socialist, journalist, and prolific author of novels and nonfiction books. Eight of his novels or short stories were made into motion pictures. In "Why Is Coney?" published in *Hampton's Magazine* in August 1909, Kauffman describes Coney's attractions, with particular emphasis on the three big amusement parks. His main interest, however, is in the philosophies of the operators of these parks for attracting and entertaining visitors. Their reasons for the popularity of Coney include the desire of adults to feel like children, the demand of a weary mind to be thrilled or amused, and the need for novelty.

CONEY IS AN EMPIRE AMONG ITS KIND. As the Parisians have their carnival in every mid-Lent, so do New Yorkers have at Coney a carnival all summer long. Broadly speaking, the amusement park is already a great American industry. Large fortunes have been made in it, and some fortunes, almost as large, have been squandered there. It is a national institution, but it is also a national mystery. How have the men who made it come to the making? How do any men ever invent the nerve-racking, breath-snatching machines upon which it is founded? And what, in the name of all obscurity, is it in the breast or brain of the average human being that makes such devices popular?

Go as you will, and come from what surroundings you may, no sooner have you entered upon that one long street, Surf Avenue, which is at once the heart and the aorta of Coney, than you have entered upon the Land of Carnival. The broad but crowded way is dancing with the noise of festival, with the clangor of brass bands, the cries of venders, the smell of the circus, the tang of the sea. [...]

Every nook has something to sell—and sells it. There are miles of scenic railways, panoramas depicting every disaster from the San Francisco fire to the Messina earthquake. There are the familiar canes to be caught with a ring; the familiar chutes to be shot, and the familiar "galleries" where the rattle of rifles recalls the battle of the Yalu. Down on the beach an army is shouting in the surf, and on every hand along the jostling, good-natured street are peanuts and popcorn, "crispettes" and "hot dogs." Upon dozens of polished floors dancers are slowly revolving with a marvelous ability to distinguish between the time of their own orchestra and that of the band in the café opposite, and everywhere, are picture machines and singing machines. [. . .]

These are, then, the sorts of things hundreds of thousands of persons pay to see and to do. Why they want to see and do them, and, still more, why they want to pay for their pains, presents, as I have said, more than a little mystery. The solution of the riddle involves a study of personalities.

Once a mere city of dives and dance halls, Coney Island is now, after thirteen years, a fairly orderly, almost harmless and altogether amusing community of men who get your nickels and the other fellow's dimes by providing a legion of chances to be ridiculous. Of course, you are probably quite as ridiculous at all times as you are at Coney, but at Coney you are a little more egregiously and much more merrily ridiculous.

And Coney, barring the independents and the free-lances [. . .] is now, so far as its amusement parks are concerned, under the control of three men: Frederic Thompson, of Luna Park; George C. Tilyou, of Steeplechase; and William H. Reynolds, whose prime minister is Samuel W. Gumpertz, General Manager of Dreamland. [. . .]

A short, slim, alert man of thirty-six, with gray eyes, light-brown hair and a quick, decisive manner, Frederic Thompson [. . .] knows what he is doing. He has no park save the Luna Park of Coney. He invents, patents, and owns almost all of the devices in that park. And his success is the product of hard work. All summer long he lives in a little apartment over the Japanese roof garden in the heart of the park. Waking and sleeping he is "on the job," and he sleeps only in the mornings. It is no uncommon thing for him to rush into a group of workmen twenty-four hours before some "amusement" is to "open" and there, slipping off his coat and collar, get to work with them, reconstructing the whole affair.

But how has Thompson discovered the secret of popularity in amusement devices? He does not study rival parks; he studies people. Setting originality above everything else, he refuses to visit any place where he may be subjected to suggestion. Instead, he mixes with the Luna crowds until he is a part of them and it was there that he acquired his theory that what grown men most want is to be transformed into children. [. . .]

Like Frederic Thompson, George C. Tilyou, who has been an "amusement man" since 1897, became one by accident; but, unlike Thompson, he was virtually born to Coney. A native of New York, and now only forty years old, he was a real estate operator, and he began his work in the world when, at the age of fourteen, he took to selling souvenir shells on the Island, where he had lived since his third birthday. He soon established the first real estate office on the Island, and then, having some money to invest, built the Surf Theater on the Bowery, which he himself had laid out—then the only playhouse in Coney. [. . .]

"Generally speaking," Mr. Tilyou told me, "I would say that any success in the amusement business is unaccountable. But from particular instances I've come to the broad theory that what attracts the crowd is the wearied mind's demand for relief in unconsidered muscular action. Certainly the success of a device does not depend on the amount of money invested. I have seen instant failure meet machines which cost thousands of dollars each. Yet, after the original Steeplechase race course, my big hit was what we called the California Red Bats, and that was as cheap as anything could be.

"I calculated that the American people didn't mind an occasional joke on themselves if it was a good-natured joke. I built a flight of six steps up to a table, placed a box in this and in the box put three broken bricks. Then I charged ten cents a look at these bricks. Everybody was curious and everybody looked but nobody told what they saw. Naturally the curiosity spread like the measles and in that season 300,000 people came to see an exhibit that had cost me precisely $5. To sum up my opinion of the whole thing, we Americans want either to be thrilled or amused, and we are ready to pay well for either sensation."

In point of service, the oldest amusement park man in the business, though he is still in his early forties, Samuel W. Gumpertz, of Dreamland—black-mustached with snapping eyes—differs widely in his methods from both Frederic Thompson and George Tilyou. He frankly follows the trail, and his specialty is not so much inventing attractions as it is securing them. At that, however, he is without an equal. [. . .]

Gumpertz packs into one word the psychology of his business success. "Novelty," he said to me, "that's the answer. None of these park amusements is lasting. Few people try one more than half a dozen times in a visit and almost nobody wants the same thing the next season. The only way to make an old show go is to hang out a new sign—and that won't work more than one time with the audience."

Here, then, you have the three men who have made successes of the amusement park, and here you have their three explanations—each different from the others. I have stated the riddle and I have set down the replies of those whose careers have proved them to be experts. You may take your choice—if you want to. For my part, I am still in the position of the parent whose little girl suddenly inquired of him: "Daddy, what becomes of the stocking that was where the hole is now?"

But of one thing there can be no doubt. It is blatant, it is cheap, it is the apotheosis of the ridiculous. But it is something more: it is like Niagara Falls, or the Grand Canyon, or Yellowstone Park; it is a national playground; and not to have seen it is not to have seen your own country.

THE CONEY ISLAND EXCURSION

Kathy Peiss

Kathy Peiss (b. 1953) is the Roy F. and Jeannette P. Nichols Professor of American History at the University of Pennsylvania. In addition to *Cheap Amusements: Working Women and Leisure in Turn-of-the-Century New York* (1986)—from which "The Coney Island Excursion" is taken—she is the author of *Hope in a Jar: The Making of America's Beauty Culture* (1998) and *Zoot Suit: The Enigmatic Career of an Extreme Style* (2011). Peiss notes that "an excursion to Coney Island was the apotheosis of summer entertainment" for young working women at the turn of the twentieth century, offering them a feeling of freedom and excitement. On the Bowery, in the amusement parks and dancing pavilions, and on the boardwalk, women could meet men for "flirtations and adventure." Many of the rides promoted familiarity between the sexes, as exemplified in Peiss's description of those at Steeplechase Park.

WORKING WOMEN'S CULTURE AT CONEY ISLAND

For young working women, an excursion to Coney Island was the apotheosis of summer entertainment. The diversions ranged from sideshow attractions and vaudeville shows to restaurants and the boardwalk. Not unexpectedly, the most popular gathering places were dancing pavilions, open-air structures built on piers or on the beach, which rollicked with music and spieling from 7:00 p.m. until the last boat back to the city each night. The pavilions attracted "pivoters," those "thousands of girls who are seized with such madness for dancing that they spend every night in the dance halls and the picnic parks."[1] Working women could find eight large dance halls at Coney Island, ranging from regulated places to more disreputable saloons with a dance floor, each having a discernible cultural style.

Beatrice Stevenson, examining the working girls' amusements at Coney Island, catalogued these halls:

> At the largest and most exclusive, Saturday night sees an enormous crowd of elaborately dressed girls and men of good appearance and grooming. At other places girls are more plainly dressed, wear shirt waists and street hats, and at still others the girls are of coarse appearance and are flashily dressed. The forms of dancing and behavior vary at the three grades of halls; in the most fashionable there is a good deal of promiscuous intercourse, flirting and picking up of acquaintances, but the dancing itself is usually proper and conventional; in the most Bohemian, behavior is free and pronouncedly bad forms of dancing are seen.[2]

Even after the new amusement parks were built, numerous dance houses and concert halls could be found in the seedy places of the Bowery that continued to attract young working women on Saturday and Sunday nights. [...]

Many of the social forms so familiar to young women in the city's dance halls and streets simply carried over to Coney Island. By relying on the system of treating, women could enjoy a day at Coney's resorts with their only expense being transportation. [...] Some working women's manipulation of this relationship was suggested by a journalist, who overheard two young women at an unguarded moment discussing their male escorts:

"What sort of a time did you have?"

"Great. He blew in $5.00 on the blow-out."

"You beat me again. My chump only spent $2.55."[3]

Such customary practices as picking up a date and breaking dancers could be seen in the dancing pavilions of West Brighton. "Any well-seeming youngster may invite any girl to dance" at Coney Island, observed one journalist, "an arrangement long since sanctioned by that maelstrom of proletarian jollity, the 'social,' where tickets . . . connote partners and more partners, till everybody knows everybody else." Lillian Betts concurred, noting that at dancing pavilions "the buying of a drink gives the right of the floor to any man."[4]

West Brighton's Bowery, the dancing pavilions, and the boardwalk were social spaces women used for flirtations and adventure, but like their urban counterparts, they held sexual risks. The typical shopgirl at Coney, one journalist asserted, was "keen and knowing, ever on the defensive, she discourages such advances as perplex her. . . . Especially she distrusts cavaliers not of her own station." At other amusement parks, too, unescorted women could expect verbal harassment and advances. At Fort George, claimed [Belle Linder] Israels, "no girl or group of girls can walk along the street there or through the park without being repeatedly accosted by men."[5] Young women sought Coney's diversions with a friend of the same sex, the protective arrangement that better allowed them to strike up innocuous acquaintances with young men. [. . .]

SEXUAL CULTURE AT CONEY

Luna and Dreamland based much of their appeal on spectacle and sensation, inspiring surprise, awe, laughter, and delight in the experiences they orchestrated for the public. They intentionally rejected the "old" Coney Island's sexual culture. Still, many of Coney's visitors, including working women, continued to gravitate to the rowdy streets, alluring concession stands, and bawdy sideshows that flourished under the shadow of the big amusement parks. [. . .]

While journalists touted the wholesome respectability of the "new" Coney Island, middle-class reform groups found much to criticize. In 1901, the Women's Branch of the Brooklyn City Mission crusaded against immorality and prostitution at Coney. When police denied that such activities occurred, a New York *Tribune* reporter investigated the moral condition of the resort. He condemned the "disgusting photographs" displayed in kinetoscope shows, noting that "the most pathetic sight was the number of women with daughters and sons that patronized the places where these machines were."[6] Another study of vice at the island's resorts was conducted in 1910, while in 1912, a reform group called the West End Improvement League of Coney Island crusaded for more beach front, a boardwalk, and an improved moral tone. One Reverend Mortenson, of the Society of Inner Mission and Rescue Work, was outraged by the rowdyism at night, the sideshows and bawdy concert halls, the suggestive moving picture machines, and, not least, the immorality of the beach on Sunday afternoons: "The nudity and unproper behavior of many of the people there are, mildly speaking, shocking."[7] Indeed, some New York City guidebooks continued to advise middle-class tourists to stick to the safe and refined Manhattan and Brighton Beaches, warning that the individual who went to West Brighton "should look out for his pocket-book and not be too curious to visit all the 'midway attractions,' some of which are to be avoided."[8]

The freer sexual expression of the dance halls, beaches, and boardwalk, which had long appealed to working women, increasingly became commodified in the amusement concessions of West Brighton. Many sideshows promoted familiarity between the sexes, romance, and titillation to attract crowds of young women and men. Penny arcades, for example, had machines to measure the ardor of a couple's kiss. The Cannon Coaster, which shot people out of a cannon onto a slide, advertised itself with the come-on, "Will she throw her arms around your neck and yell? Well, I guess, yes." Rides that sent their patrons into dark, winding passages—the Canals of Venice and the Tunnel of Love, for example—proliferated. Said the manager of one of these mazes, "The men like it because it gives them a chance to hug the girls, the girls like it because it gives them a chance to get hugged."[9] [...]

STEEPLECHASE

George Tilyou's Steeplechase Park, the third of the large amusement parks of Coney Island, exemplifies the commercial potential of making sexuality and romance the focal point of amusement. Tilyou's inspiration came as much from the world of cheap amusements as it did from the middle-class exposition. He built Steeplechase in 1897 on different principles from those underlying Luna and Dreamland, being much less concerned with grandeur, artistic design, and awe-inspiring sensation. Advertised as "The Funny Place," Steeplechase featured hilarity, symbolized by a vulgar, grinning, slightly sinister clown face above its entrance gates, which by 1905 "was causing sensitive folk to wince as they walked by."[10] With none of the attractions of Luna Park or Dreamland—no exotic villages, scenes of natural disasters, or re-enactments of current events[—]Steeplechase relied on fun houses, mechanical sensations, and circus-type sideshow attractions. Tilyou rarely allowed his patrons to be passive viewers. Instead, the patrons were whirled through space and knocked off balance, their hats blown off, skirts lifted, sense of humor tried. The patrons themselves became the show, providing interest and hilarity to each other.

At Steeplechase, visitors often experienced the unexpected in a sexual context. Some attractions simply encouraged closeness and romance. Men and women customarily sat together on the mechanical horses for the Steeplechase Ride. More inventive were such novelties as the Razzle-Dazzle, also known as the Wedding Ring. This attraction was simply a large circle of laminated wood suspended from a pole, which would be rocked back and forth, causing the patrons to lose their balance. The Wedding Ring made instant acquaintances of strangers and gave women and men a perfect excuse to clutch each other. Similarly, the Barrel of Love was a slowly revolving drum that forced those in it to tumble into each other. Tilyou's intentions were made clear in the advertisement, "Talk about love in a cottage! This has it beat a mile." Meanwhile, the Dew Drop, a parachute ride, never failed to lift women's skirts to the delight of onlookers.[11] Audience participation, the interaction of strangers, and voyeurism were incorporated into Tilyou's conception of mass entertainment.

Significantly, Tilyou never changed this formula, even with the moral cleansing of Coney Island and competition from the other amusement parks after 1900. Fire destroyed much of Steeplechase in 1907, and Tilyou energetically rebuilt it, playfully constructing a temple to exhibitionism, humor, and heterosocial relations called the Pavilion of Fun. The Pavilion featured novel and ingenious methods of placing people in compromising positions, never giving its victims any relief. The human pool table, for example, was placed at the foot of the Dew Drop. Instead of landing safely on solid ground after the parachute ride, the patrons found themselves on a spinning disk that threw them wildly into one another, with the expected results of flying clothes and revealed limbs.[12] [...]

While social classes mingled at the different amusement parks, Steeplechase attracted a less well-to-do crowd than Luna or Dreamland. Indeed, Tilyou actively promoted it among laboring women and men, advertising in working-class newspapers, including the New York *Call,* a socialist paper, as well as the regular dailies. Affordable entrance fees offered "10 hours of fun for 10 cents," and Tilyou alone offered a combination ticket that for twenty-five cents admitted visitors to the park and sixteen attractions as well.[13] Moreover, Steeplechase incorporated into its notion of mass entertainment cultural patterns derived from working-class amusements, street life, and popular entertainment. Like them, the park encouraged familiarity between strangers, permitted a free-and-easy sexuality, and structured heterosocial interaction. This culture was not adopted wholesale, but was transformed and controlled, reducing the threatening nature of sexual contact by removing it from the street, workplace, and saloon. Within the amusement park, familiarity between women and men could be acceptable if tightly structured and made harmless through laughter. At Steeplechase, sexuality was constructed in terms of titillation, voyeurism, exhibitionism, and a stress on couples and romance.

Steeplechase was the most enduring of the three parks. The more pretentious Dreamland was never as popular as Luna Park and Steeplechase, and Luna's fortunes declined after 1920. In part, this was due to the financial and personal problems of its founders, but in many ways, Luna emerged at the end, not the beginning, of an era. Its scenic railways and re-enactments of current events were the culmination of Victorian ways of seeing and experiencing. With the rise of the movies and the automobile, Luna's spectacles seemed increasingly old-fashioned, until the amusement park finally closed in the 1940's. Steeplechase, however, remained popular through much of the twentieth century.[14]

NOTES

Notes are by Kathy Peiss. The numbering has been changed to fit the excerpt in this anthology.

1   [Belle Lindner] Israels, ["Way of the Girl," *Survey* 22 (3 July 1909): 492, 491]; [Julian] Ralph, "Coney Island," [*Scribner's* 20 (July 1896)]: 18.

2   Beatrice L. Stevenson, "Working Girls' Life at Coney Island," *Yearbook of the Women's Municipal League*, Nov. 1911, p. 19. See also Lindsay Denison, "The Biggest Playground in the World," *Munsey's* 33 (Aug. 1905): 566.

3   Edwin E. Slosson, "The Amusement Business," *Independent* 57 (21 July 1904): 139.

4   Rollin Lynde Hartt, "The Amusement Park," *Atlantic* 99 (May 1907): 676; [Lillian W.] Betts, ["Tenement-House Life and Recreation," *Outlook* 61 (11 Feb. 1899)]: 365.

5   Hartt, "Amusement Park," p. 676; Israels, "Way of the Girl," p. 490.

6   "Coney Needs Cleansing," New York *Tribune*, 15 July 1901, p. 12. For the police department's response, see "Coney Island Decent Now," New York *Tribune*, 19 July 1901; cf.

[Albert Bigelow] Paine, ["The New Coney Island," *Century Magazine* 68 (Aug. 1904)]: 533.

7 West End Improvement League of Coney Island, *Neglected Coney Island* (New York, [1912]), p. 25; see in particular photographs on pp. 19, 28–29, which show women and men on the beach holding each other around the shoulders or waist, chasing each other, and generally assuming relaxed and joyous postures. See also [Oliver] Pilot and [Jo] Ransom, *Sodom by the Sea[: An Affectionate History of Coney Island* (Garden City, N.Y., 1941)], pp. 126–127.

8 Brooklyn Daily Eagle, *Visitor's Guide to New York*, p. 38; [Richard Henry] Edwards, *Popular Amusements* [New York, 1915], p. 107.

9 *History of Coney Island[: Lists and Photographs of Main Attractions* (New York, 1904], p. 44; Hartt, "Amusement Park," pp. 676–677. For similar rides and sideshows, see the photographs in *Souvenir of Coney Island* (New York, n.d.).

10 [Edo] McCullough, *Good Old Coney Island[: A Sentimental Journey into the Past* (New York, 1957)], p. 311. While largely anecdotal, McCullough's history clearly identifies the alternative conception of amusement that Steeplechase embodied.

11 See *ibid.*, pp. 309–310, for a description of these amusements.

12 *Ibid.*, 311–313.

13 *Glimpses of the New Coney Island: America's Most Popular Pleasure Resort* (New York, 1904), n. pag. *History of Coney Island*, p. 36, lists the sixteen attractions. On the three amusement parks' appeal to different audiences, see Pilot and Ransom, *Sodom by the Sea*, p. 157.

14 McCullough, *Good Old Coney Island*, p. 316; Pilot and Ransom, *Sodom by the Sea*, p. 157.

SAMANTHA AT CONEY ISLAND AND A THOUSAND OTHER ISLANDS

Marietta Holley

Marietta Holley (1836–1926) was born on a farm in Jefferson County, New York. She is important for the creation of her female protagonist, Samantha Smith Allen, who appears in more than fifteen of her books. Many of the novels were written using the pen name Josiah Allen's Wife. All these books employ dialect and humor, and feature the good-natured, country philosopher Samantha. In this excerpt from *Samantha at Coney Island and a Thousand Other Islands* (1911), the protagonist comes to the rescue of her husband, Josiah, lost in the wilds of Coney Island.

THE WONDERFUL AND MYSTERIOUS SIGHTS I SAW IN STEEPLE CHASE PARK, AND MY SEARCH THERE FOR MY PARDNER

Steeple Chase Park is most as big as Luny Park, but is mostly one huge buildin' covered with glass, and every thing on earth or above, or under the earth, is goin' on there, acres and acres of amusements (so-called) in one glass house.

As I went in, I see a immense mirror turnin' round and round seemin'ly invitin' folks to look. But as I glanced in, I tell the truth when I say, I wuzn't much bigger round than a match, and the thinness made me look as tall as three on me.

"Oh," sez I, "has grief wore my flesh away like this? If it keeps on I shan't dast to take lemonade, for fear I shall fall into the straw and be drowned."

A bystander sez, "Look agin, mom!"

I did and I wuzn't more'n two fingers high, and wide as our barn door.

I most shrieked and sez to myself, "It has come onto me at last, grief and such doin's as I've seen here, has made me crazy as a loon." And I started away almost on a run.

All of a sudden the floor under me which looked solid as my kitchen floor begun to move back and forth with me and sideways and back, to and fro, fro and to, and I goin' with it, one foot goin' one way, and the other foot goin' somewhere else; but by a hurculaneum effort I kep' my equilibrium upright, and made out to git on solid floorin'. But a high-headed female in a hobble skirt, the hobbles hamperin her, fell prostrate. I felt so shook up and wobblin' myself, I thought a little Scripter would stiddy me, and I sez, "Sinners stand on slippery places." [...]

I scrambled to my feet quick as I could, and as I riz up I see right in front on me the gigantick, shameless female Bildad had as good as told me Josiah had been flirtin' with. I knowed her to once, the gaudy, flashin' lookin' creeter, bigger than three wimmen ort to be; she wuz ten feet high if she wuz a inch. As she came up to me with mincin' steps, I sez to her in skathin' axents:

"What have you done with my innocent pardner? Where is Josiah Allen? Open your guilty breast and confess." And now I'm tellin' the livin' truth, as she towered up in front on me, her breast did open and a man's face looked out on me. My brain tottled, but righted itself with relief, for it wuz not Josiah; it wuz probable some other woman's husband. But I sez to myself, let every woman take care of her own husband if she can; it hain't my funeral.

And I hurried off till I come out into a kinder open place with some good stiddy chairs to set down on, and some green willers hangin' down their verdant boughs over some posy beds. Nothin' made up about 'em. Oh how good it looked to me to see sunthin' that God had made, and man hadn't dickered with and manufactured to seem different from what it wuz. Thinks I, if I should take hold of one of these feathery green willer sprays it wouldn't turn into a serpent or try to trip me up, or wobble me down. They looked beautiful to me, and beyond 'em I could see the Ocean, another and fur greater reality, real as life, or death, or taxes, or anything else we can't escape from.

Settin' there lookin' off on them mighty everlastin' waves, forever flowin' back and forth, forth and back, the world of the flimsy and the false seemed to pass away and the Real more nigh to me than it did in the painted land of shams and onreality I had been passin' through. And as I meditated on the disgraceful sight I had seen—that gaudy, guilty creeter with a man concealed in her breast. For if it wuzn't a guilty secret, why wuz the door shet and fastened tight, till the searchlight of a woman's indignant eyes brought him to light?

Thinkin' it over calmly and bein' reasonable and just, my feelin's over that female kinder softened down, and I sez to myself, what if there wuz a open winder or door into all our hearts, for outsiders to look in, what would they see? Curious sights, homely ones and beautiful, happy ones and sorrowful, and some kinder betwixt and between. Sacred spots that the nearest ones never got a glimpse on. Eyes that look acrost the coffee pot at you every mornin' never ketched sight on 'em, nor the ones that walk up and down in them hidden gardens. Some with veiled faces mebby, some with reproachful orbs, some white and still, some pert and sassy.

Nothin' wicked, most likely; nothin' the law could touch you for; but most probable it might make trouble if them affectionate eyes opposite could behold 'em, for where love is there is jealousy, and a lovin' woman will be jealous of a shadder or a scare-crow. It is nateral nater and can't be helped. But if she stopped to think on't, she herself has her hid-away nooks in her heart, dark or pleasant landscapes, full of them, you never ketch a glimpse on do the best you can. And jealous curosity goes deep. What would Josiah see through my heart's open door? What would I see in hisen? It most skairs me to think on't. No, it hain't best to have open doors into hearts. Lots of times it would be resky; not wrong, you know, but jest resky.

Thus I sot and eppisoded, lookin' off onto the melancholy ocean, listenin' to her deep sithes, when onbid come the agonizin' thought, "Had Josiah Allen backslid so fur and been so full of remorse and despair, that his small delicate brain had turned over with him, and he had throwed himself into the arms of the melancholy Ocean? Wuz her deep, mournful sithes preparin' me for the heart-breakin' sorrow?" I couldn't abear the thought, and I riz up and walked away. As I did so a bystander sez, "Have you been up on the Awful Tower?"

"No," sez I, "I've been through awful things, enough, accidental like, without layin' plans and climbin' up on 'em." But Hope will always hunch Anxiety out of her high chair in your head and stand up on it. I thought I would go upstairs into another part of the buildin' and mebby I might ketch a glimpse of my pardner in the dense crowd below.

And if you'll believe it, as I wuz walkin' upstairs as peaceful as our old brindle cow goin' up the south hill paster, my skirts begun to billow out till they got as big as a hogsit. I didn't care about its bein' fashion to not bulge out round the bottom of your skirts but hobble in; but I see the folks below wuz laughin' at me, and it madded me some when I hadn't done a thing, only jest walk upstairs peaceable. And I don't know to this day what made my clothes billow out so.

But I went on and acrost to a balcony, and after I went in, a gate snapped shet behind me and I couldn't git back. And when I got to the other side there wuzn't any steps, and if I got down at all I had to slide down. I didn't like to make the venter, but had to, so I tried to forgit my specs and gray hair and fancy I wuz ten years old, in a pigtail braid, and pantalettes tied on with my stockin's, and sot off. As I went down with lightnin' speed I hadn't time to think much, but I ricollect this thought come into my harassed brain:

Be pardners worth all the trouble I'm havin' and the dretful experiences I'm goin' through? Wouldn't it been better to let him go his length, than to suffer what I'm sufferin'? I reached the floor with such a jolt that my mind didn't answer the question; it didn't have time.

All to once, another wind sprung up from nowhere seemin'ly, and tried its best to blow off my bunnet. But thank Heaven, my good green braize veil tied round it with strong lutestring ribbon, held it on, and I see I still had holt of my trusty cotton umbrell, though the wind had blowed it open, but I shet it and grasped it firmly, thinkin' it wuz my only protector and safeguard now Josiah wuz lost, and I hastened away from that crazy spot.

As I passed on I see a hull lot of long ropes danglin' down. On top of 'em wuz a trolley, and folks would hang onto the handle and slide hundred of feet through the air. But I didn't venter. Disinclination and rumatiz both made me waive off overtures to try it.

Pretty soon I come to a huge turn-table, big as our barn floor. It wuz still and harmless lookin' when I first see it, and a lot of folks got onto it, thinkin' I spoze it looked so shiny and good they'd like to patronize it. But pretty soon it begun to move, and then to turn faster and faster till the folks couldn't keep their seats and one by one they wuz throwed off, and went down through a hole in the floor I know not where.

As I see 'em disappear one by one in the depths below, thinks I, is that where Josiah Allen has disappeared to? Who knows but he is moulderin' in some underground dungeon, mournin' and pinin' for me and his native land. Of course Reason told me that he couldn't moulder much in two days, but I wuz too much wrought up to listen to Reason, and as I see 'em slide down and disappear, onbeknown to myself I spoke out loud and sez:

"Can it be that Josiah is incarcerated in some dungeon below? If he is, I will find and release him or perish with him."

A woman who looked as if she belonged there, hearn me and sez, "Who is Josiah?" "My pardner," sez I, and I continued, "You have a kind face, mom; have you see him? Have you seen Josiah Allen?"

"Describe him," sez she, "there wuz a man here just now hunting for some woman."

"Oh, he is very beautiful!"

"Young?" sez she.

"Well, no; about my age or a little older."

"Light complexion? Dark hair and eyes? Stylish dressed?"

"No, wrinkled complexion, bald, and what few hairs he's got, gray."

She smiled; she couldn't see the beauty Love had gilded his image with.

Sez I, "If he's incarcerated in some dungeon below, I too will mount the turn-table of torture, and share his fate or perish on the turn table."

Sez she, "There is no dungeons below; the folks come out into a vast place as big as this. There is just as much to see down there as there is here, just as many people and just as much amusement."

"Amusement!" sez I in a holler voice.

After I left her, I see a whisk broom hangin' up in a handy place, and it had a printed liebill on it, "This whisk broom free." And as my parmetty dress had got kinder dusty a slidin' and wobblin' as I had slode and wobbled, I went to brush off my skirt with it, when all of a sudden somebody or sunthin' gin me a stunnin' blow right in my arm that held the brush. I dropped it without waitin' to argy the matter, and I don't know to this day who or what struck me and what it wuz for. But my conscience wuz clear; I hadn't done nothin' [. . .]

I hastened away and thought I would go up into the second story agin and mebby ketch sight of my pardner, for the crowd had increased. And as I stood there skannin' the immense crowd below to try to ketch a glimpse of my lawful pardner, all to once I see the folks below wuz laughin' at me. I felt to see if my braize veil hung down straight and graceful, and my front hair wuz all right, and my cameo pin fastened. But nothin' wuz amiss, and I wondered what could it be. The balcony wuz divided off into little spaces, five or six feet square, and I stood in one, innocent as a lamb (or mebby it would be more appropriate to say a sheep), and leanin' on the railin', and one sassy boy called out:

"Where wuz you ketched? Are you tame? Wuz you ketched on the Desert of Sara? Did Teddy ketch you for the Government?" and I never knowed till I got down what they wuz laughin' at.

The little boxes in the balcony wuz painted on the outside to represent animal cages. On the one where I had been wuz painted the sign Drumedary. Josiah Allen's wife took for a drumedary—The idee!

But the view I got of the crowd below wuz impressive, and though it seemed to me that everybody in New York and Brooklyn and the adjacent villages and country, wuz all there a Steeple Chasin', yet I knowed there wuz jest as many dreamin' in Dreamland and bein' luny in Luny Park. And Surf Avenue wuz full, and what they called the Bowery of Coney Island, and all the amusement places along the shore. And all on 'em on the move, jostlin' and bein' jostled, foolin' and bein' fooled, laughin' and bein' laughed at.

Why, I wuz told and believe, that sometimes a million folks go to Coney Island on a holiday. And I wuz knowin' myself to over three thousand orphan children goin' there at one time to spend a happy day, the treat bein' gin 'em by some big-hearted men. Plenty to eat and drink, and a hull day of enjoyment, candy, pop corn, circus, etc., bright day, happy hearts, how that day will stand out against the dull gray background of their lives! And them men ort to hug themselves thinkin' the thought, over three thousand happinesses wuz set down to their credit in the books of the Recordin' Angel. And I sez to myself, "Samantha, you ort to speak well of anything that so brightens the lives of the children of the great city."

CONEY ISLAND

Sara Teasdale

Sara Teasdale (1884–1933) was born in St. Louis, Missouri. She became part of the circle of *Poetry* magazine and its founder, Harriet Monroe, in Chicago. In 1916, she moved to New York City and two years later was awarded the Columbia University Poetry Society Prize (which became the Pulitzer Prize for poetry). "Coney Island" is from her second collection, *Helen of Troy and Other Poems* (1911). The poem, set in the off-season, concerns a love that has passed its time and is gone, like June at the amusement area. It is marked, as are her other poems, by its simplicity and clarity.

Why did you bring me here?
The sand is white with snow,
Over the wooden domes
The winter sea-winds blow—
There is no shelter near,
   Come, let us go.

With foam of icy lace
The sea creeps up the sand,
The wind is like a hand
That strikes us in the face.
Doors that June set a-swing
Are bolted long ago;
We try them uselessly—
Alas, there cannot be
For us a second spring;
   Come, let us go.

THE GREATER CONEY

O. Henry

O. Henry was the pen name of William Sydney Porter (1862–1910), the author of short stories best known for their surprise endings. Born in North Carolina, as a young man he moved to Texas, where he held various jobs, including bank clerk, reporter, and publisher. While in prison on a charge of embezzlement, he began to write and sell short stories, a genre of which he became a master. After being released from prison, in 1902 he moved to New York, where his writing career flourished. In "The Greater Coney," published in *Sixes and Sevens* (1911), laborer Dennis Carnahan tells about his recent visit to Coney, where he encounters his girlfriend, Norah Flynn, and they patch up a lover's quarrel. Dennis sarcastically refers to the "moral reconstruction" of Coney Island, explaining "that the reprehensible and degradin' resorts that disgraced old Coney are said to be wiped out." In a reference to the advent of the enclosed amusement parks, Dennis claims that people now go to Coney to "give up their quarters to squeeze through turnstiles and see imitations of city fires and floods painted on canvas."

"**NEXT SUNDAY,**" said Dennis Carnahan, "I'll be after going down to see the new Coney Island that's risen like a phoenix bird from the ashes of the old resort. I'm going with Norah Flynn, and we'll fall victims to all the dry goods deceptions, from the red-flannel eruption of Mount Vesuvius to the pink silk ribbons on the race-suicide problems in the incubator kiosk.

"Was I there before? I was. I was there last Tuesday. Did I see the sights? I did not.

"Last Monday I amalgamated myself with the Bricklayers' Union, and in accordance with the rules I was ordered to quit work the same day on account of a sympathy strike with the Lady Salmon Canners' Lodge No. 2, of Tacoma, Washington.

"'Twas disturbed I was in mind and proclivities by losing me job, bein' already harassed in me soul on account of havin' quarrelled with Norah Flynn a week before by reason of hard words spoken at the Dairymen and Street-Sprinkler Drivers' semi-annual ball, caused by jealousy and prickly heat and that divil, Andy Coghlin.

"So, I says, it will be Coney for Tuesday; and if the chutes and the short change and the green-corn silk between the teeth don't create diversions and get me feeling better, then I don't know at all.

"Ye will have heard that Coney has received moral reconstruction. The old Bowery, where they used to take your tintype by force and give ye knockout drops before having your palm read, is now called the Wall Street of the island. The wienerwurst stands are required by law to keep a news ticker in 'em; and the doughnuts are examined every four years by a retired steamboat inspector. The nigger man's head that was used by the old patrons to throw baseballs at is now illegal; and, by order of the Police Commissioner the image of a man drivin' an automobile has been substituted. I hear that the old immoral amusements have been suppressed. People who used to go down from New York to sit in the sand and dabble in the surf now give up their quarters to squeeze through turnstiles and see imitations of city fires and floods painted on canvas. The reprehensible and degradin' resorts that disgraced old Coney are said to be wiped out. The wipin'-out process consists of raisin' the price from 10 cents to 25 cents, and hirin' a blonde named Maudie to sell tickets instead of Mickey, the Bowery Bite. That's what they say—I don't know.

"But to Coney I goes a-Tuesday. I gets off the 'L' and starts for the glitterin' show. 'Twas a fine sight. The Babylonian towers and the Hindoo roof gardens was blazin' with thousands of electric lights, and the streets was thick with people. 'Tis a true thing they say that Coney levels all rank. I see millionaires eatin' popcorn and trampin' along with the crowd; and I see eight-dollar-a-week clothin'-store clerks in red automobiles fightin' one another for who'd squeeze the horn when they come to a corner.

"'I made a mistake,' I says to myself. 'Twas not Coney I needed. When a man's sad 'tis not scenes of hilarity he wants. 'Twould be far better for him to meditate in a graveyard or to attend services at the Paradise Roof Gardens. 'Tis no consolation when a man's lost his sweetheart to order hot corn and have the waiter bring him the powdered sugar cruet instead of salt and then conceal himself, or to have Zozookum, the gipsy palmist, tell him that he has three children and to look out for another serious calamity; price twenty-five cents.

"I walked far away down on the beach, to the ruins of an old pavilion near one corner of this new private park, Dreamland. A year ago that old pavilion was standin' up straight and the old-style waiters was slammin' a week's supply of clam chowder down in front of you for a nickel and callin' you 'cully' friendly, and vice was rampant, and you got back to New York with enough change to take a car at the bridge. Now they tell me that they serve Welsh rabbits on Surf Avenue, and you get the right change back in the movin'-picture joints.

"I sat down at one side of the old pavilion and looked at the surf spreadin' itself on the beach, and thought about the time me and Norah Flynn sat on that spot last summer. 'Twas before reform struck the island; and we was happy. We had tintypes and chowder in the ribald dives, and the Egyptian Sorceress of the Nile told Norah out of her hand, while I was waitin' in the door, that 'twould be the luck of her to marry a red-headed gossoon with two crooked legs, and I was overrunnin' with joy on account of the illusion. And 'twas there that Norah Flynn put her two hands in mine a year before and we talked of flats and the things she could cook and the love business that goes with such episodes. And that was Coney as we loved it, and as the hand of Satan was upon it, friendly and noisy and your money's worth, with no fence around the ocean and not too many electric lights to show the sleeve of a black serge coat against a white shirtwaist.

"I sat with my back to the parks where they had the moon and the dreams and the steeples corralled, and longed for the old Coney. There wasn't many people on the beach. Lots of them was feedin' pennies into the slot machines to see the 'Interrupted Courtship' in the movin' pictures; and a good many was takin' the air in the Canals of Venice and some was breathin' the smoke of the sea battle by actual warships in a tank filled with real water. A few was down on the sands enjoyin' the moonlight and the water. And the heart of me was heavy for the new morals of the old island, while the bands behind me played and the sea pounded on the bass drum in front.

"And directly I got up and walked along the old pavilion, and there on the other side of, half in the dark, was a slip of a girl sittin' on the tumble-down timbers, and unless I'm a liar she was cryin' by herself there, all alone.

"'Is it trouble you are in, now, Miss,' says I; 'and what's to be done about it?'

"'Tis none of your business at all, Denny Carnahan,' says she, sittin' up straight. And it was the voice of no other than Norah Flynn.

"'Then it's not,' says I, 'and we're after having a pleasant evening, Miss Flynn. Have ye seen the sights of this new Coney Island, then? I presume ye have come here for that purpose,' says I.

"'I have,' says she. 'Me mother and Uncle Tim they are waiting beyond. 'Tis an elegant evening I've had. I've seen all the attractions that be.'

"'Right ye are,' says I to Norah; and I don't know when I've been that amused. After disportin' meself among the most laughable moral improvements of the revised shell games I took meself to the shore for the benefit of the cool air. 'And did ye observe the Durbar, Miss Flynn?'

"'I did,' says she, reflectin'; 'but 'tis not safe, I'm thinkin', to ride down them slantin' things into the water.'

"'How did ye fancy the shoot the chutes?' I asks.

"'True, then, I'm afraid of guns,' says Norah. 'They make such noise in my ears. But Uncle Tim, he shot them, he did, and won cigars. 'Tis a fine time we had this day, Mr. Carnahan.'

"'I'm glad you've enjoyed yerself,' I says. 'I suppose you've had a roarin' fine time seein' the sights. And how did the incubators and the helter-skelter and the midgets suit the taste of ye?'

"'I—I wasn't hungry,' says Norah, faint. 'But mother ate a quantity of all of 'em. I'm that pleased with the fine things in the new Coney Island,' says she, 'that it's the happiest day I've seen in a long time, at all.'

"'Did you see Venice?' says I.

"'We did,' says she. 'She was a beauty. She was all dressed in red, she was, with—'

"I listened no more to Norah Flynn. I stepped up and gathered her in my arms.

"''Tis a story-teller ye are, Norah Flynn,' says I. 'Ye've seen no more of the greater Coney Island than I have meself. Come, now, tell the truth—ye came to sit by the old pavilion by the waves where you sat last summer and made Dennis Carnahan a happy man. Speak up, and tell the truth.'

"Norah stuck her nose against me vest.

"'I despise it, Denny,' she says, half cryin'. 'Mother and Uncle Tim went to see the shows, but I came down here to think of you. I couldn't bear the lights and the crowd. Are you forgivin' me, Denny, for the words we had?'

"''Twas me fault,' says I. 'I came here for the same reason meself. Look at the lights, Norah,' I says, turning my back to the sea—'ain't they pretty?'

"'They are,' says Norah, with her eyes shinin'; 'and do ye hear the bands playin'? Oh, Denny, I think I'd like to see it all.'

"'The old Coney is gone, darlin','' I says to her. 'Everything moves. When a man's glad it's not scenes of sadness he wants. 'Tis a greater Coney we have here, but we couldn't see it till we got in the humor for it. Next Sunday, Norah darlin', we'll see the new place from end to end.'"

"IN DREAMLAND," CONEY ISLAND, 1905. (PHOTOGRAPH PUBLISHED BY DETROIT PUBLISHING COMPANY. LIBRARY OF CONGRESS, PRINTS AND PHOTOGRAPHS DIVISION)

DREAMLAND

Kevin Baker

Kevin Baker (b. 1958) was born in Englewood, New Jersey. He is a journalist and a contributing editor at *Harper's*. Baker has written several novels, including *The Big Crowd* (2013) and the City of Fire trilogy: *Dreamland* (1999), *Paradise Alley* (2002), and *Strivers Row* (2006). *Dreamland*, a sprawling historical novel loaded with Yiddish phrases and gangland slang, describes Coney as both a brutally violent place and a source of solace for those who cannot find comfort in the outside world. The novel features a wide variety of colorful characters, including Trick the Dwarf, who lives in the midget village in Dreamland; the kind-hearted criminal Kid Twist; and his factory-worker girlfriend, Esther Abramowitz. Baker also wrote about Coney in his graphic novel (with illustrator Daniel Zezelj), *Luna Park* (2010).

TRICK THE DWARF

I took them straight out to the old Tin Elephant. I could have put them up in my town—after all, I had a palace!—but they would have stood out like, well, like two sore thumbs.

Fortunately, even Coney Island has never been short on places where you could hang yourself in complete solitude and anonymity. It was easy to get a room in the Elephant's arse at that hour. It was almost dawn by the time we got there, and the last tricks of the night were just stumbling out, hats pulled down over their eyes, reeking of sausage, and gin, and bed sweat.

The whores were still up, washing themselves in their room basins. We could hear them calling, each to each, as we climbed the winding, spiral staircase; lovely, bright voices, twittering like songbirds, happy to be at the end of the night. Though it was at this hour, too, that they tended to kill themselves, when all the sensation of the early evening—the promise of the brightly lit parlor, and the piano music downstairs and the smell of a first, freshly poured beer—had metamorphosed into nothing more than one more grunting, sweaty, two-hundred-fifty-pound brush salesman. One of the songbirds' voices would be missing, and they would find her in her room, hung with her own kimono sash or doused with opium.

I took my new friends back to the last room—the one where I used to live, before I persuaded Matty Brinckerhoff to build The Little City for me and mine. Some mad predecessor to Brinckerhoff had put it up thirty years before, back when that sort of thing was the rage: an entire hotel constructed in the image of an elephant. Complete with tusks and a trunk, an observation deck up in its howdah, shops and penny arcades and entire shows and dance halls jammed into its immense legs. At night its yellow eyes shined out over the boardwalk and the ocean, some rough beast lurking amidst the more respectable hotels.

It had been slowly chipped away over the years, like everything else at Coney: a wonder surpassed by many other wonders, its rooms filled up with whores and other human flotsam. I had lived in my little room with only the bed, a basin, a table and chair I sawed off myself—the management didn't care much what you did, so long as you paid every week—and the black steamer trunk I had hauled through thirty seasons of grand expositions and international spectaculars and other such degradations.

It was too noisy to actually sleep at night, with the mabs and their customers. The tin roof broiled when the sun was out, and it rang like hammers on an anvil when it rained. Fortunately, I had work: barker for a Son of Ham act among the Luna Park sideshows:

"Hit the nigger Hit the nigger in the head Three balls for the price of five Three balls and a big prize if you can hit the nigger in the head!"

Luke, the poor, addled Negro they had for the act, would stick his head through a crude yellow drawing of the moon, and grin a great, toothless grin at the crowd. It was a terrifying sight: his old prizefighter's head, gnarled as an apple branch, odd lumps and contusions sticking up on all sides. Let's face it, you could never get a man to do such work if he wasn't more than a little punch-drunk already.

It wasn't hard work—for me, anyway. I didn't have to do very much, and how quickly and viciously the baseballs would start to fly! Real, hard-cored baseballs, too, tight as the ones Christy Mathewson threw up at the Polo Grounds. The rubes so excited to score a hit that half the time they didn't even remember their prizes, and every hour or so I had to take old Luke back behind the stand and wash him down so the whole thing didn't get too gory for the family crowd. Well, let's just say that it was a less than edifying profession.

There were worse jobs on Coney Island, believe it or not—at least, worse jobs for me. Over at Steeplechase Park, where the paying customers came off the mechanical horses, there was another one of my kind: a smirking, demonic caricature of a dwarf, done up in a harlequin's suit and hat and painted face.

I had watched him, chasing all the flushed-faced clerks, and the day laborers, and the factory girls, with a cattle prod, driving them back across the blowholes that sent the women's skirts billowing up around their ears—and all for the benefit of their fellow patrons, sitting up in the bleachers of the Laughing Gallery. He made them howl: the men high-stepping through the air, holding their hands on their backsides like Mack Sennett's Keystones—the women running and squeaking in fear, holding their hands over their sexes. [. . .]

As I watched, a once-innocent young girl tried to get by. She looked unsettled already by the shenanigans on the Steeplechase, plump, greasy fingerstains visible on the bosom of her white shirtwaist. The crowd screamed as he advanced on her, oversized clown's head lolling grotesquely. He drove her backwards, terrified, the girl clutching her hands to her chest—her fellow passengers scurrying by, just glad to be unnoticed. Once outside, they exhaled in relief—and took their own seats among the screaming faces in the Laughing Gallery.

I had to turn away. That was my greatest fear, before the construction of The Little City, that I could be compelled by necessity to take such a situation. That is always the thing with depravity: just when you think you've plumbed the very depths, there's always someplace lower to fall. [. . .]

ON THE BOARDWALK

They met on the beach at Coney. He was making his way through the Sunday crowd, looking out for his opportunities, and when he happened to glance down there she was: buried up to her thighs in the sand like a child, wearing a shiny green mermaid's bathing suit, still wet from the sea, and brushing out her hair with a silver brush.

Esther felt him over her, blocking the sun. She looked up and smiled to see him there—looking so solemn, in his flashy suit the color of peach ice cream and a brilliant blue bow tie. He tipped his hat to her, and held out his arm, and without even thinking about it she reached up and took it, and let him guide her back toward the parks.

Anyplace else, she would never have done such a thing. Anyplace else but on the beach on Coney Island, on a beautiful Sunday morning. She put the cheap, silver-painted brush she had bought at Wanamaker's away, and took his arm, and let him lift her up, watching him watch the skirt of her costume slip slowly down over her bare, white legs.

"Let me treat you," Kid told her.

Esther laughed at him, but there was something very serious in his face. "Treat me?"

"Anything you want," he told her impulsively. "The best piece of goods there is!"

"My Rockefeller prince!"

She laughed again, and let him take her back up the beach, toward the pavilions of fun, trying discreetly to brush the last of the sand off her legs, the green-gold imitation scales of her suit glistening in the sunlight.

Up on the boardwalk, up on the breezeway at Feltman's they ate lobster and clams and corn on the cob, until their tiny white-tableclothed table was drenched in melted butter and warm sea brine. A band in lederhosen was playing Viennese waltzes, and everyone was laughing. Esther even let him give her some of his beer; she thought it tasted awful, but she wanted to know what the goyim went padding down into the German saloon beneath their tenement for.

"You like it?" Kid asked, nudging her. "Beer agrees with you, moon?"

She shook her head, and smiled secretly to herself.

"*Herzalle meine*" [my heart], he beseeched her. The usual seducer's words, but he said them flatly, as if he were trying to convince himself more than her. A hand lay on her knee under the little table, the fingers trembling slightly. Esther pushed it casually aside, used to much more from the factory foremen, and there was no resistance.

"How can you be here with me?" he asked her—trying to smile, but actually very serious again. "How do you know what kind of man I am?"

"I like you," Esther shrugged, trying to sound bold, and brazen, groping for reasons. "I like how you laugh. And you have kind eyes."

Why was she there?

"But I could be the worst *yentzer* [crook] in the whole world!"

"I can take care of myself."

"But you don't know what I am." Completely serious again, his eyes large dark circles. *He did have nice eyes—*

"What does it matter?" she said, as bluff as she could manage. *What a strange seducer, warning her to look out.* "What does it matter, here and now?"

"I guess you're right there," he laughed uncertainly, and went back to tearing up his lobster.

After lunch, they walked hand-in-hand to the Steeplechase, past the chop suey joints and the shooting galleries. Past the player pianos and the beef dripping from a spit and wash-boilers full of green corn, and the men taunting them from the quick-lunch stands:

"Who's your sweetie?"

"Where're you two goin'? Off to see the elephant?"

He only glowered at them and pulled her on, through the shuffling, indifferent crowds.

A million encounters, she thought. *A million encounters every day, all meaning nothing—*

He towed her through the Gates of Mirth, into the glassed-in Pavilion of Fun, with its sheared-off, manic head, grinning from ear to ear:

STEEPLECHASE—FUNNY PLACE

The track wound around the entire park, long and undulant, and lined with American flags. He paid her quarter fare, and a grinning youth in blackface and tattered jockey's silks stepped forward, to help her mount the mechanical horse.

"Up you go—"

"No, you don't!"

He pushed the attendant away and helped her on himself—staring at the white flesh of her ankles again, as she swung her leg over. He climbed on behind her, and she didn't protest. All around them other men were bowing and smiling, helping other women they had just met onto their mounts.

A million encounters, meaning nothing

"Better hold on, little dove."

She could feel his warm breath on her cheek, murmuring into her ear.

"It gets going."

But it didn't. The horses didn't go very fast at all, that was the attraction. Another youth in checkerboard silks and painted darkie face blew a trumpet, and bells clanged, and the horses shot off—just fast enough to send the women squealing into their escorts' arms. They moved so slowly the men didn't even need a hand to hang onto their hats. They could devote both arms to the work, hands sliding and grabbing and caressing.

The horse soared effortlessly up and the whole expanse of the parks spread out beneath her, inexpressibly beautiful. It was the smoothest ride she had every felt—as smooth as air, smooth as pudding under her feet. She had gone fast before. She had felt the speed in one of her brother's new automobiles, or when some idiot of a conductor took the el, fast as he could hold her, around the Dead Man's Curve on 110th Street. But she had never known anything like this—fast enough but smooth, too, as smooth as fine lawn—

They glided back down, the rest of the park beneath her, all the rides and attractions shining beneath its glass trellis like jewels through ice. The Mixer, and the Barrel of Fun, and the Bounding Billows, and the Golden Stairs, and the Razzle Dazzle and the Cave of the Winds. And around them, all the distended men and women, still shuffling relentlessly forward—

A million encounters, all useless

He slid his arms around her waist, and leaned them expertly into the curves. Soon they were out ahead of the rest, a small breeze blowing pleasantly across her face. At her waist, she could feel his hands beginning to move on her: still hesitant, awkward but gentle now, caressing her through the mermaid costume.

"You're all soft silk and fine velvet," he murmured in her ear, and she wanted to laugh to hear him say it.

He moved his hands slowly up her waist, her belly, to places where she had never felt a man's hands before, and she let him—glad that he had pushed them ahead of the other, groping men, away from their leering eyes. They rose again, and she could see the ocean turning toward them, and the mobs along the beach: the pleasure boats, graceful as swans, with their huge white decks and romantic names—the *Pegasus* and the *Prometheus* and *Anacreon in Heaven*.

They encompassed half the earth in a matter of seconds—then they were down again: the other riders chortling and cursing on their own horses, the women screaming. His hands, his hands slid up almost to her breasts, stopping when she flinched, sliding, stroking down her again, and she let him. They were moving too quickly, too high up for anyone else to see, alone among the millions.

"You're finer than silk and velvet, I'll give you only dove's milk to drink—" The seducer's voice gone now. Only his own words remaining, eager, and uncertain, and a little desperate.

They made the final turn, past the pier, heading in toward the land, the streets and the slouching summer houses on Brighton Beach. Houses of easy virtue, she remembered—like going to see the elephant. He was lowering his face to the open collar of her mermaid's bathing costume, nuzzling his lips down her neck.

Like a horse, Esther thought, ludicrously, his lips wet and soft as a horse's.

He kissed her ear, stroked his hand along her neck, and she let him. They were going a little faster now, coming into the finish, and she knew that she ought to stop him but she was not sure that she could push him away and hang on. She did not want to fall off, plummeting out on the mechanical track on her bottom. She could get electrocuted, she could get run down like that poor woman she had seen in the nickelodeon at Union Square, running out before the King's horse at the Derby for women's rights—

Run down by a horse

She leaned her head back into him at the home stretch, looked at him there. His eyes were closed, to her surprise, his face boyish and sweet. She leaned back, and held onto his arms, let him hold her as they swooped down past the last American flags, over the finish line, to another, mocking jockey in blackface who pinned a blue ribbon on both their chests.

Esther struggled off the horse, her legs weak, bare white ankles flashing in front of him again. Kid struggled to get off himself, the burnt-cork jockey jeering:

"Whatsa matta? Too many legs?"

"Wait for me!"

It was too late. She was already wandering out past the finish line. She stopped to find herself on a stage—row after row of bleachers in front of her, every seat filled with laughing men and women, pointing at *her*.

A terrible little man in a clown suit rushed up to her waving some kind of club in his hands, mongoloid face grinning hideously. He swung it at her, and she backed away, holding out her hands. He only kept advancing on her, swinging the cattle prod like a baseball bat.

"Piece of wretch!" she shrieked, barely dodging away in time. "Wild animal!"

He laughed, yelling her words back at her in his ridiculous, high, dwarf's voice while he jabbed at her legs:

"Piece of wretch! Wild animal!"

She felt a terrible shock run through her body, as if a hand had wrapped itself around her heart. She fell back—and cold air rushed mortifyingly up her backside, blowing up the skirt of her mermaid bathing suit and making her jump in the air before the laughing crowd.

"Filth! Get away!"

Kid came running out on the stage, shooing away the dwarf. The mongoloid clown smirked, and scooted around him—but there was something in his face that made him go on to torture the other riders. Kid wrapped his arms protectively around her, guided her out past the Laughing Gallery and its barker:

"Come on in! Only a penny! *You* be the one laughing this time!"

"Little dove, are you all right?"

"Sure, sure," she said, smiling to reassure him—enjoying how he looked at her so solicitously, so sweetly now.

It was fun, Esther told herself, feeling her heart pounding wildly. It was terrifying, she had beat it, she had got past the awful little man, had gone through it all and survived.

It was fun, and I liked it!

That night Kid took her to Stauch's for a steak, and they sat in the balcony and watched the dancers shuffling around the huge ballroom under a giant, electrified American flag. Afterwards he wanted her to go to a moving picture at the Sunken Gardens or a show at Henderson's but it was late, she should have left for home already. The park was already beginning to take on a spectral look, as the music lowered, and the crowds wandered out. Little clumps of debris swirled around their feet like tumbleweeds: used paper napkins, and wax paper, and half-eaten hot-dog buns.

She could *hear* the lights now, the million bulbs, hissing loud as snakes. Couples hurried past, and in the darkness she could see a man's straw hat bent furtively over a dress, both faces hidden in the darkness.

He walked her over to the train platform, pleading good-naturedly, not really expecting her to stay, but wanting her to—she could *tell*, underneath it all.

"Just a little longer, bridie mine."

"No. It's late, I got to get back."

Fiery geysers of light shot up into the night—the closing fireworks, raining down in sizzling streams of red, white and blue. The bands struck up a patriotic air.

Distracted, just for a moment, Kid turned back to look for her—and she was gone. Only at the last moment did he spot her again, waving from the train window, holding her shoes in one hand. She had taken them off for speed and run onto the train barefoot.

"My little dove!" he yelled at her, half smiling, his face falling flatteringly. "My little dove. Next Sunday—over at Dreamland!" he hollered, running along the platform, smiling and frowning, unsure if she could even hear him.

"Next Sunday—by the archangel—"

But she only waved at him, smiling, until the packed train pulled out of the station, its passengers smashed right up against the windows, waving frantically to their own Sunday lovers; and the next train pulled in.

IN DREAMS BEGIN RESPONSIBILITIES

Delmore Schwartz

Delmore Schwartz (1913–1966) was born in Brooklyn, New York. The success of his story "In Dreams Begin Responsibilities," published in *Partisan Review* in December 1937, helped launch Schwartz into the literary world at an early age. This semi-autobiographical rendering of his parents' failed marriage and its ill-fated consequences remains the most famous of Schwartz's fictional works. He wrote numerous other stories, poems, plays, and essays and was the editor of *Partisan Review* (1943–1955) and the *New Republic*. Schwartz was the youngest recipient of the Bollingen Prize for his poetry collection *Summer Knowledge: New and Selected Poems* (1959). Despite the enormous talent displayed in his early work, Schwartz, because of mental illness and alcoholism, was never able to fulfill this youthful promise.

I

I think it is the year 1909. I feel as if I were in a motion picture theatre, the long arm of light crossing the darkness and spinning, my eyes fixed on the screen. This is a silent picture as if an old Biograph one, in which the actors are dressed in ridiculously old-fashioned clothes, and one flash succeeds another with sudden jumps. The actors too seem to jump about and walk too fast. The shots themselves are full of dots and rays, as if it were raining when the picture was photographed. The light is bad.

It is Sunday afternoon, June 12, 1909, and my father is walking down the quiet streets of Brooklyn on his way to visit my mother. His clothes are newly pressed and his tie is too tight in his high collar. He jingles the coins in his pockets, thinking of the witty things he will say. I feel as if I had by now relaxed entirely in the soft darkness of the theatre; the organist peals out the obvious and approximate emotions on which the audience rocks unknowingly. I am anonymous, and I have forgotten myself. It is always so when one goes to the movies, it is, as they say, a drug.

My father walks from street to street of trees, lawns and houses, once in a while coming to an avenue on which a street-car skates and gnaws, slowly progressing. The conductor, who has a handle-bar mustache[,] helps a young lady wearing a hat like a bowl with feathers on to the car. She lifts her long skirts slightly as she mounts the steps. He leisurely makes change and rings his bell. It is obviously Sunday, for everyone is wearing Sunday clothes, and the street-car's noises emphasize the quiet of the holiday. Is not Brooklyn the City of Churches? The shops are closed and their shades drawn, but for an occasional stationery store or drug-store with great green balls in the window.

My father has chosen to take this long walk because he likes to walk and think. He thinks about himself in the future and so arrives at the place he is to visit in a state of mild exaltation. He pays no attention to the houses he is passing, in which the Sunday dinner is being eaten, nor to the many trees which patrol each street, now coming to their full leafage and the time when they will room the whole street in cool shadow. An occasional carriage passes, the horse's hooves falling like stones in the quiet afternoon, and once in a while an automobile, looking like an enormous upholstered sofa, puffs and passes.

My father thinks of my mother, of how nice it will be to introduce her to his family. But he is not yet sure that he wants to marry her, and once in a while he becomes panicky about the bond already established. He reassures himself by thinking of the big men he admires who are married: William Randolph Hearst, and William Howard Taft, who has just become President of the United States.

My father arrives at my mother's house. He has come too early and so is suddenly embarrassed. My aunt, my mother's sister, answers the loud bell with her napkin in her hand, for the family is still at dinner. As my father enters, my grandfather rises from the table and shakes hands with him. My mother has run upstairs to tidy herself. My grandmother asks my father if he has had dinner, and tells him that Rose will be downstairs soon. My grandfather opens the conversation by remarking on the mild June weather. My father sits uncomfortably near the table, holding his hat in his hand. My grandmother tells my aunt to take my father's hat. My uncle, twelve years old, runs into the house, his hair tousled. He shouts a greeting to my father, who has often given him a nickel, and then runs upstairs. It is evident that the respect in which my father is held in this household is tempered by a good deal of mirth. He is impressive, yet he is very awkward.

II

Finally my mother comes downstairs, all dressed up, and my father being engaged in conversation with my grandfather becomes uneasy, not knowing whether to greet my mother or continue the conversation. He gets up from the chair clumsily and says "hello" gruffly. My grandfather watches, examining their congruence, such as it is, with a critical eye, and meanwhile rubbing his bearded cheek roughly, as he always does when he reflects. He is worried; he is afraid that my father will not make a good husband for his oldest daughter. At this point something happens to the film, just as my father is saying something funny to my mother; I am awakened to myself and my unhappiness just as my interest was rising. The audience begins to clap impatiently. Then the trouble is cared for but the film has been returned to a portion just shown, and once more I see my grandfather rubbing his bearded cheek and pondering my father's character. It is difficult to get back into the picture once more and forget myself, but as my mother giggles at my father's words, the darkness drowns me.

My father and mother depart from the house, my father shaking hands with my mother once more, out of some unknown uneasiness. I stir uneasily also, slouched in the hard chair of the theatre. Where is the older uncle, my mother's older brother? He is studying in his bedroom upstairs, studying for his final examination at the College of the City of New York, having been dead of rapid pneumonia for the last twenty-one years. My mother and father walk down the same quiet streets once more. My mother is holding my father's arm and telling him of the novel which she has been reading; and my father utters judgments of the characters as the plot is made clear to him. This is a habit which he very much enjoys, for he feels the utmost superiority and confidence when he approves and condemns the behavior of other people. At times he feels moved to utter a brief "Ugh,"—whenever the story becomes what he would call sugary. This tribute is paid to his manliness. My mother feels satisfied by the interest which she has awakened; she is showing my father how intelligent she is, and how interesting.

They reach the avenue, and the street-car leisurely arrives. They are going to Coney Island this afternoon, although my mother considers that such pleasures are inferior. She has made up her mind to indulge only in a walk on the boardwalk and a pleasant dinner, avoiding the riotous amusements as being beneath the dignity of so dignified a couple.

My father tells my mother how much money he has made in the past week, exaggerating an amount which need not have been exaggerated. But my father has always felt that actualities somehow fall short. Suddenly I begin to weep. The determined old lady who sits next to me in the theatre is annoyed and looks at me with an angry face, and being intimidated, I stop. I drag out my handkerchief and dry my face, licking the drop which has fallen near my lips. Meanwhile I have missed something, for here are my mother and father alighting at the last stop, Coney Island.

III

They walk toward the boardwalk, and my father commands my mother to inhale the pungent air from the sea. They both breathe in deeply, both of them laughing as they do so. They have in common a great interest in health, although my father is strong and husky, my mother frail. Their minds are full of theories of what is good to eat and not good to eat, and sometimes they engage in heated discussions of the subject, the whole matter ending in my father's announcement, made with a scornful bluster, that you have to die sooner or later anyway. On the boardwalk's flagpole, the American flag is pulsing in an intermittent wind from the sea.

My father and mother go to the rail of the boardwalk and look down on the beach where a good many bathers are casually walking about. A few are in the surf. A peanut whistle pierces the air with its pleasant and active whine, and my father goes to buy peanuts. My mother remains at the rail and stares at the ocean. The ocean seems merry to her; it pointedly sparkles and again and again the pony waves are released. She notices the children digging in the wet sand, and the bathing costumes of the girls who are her own age. My father returns with the peanuts. Overhead the sun's lightning strikes and strikes, but neither of them are at all aware of it. The boardwalk is full of people dressed in their Sunday clothes and idly strolling. The tide does not reach as far as the boardwalk, and the strollers would feel no danger if it did. My mother and father lean on the rail of the boardwalk and absently stare at the ocean. The ocean is becoming rough; the waves come in slowly, tugging strength from far back. The moment before they somersault, the moment when they arch their backs so beautifully, showing green and white veins amid the black, that moment is intolerable. They finally crack, dashing fiercely upon the sand, actually driving, full force downward, against the sand, bouncing upward and forward, and at last petering out into a small stream which races up the beach and then is recalled. My parents gaze absentmindedly at the ocean, scarcely interested in its harshness. The sun overhead does not disturb them. But I stare at the terrible sun which breaks up sight, and the fatal, merciless, passionate ocean, I forget my parents. I stare fascinated and finally, shocked by the indifference of my father and mother, I burst out weeping once more. The old lady next to me pats me on the shoulder and says "There, there, all of this is only a movie, young man, only a movie," but I look up once more at the terrifying sun and the terrifying ocean, and being unable to control my tears, I get up and go to the men's room, stumbling over the feet of the other people seated in my row.

IV

When I return, feeling as if I had awakened in the morning sick for lack of sleep, several hours have apparently passed and my parents are riding on the merry-go-round. My father is on a black horse, my mother on a white one, and they seem to be making an eternal circuit for the single purpose of snatching the nickel rings which are attached to the arm of one of the posts. A hand-organ is playing; it is one with the ceaseless circling of the merry-go-round.

For a moment it seems that they will never get off the merry-go-round because it will never stop. I feel like one who looks down on the avenue from the 50th story of a building. But at length they do get off; even the music of the hand-organ has ceased for a moment. My father has acquired ten rings, my mother only two, although it was my mother who really wanted them.

They walk on along the boardwalk as the afternoon descends by imperceptible degrees into the incredible violet of dusk. Everything fades into a relaxed glow, even the ceaseless murmuring from the beach, and the revolutions of the merry-go-round. They look for a place to have dinner. My father suggests the best one on the boardwalk and my mother demurs, in accordance with her principles.

However they do go to the best place, asking for a table near the window, so that they can look out on the boardwalk and the mobile ocean. My father feels omnipotent as he places a quarter in the waiter's hand as he asks for a table. The place is crowded and here too there is music, this time from a kind of string trio. My father orders dinner with a fine confidence.

As the dinner is eaten, my father tells of his plans for the future, and my mother shows with expressive face how interested she is, and how impressed. My father becomes exultant. He is lifted up by the waltz that is being played, and his own future begins to intoxicate him. My father tells my mother that he is going to expand his business, for there is a great deal of money to be made. He wants to settle down. After all, he is twenty-nine, he has lived by himself since he was thirteen, he is making more and more money, and he is envious of his married friends when he visits them in the cozy security of their homes, surrounded, it seems, by the calm domestic pleasures, and by delightful children, and then, as the waltz reaches the moment when all the dancers swing madly, then, then with awful daring, then he asks my mother to marry him, although awkwardly enough and puzzled, even in his excitement, at how he had arrived at the proposal, and she, to make the whole business worse, begins to cry, and my father looks nervously about, not knowing at all what to do now, and my mother says: "It's all I've wanted from the moment I saw you," sobbing, and he finds all of this very difficult, scarcely to his taste, scarcely as he had thought it would be, on his long walks over Brooklyn Bridge in the revery of a fine cigar, and it was then that I stood up in the theatre and shouted: "Don't do it. It's not too late to change your minds, both of you. Nothing good will come of it, only remorse, hatred, scandal, and two children whose characters are monstrous." The whole audience turned to look at me, annoyed, the usher came hurrying down the aisle flashing his searchlight, and the old lady next to me tugged me down into my seat, saying: "Be quiet. You'll be put out, and you paid thirty-five cents to come in." And so I shut my eyes because I could not bear to see what was happening. I sat there quietly.

V

But after awhile I begin to take brief glimpses, and at length I watch again with thirsty interest, like a child who wants to maintain his sulk although offered the bribe of candy. My parents are now having their picture taken in a photographer's booth along the boardwalk. The place is shadowed in the mauve light which is apparently necessary. The camera is set to the side on its tripod and looks like a Martian man. The photographer is instructing my parents in how to pose. My father has his arm over my mother's shoulder, and both of them smile emphatically. The photographer brings my mother a bouquet of flowers to hold in her hand but she holds it at the wrong angle. Then the photographer covers himself with the black cloth which drapes the camera and all that one sees of him is one protruding arm and his hand which clutches the rubber ball which he will squeeze when the picture is finally taken. But he is not satisfied with their appearance. He feels with certainty that somehow there is something wrong in their pose. Again and again he issues from his hidden place with new directions. Each suggestion merely makes matters worse. My father is becoming impatient. They try a seated pose. The photographer explains that he has pride, he is not interested in all of this for the money, he wants to make beautiful pictures. My father says: "Hurry up, will you? We haven't got all night." But the photographer only scurries about apologetically, and issues new directions. The photographer charms me. I approve of him with all my heart, for I know just how he feels, and as he criticizes each revised pose according to some unknown idea of rightness, I become quite hopeful. But then my father says angrily: "Come on, you've had enough time, we're not going to wait any longer." And the photographer, sighing unhappily, goes back under his black covering, holds out his hand, says: "One, two, three, Now!", and the picture is taken, with my father's smile turned to a grimace and my mother's bright and false. It takes a few minutes for the picture to be developed and as my parents sit in the curious light they become quite depressed.

VI

They have passed a fortune-teller's booth, and my mother wishes to go in, but my father does not. They begin to argue about it. My mother becomes stubborn, my father once more impatient, and then they begin to quarrel, and what my father would like to do is walk off and leave my mother there, but he knows that would never do. My mother refuses to budge. She is near to tears, but she feels an uncontrollable desire to hear what the palm-reader will say. My father consents angrily, and they both go into a booth which is in a way like the photographer's, since it is draped in black cloth and its light is shadowed. The place is too warm, and my father keeps saying this is all nonsense, pointing to the crystal ball on the table. The fortune-teller, a fat, short woman, garbed in what is supposed to be Oriental robes, comes into the room from the back and greets them, speaking with an accent. But suddenly my father feels that the whole thing is intolerable; he tugs at my mother's arm, but my mother refuses to budge. And then, in terrible anger, my father lets go of my mother's arm and strides out, leaving my mother stunned. She moves to go after my father, but the fortune-teller holds her arm tightly and begs her not to do so, and I in my seat am shocked more than can ever be said, for I feel as if I were walking a tight-rope a hundred feet over a circus-audience and suddenly the rope is showing signs of breaking, and I get up from my seat and begin to shout once more the first words I can think of to communicate my terrible fear and once more the usher comes hurrying down the aisle flashing his searchlight, and the old lady pleads with me, and the shocked audience has turned to stare at me, and I keep shouting: "What are they doing? Don't they know what they are doing? Why doesn't my mother go after my father? If she does not do that, what will she do? Doesn't my father know what he is doing?"—But the usher has seized my arm and is dragging me away, and as he does so, he says: "What are *you* doing? Don't you know that you can't do whatever you want to do? Why should a young man like you, with your whole life before you, get hysterical like this? Why don't you *think* of what you're doing? You can't act like this even if other people aren't around! You will be sorry if you do not do what you should do, you can't carry on like this, it is not right, you will find that out soon enough, everything you do matters too much," and he said that dragging me through the lobby of the theatre into the cold light, and I woke up into the bleak winter morning of my 21st birthday, the windowsill shining with its lip of snow, and the morning already begun.

SUNDAY

Robert Olen Butler

Robert Olen Butler was born in 1945 in Granite City, Illinois. He is a novelist and short story writer who won the Pulitzer Prize in fiction in 1993 for his collection *A Good Scent from a Strange Mountain* (1992). "Sunday" was published in *Had a Good Time: Stories from American Postcards* (2004), a collection of tales based on the greetings written on postcards that Butler had collected over the years. The postcard that inspired "Sunday" portrays a group of ocean bathers. The story is set on August 7, 1910, and imagines the death of the protagonist—a successful middle-aged insurance salesman newly married to a young woman—from a heart attack while lying peacefully and reading his newspaper on the beach at Coney Island. Ironically, "his demise went unnoticed for some time, in spite of being surrounded by Coney's largest crowd of the season."

SUNDAY, AUG 7TH 1910

I love *The New York Times* here on my lap, I love this canvas chair I'm sitting on and I love this beach and I love all of Coney Island—the press of this multitude of bodies about me, each set free in bathing flannels, not to mention Coney's temples and pagodas and fountains strung with a million and a half electric lights—I love the nickel red hots in buns with mustard, especially the several I've recently consumed—though they are not loving me in return, they are clogging the center of my chest and whispering slithery hot little sausagey secrets—I love the Fourth of July, the rockets' red glare, which now will mark forever, year after year, not only the birth of our country, which I also love, but also my wedding day, which I had long since given up hope ever to have, and of course I love my sweet young wife—I especially love her—my Lillian, my Lily. I don't love the thought that she will one day be a widow before being an old woman—I am forty-eight years old and she is twenty-three—but she loves me and says this is all right, and I wonder at how I came to find the nerve to ask her if this might be so. Presently she is out somewhere laughing and splashing amidst the throng, amidst ten thousand temporary exiles from the city, out in the Atlantic Ocean with her friends and former fellow type-writers, most of whom still work under my direction.

A short time ago, we all stood together in the ocean, up to our waists, all of us from the Manhattan Life Insurance Company, along with dozens of strangers, and a young man, one of the strangers, took our photo from the lifeguard's perch and we cried together, "Hurrah!" as if it were the Fourth of July. We were countrymen, all of us. How I love my United States of America. I began with so very little. I passed through Castle Garden, long before Ellis Island opened—though I barely remember it, which is all right with me because in fact my life began that day—an official who could not write our family name even gave us a new one, which we gladly took on—and my parents and I were soon stuffed with two hundred others and a dozen languages and a thousand rats into the tiny spaces of a tenement on the Lower East Side and there was no light and there was no air and there was only the stink of the water closet down the hall and the garbage down the air shaft and cholera took my mother soon after, though I clearly remember my mother, the vast sheltering bosom of her, her unblinking eyes fixed admiringly on me with the flicker of candlelight there, her long hair always gathered up in a knot—I don't remember ever seeing her hair unloosed, which I regret—and then there was another mother, who was a good woman, and there were years of striving, and I love my country because now I am an office manager at the Manhattan Life Insurance Company and I have an apartment uptown nearly to Houston Street and it's on the first floor and it has windows and I have at last married a woman and she loves me.

An eddy of people swirls by me now, a party bearing wicker baskets and blankets and already-squalling children. I will welcome such a squall one day. These are my countrymen too, and I smile at them as they pass, though they are unaware of it, for they do not give me a glance. I lift my smile to the sunny sky above me. And the red hots shift in my chest. I resolve to revisit the red-hot stand later, to push these along with more of their kind. It is Sunday. I am at leisure. My wife is somewhere nearby. I lift my paper. *The New York Times, New York, Sunday, August 7, 1910. 64 pages.*

Why do I love so much to read the newspapers? They are always full of clouds. At the top of the page to the right, however, Sunday has no clouds: *The Weather. Fair Sunday.* But of course there's always tomorrow. *Unsettled Monday.* I'm happy there are sixty-four pages. Tomorrow is unsettled. Yesterday was full of well-chronicled strife. But I can sit safely here in the middle and read my newspaper in the bright sunlight and let all these lives full of striving flow around me. Tomorrow I will have been married for five weeks. On Independence Day we held hands, Lily and I, and I placed a ring on her finger and we kissed and that night we sat in the Battery and watched the sky light up for us. Later, in the light from the gas-mantle lamp of my apartment, my wife unfastened her hair, slowly pulling out the pins and placing each one between her lips and I could hardly breathe, but I asked if she would turn her back to me so I could see her hair, and she did, and the last pin was gone and her hair rushed free and fell, breaking for a moment on her shoulders and then cascading far down her back. Thinking now of her hair, I once again am struggling to draw a breath.

I close my eyes and I wait. The joy in me finally settles down and I open my eyes. I lift my *Times* and begin to read. The lead story headline first, directly beneath the unsettled Monday: SOLDIERS DISPERSE PRIEST-LED RUS-TICS. The dateline is San Sebastian, in Spain. I've been following this. The government of Spain and the Vatican are struggling for power. Under their present Church-State agreement, public expressions of any faith besides Catholicism are illegal. And there is a heavy national tax for the Church. The new premier José Canalejas and the young King Alfonso are trying to disengage the State from the Church and ease the tax and allow other religions to express themselves, and as a result there are great political struggles and even cleric-inspired public uprisings. It seems so much of my life that I remember is by artificial light in a small room. My father with the kerosene lamp trimmed low on the table between us. "More people have murdered each other in the name of God than anything else," he said to me. "Harold," he said, "give me your hand." And he laid his own hand, palm up, in the center of the table, next to the lamp. I put mine on his and he closed his hand, holding me tight. "You must think clearly," he said. "Always. If God exists, he is either too savage for our respect or no one in this world knows the first thing about him."

Lily and I go to a church on Avenue C most Sundays. But we married at City Hall. We pray, each of us, at times, but I'm not sure who it is I'm speaking to and he does not fill me with as much joy as holding Lily or bathing in the Atlantic Ocean or watching the Stars and Stripes flying up over the grandstand at the Polo Grounds. Or seeing the Giants win, for that matter. I can wait no longer. I thumb back to Section C of the *Times* and my heart is fluttering as I head for yesterday's game. I pass by a full-page announcement of Macy's Furniture Sale where *The Prices Do the Talking* and by news of the *New Ruler of Morocco, Who Is Torturing and Killing His Subjects* and an *Opera War in London* and tourists turning away from Paris in favor of Berlin and stories on Mahler's new symphony and dwarfs in New Guinea and the divorce rate in France, and at last I arrive at the sports page to find that my Giants, who I love, have won, beating the St. Louis Cardinals 5–4 in eleven innings with Fred Snodgrass slashing the winning single to right field.

I am about to return to the front page—my habits are fixed with my daily newspaper, to skim all the news stories commencing with page one and then return later to read them in full until I take in every word—but first I seek out a story a few pages back from the sports in Section C. The Giants have won. I have that to support me as I face the trials of life recorded elsewhere in *The Times*. The Moroccan king. I read the lead paragraph: *The question is being asked in Europe, and asked with more and more insistence, How long is the brute who is now the ruler of Morocco to be allowed to torture and kill his subjects?* I glance farther along. It's about politics, not religion. A struggle for power. A rival thrown to lions. The man's wife shackled and hung by her wrists for weeks. When will Europe intervene?

I close Section C. I am touchy about a wife in peril. The pressure in my chest resumes. Marriage is making me prone to strong feelings, it seems. I move back to the first section, glancing inside briefly. I'm heartened by *An Immense Purchase of Muslin Underwear* at Greenhut & Co. with the resultant savings passed on to an eager public, of course. And for those who are victims of the bad news today, the Stern Brothers have big savings on *Imported Mourning Millinery*. And I am at the front page again.

A great shout goes up and I lower the paper. On the edge of the shore three young men hold two other young men on their shoulders while another young man climbs up their backs to the peak. But half a dozen young women who stand before the construction project all turn in a perfect line and face the same way and they bend forward at the waist and lift the hems of their bathing dresses. They wag their bottoms like music hall girls and the quite considerable crowd of onlookers raises a loud, delighted cry. The pyramid strives for a better view and crumbles. I lift the veil of my front page and turn my eyes to the left-hand lead story. A tale of political corruption: HUGE BRIBE OFFERS TOLD OF BY INDIANS. A Choctaw chief and his son have testified to a Congressional investigative committee about bribes offered by lawyers holding government contracts seeking to buy 450,000 acres of Indian land rich in coal. I drop the veil to see a mound of bodies, limbs waving, the onlookers storming in. Even the vice president has been mentioned as having personal interests in the contracts. This, too, is my country.

I raise my paper. The news once again replaces the crowd, the beach, the sea, the far horizon. *The Times* is merely crowned with the blue sky above. I'm growing unusually agitated by the wider world today. I like the heat, the sun, even the crowds of August at Coney. But I'm sweating unusually and there's a restlessness in me, in my limbs, in my throat. I move my eyes across the top of the front page to the third column, and crime is flourishing in this very place where I've brought my wife. MAYOR HEARS CRIME THRIVES IN CONEY. This story I read word for word at once, continuing on even after my fears abate somewhat. It's simply a matter of pickpockets—which I know already to beware of—and short-change artists working as waiters in the less reputable eating joints at the far west end. These aren't places where we'd go anyway. But there's more corruption, as well. I follow the story to its continuation on page two. The mayor and the police commissioner are struggling. The mayor has ordered the police on duty to wear uniforms at all times, the plainclothes operations having facilitated the collection of bribes and extortion money by bad cops, he says. The commissioner says he needs the plainclothesmen to catch the short-changers.

My father whispers to me. In my right ear. Among the laughter and the calling out and the women's voices babbling behind me and an accordion playing in the distance and a dog barking. I hear his voice clearly. "Harold," he says. I turn in that direction. The door of the apartment opens wide and he stands there with blood on his left temple and a bright red abrasion on his cheek. My second mother screams. He is sitting at the table now and

I am standing near. His forearms are resting heavily before him. Then a policeman in a dark blue uniform, his buttons flashing gold in the lamplight, is standing in the doorway. My father drags himself up and crosses to the policeman and lifts his right arm and the policeman does too, and they grasp hands and they shake. "Thank you," my father says, and the policeman says, "We caught him over on Orchard. He took a beating from resisting. A severe beating." "Thank you," my father says again, lower this time, emphatic, and he shakes the policeman's hand once more. Then they both look in my direction.

I flinch. I am on the beach at Coney Island. I am surrounded by strangers. I am holding my *New York Times*. It is still lifted, wide open to pages two and three. I heard my father's voice with perfect clarity, right here beside me. I listen, but he does not speak again. I look back to the newspaper, returning to the last sentence I read at the foot of page two, a numbering of the police force. I lift my eyes to the top of the page. DENTIST SHOT DOWN TALKING IN STREET. But he seemed to know his assailant. *No Attempt to Rob Murdered Man—Police Believe the Motive Was Jealousy.* Dr. W. F. Michaelis of Chicago, what could have possessed you to do what you seem to have done? *Miss Inez Wilcox, a young stenographer employed in a downtown office, was at the office of Dr. Michaelis until within half an hour of the time of the murder. She had been employed in clerical work by the dentist, she explained, and was so occupied until 10 o'clock last night. She left the office at the same time as Dr. Michaelis, and parted from him in the street. Half an hour later he was shot to death.*

I'm starting to grind inside again, rather like I did thinking of the Moroccan wife hanging by her wrists. But I skim on. The dentist's wife was away in Indiana with their three daughters, and love letters were discovered in a mailbox at Dr. Michaelis's office. *He was dapper in his dress, always wearing gloves, both Summer and Winter.*

I put the paper down. I lean forward and peer though the passing bodies and the posing young men on the water's edge. I look out into the breakers, searching for my wife. I don't see her or her three girlfriends from Manhattan Life who took her off to splash and gossip.

My indigestion's getting worse, clutching its way up into my throat, and further, making even my jaw ache. I sit back. Lily worked for me. Typing on her Remington brilliantly, her back straight, her fingers flashing like a great pianist's. It took me a year to struggle with the impropriety of speaking to her in the way I finally did. A warm day this past May, the tenth. The windows of our office were flung open. I was a lowly clerk in this very office when our building was the tallest in the world, sixteen years ago. It still gives me great pleasure to stand beneath it. It towers up in granite and terra-cotta and brick to twin domes and then farther up still, 348 feet to its lantern top and the American flag flying above, and I am a lucky man to work high up within this wonder, on the twelfth floor.

It was during our lunch break on May the tenth and Lily was standing before the window, looking out to the west, toward the docks and the Hudson River, and then her face turned to the south. I knew what she was seeing. I had hesitated so many times before, but this time I stepped up beside her and shared her gaze: Miss Liberty in the harbor, lifting her torch. "She's beautiful," I said.

"Yes," she said.

"Did she welcome you?"

"I'm native-born," she said quickly, firmly.

I held on fast to the windowsill. I'd finally spoken and I'd instantly made a terrible mistake.

But Lily read my face. "I'm not saying that's better."

"Some do," I said.

"I don't," she said. Her hand fluttered out toward me but found nothing exactly to do to express the reassurance it intended. I'd made another mistake, pressing this issue. I wanted very badly to take her hand, but I couldn't. She withdrew it and looked at me closely. "And you?" she asked. "Was she there to welcome you?"

"No. But only because I came long ago, as a child."

She smiled. "So you've been an American longer than she has."

I laughed. Softly, and I knew how much I loved her.

"Harold," she whispers. Here beside me on the beach. She's come back from the ocean and her friends, and I turn to her, but she's not here. Passing bodies. A blur of bare arms and bathing costumes. And a white-knuckled fist is clenching in my chest. Let go, I say inside my head. Please let go.

I need simply to return to what I was doing. Harold, she says. I want to marry you, I say. Yes, she says and we are lit by moonlight on a bench in Tompkins Square and I have forgotten to go down on a knee, which I scramble to do, and she puts her hand on my shoulder. No, she says. Just sit beside me.

At the top of the page of my *Times*. My arm is hurting. A sharp pain is running down my left arm At the top of the page: AVIATION MEET AT ASBURY PARK. World-famous aeronauts. Including five professionals flying for the Wright Brothers. Brookins and Coffin and La Chapple and Johnstone and Hoxsey. I am panting with the pain inside me. I will take Lily to Asbury Park. We stood high in the air when I first knew I loved her. I will take her flying someday. The paper is quaking. The pain will pass. Please let it pass. I realize I am praying. Beside this story is another on aeroplanes. MIMIC WARFARE IN AIR. *The bombardment of a warship and two submarines before a grandstand filled with people and a long line of parked motors.*

Please let go. My newspaper falls. I try to rise up to find Lily. But my arms are very heavy and someone is squeezing the center of me *my father's arms are around me his rough cheek against mine Daddy please he hugs me too hard and now his face is very still in the flicker of a candle he is lying on the bed and I bend near to him and call for him, Papa, and he is silent and there is weeping beside me, Mama, my real mama, is here in the room and her hair is pinned up tight and I think to ask how she is still alive, where have you been, but before I do she looks at me and puts her finger to her lips and I am holding Papa's hand and leaning into the rough cloth of his coat and Mama is on my other side and the street is full of passing bodies, dark clothes, flowing skirts, the smell of coal fire and horses and rotting fruit and Lily's cheek touches mine I cannot breathe from the happiness of her cheek against mine and I look and the room is dark, this place where I live, the room is very dark and it is large and at the far end is a sudden tiny flare of light Mama lighting a candle and she straightens and her hands rise to the back of her head, the gathering there, and then her hair falls and beyond her the night sky blooms into great flashing white spirals of light, bombs bursting in air.*

DEATH AT CONEY

Amidst the revelry yesterday at Coney
Island, a man quietly died on the
beach. Harold Smith, 48 years old, an
office manager, of 173 Ludlow Street,
Manhattan, was found dead in a can-
vas chair of apparent natural causes.
His demise went unnoticed for some
time, in spite of being surrounded by
Coney's largest crowd of the season.
Smith worked for the Manhattan Life
Insurance Company. He is survived
by his wife, Lillian.

from page 3 of *The Sun*, New York

Monday, August 8, 1910

RUINS HELP DRAW 350,000 TO CONEY

On May 27, 1911, the recently bankrupted Dreamland was largely destroyed in a fire. Since the park was not insured, it was never rebuilt. However, true to the Coney traditions of resilience and making a buck from any situation, manager Samuel Gumpertz quickly opened exhibits on the site of the ruins. The Dreamland Circus Sideshow operated for years. The animals from Joseph G. Ferari's Trained Wild Animal Arena that had survived the fire were on display. The main event, however, was the sideshow, which included such human oddities as the fat lady, the elastic-skinned man, the giant, and the tattooed lady. A tent was erected to house the show, and on May 29, 1911, the *New York Times* proclaimed: "To the freaks fell the honor of reopening Dreamland."

THE FIRST OF THE BURNED-OUT SHOWS of Dreamland reopened for business at 3 o'clock yesterday afternoon, and an hour later the organ of Ferari's Animal Show struck up and the public was invited to step in and see all that remained of the wild beast collection. That is the spirit in which Coney Island is taking the big fire, and on every side yesterday were evidences of determination to make the best out of a bad business. Indeed, the great waste, five blocks square, was considered an attraction, and it was reckoned that the desire to see the piles of blackened timbers and bent steel helped bring 350,000 people to the island. A plan for clearing the debris to make room for all sorts of small shows is already being considered.

To the freaks fell the honor of reopening Dreamland. A tent was pitched on the edge of Surf Avenue, and by hard work all Saturday night a complete installation of water and electric light was accomplished, canvases displaying the fat lady and the elastic-skinned man were hung out in regular country fair style, and the spielers took their places on the platform and urged the passers-by to come in.

"All that's left of Dreamland, beautiful Dreamland," was the burden of their cry, and a good many visitors were induced to part with their dimes.

The freaks looked a little uncomfortable, each seated in a sort of loose box, but the arrangement had its advantages for the spectators. They could lean over the edge and ask the tattooed lady whether it hurt much to have a beautiful cross worked in indelible ink on the chest and American flags on the arm, and they could chaff the giant in a much more familiar way than if they had been seated in state on a dais.

The remnants of Ferari's show consisted of five lionesses, four leopards, six ponies, and an unestimated number of monkeys. Ferari sent for the traveling outfit he uses in the Winter, and set up his stage under canvas. He was able to put on a show of five acts, half as many as before the fire, and Mme. André with the leopards, Capt. Bonavista and Vincent Rivero with the lionesses, Ricardo with the leopards, and Ferari himself with the ponies, drew good houses all day long. Particularly welcome to the visitors was Marguerite, the baby lioness, seven months old, who had been reported to be dead. But there she was yesterday afternoon, about the size of a small collie, pulling at the rope to which she was tied or working herself up to a playful fury at the sight of one of her kindred in its cage. She had lost, however, her playmate, a terrier, who was stolen in the confusion.

Next door the menagerie was a tent in which the stuffed form of Sultan, the lion which was shot on the Rocky Road to Dublin was on view for a dime. The animal had been prepared for exhibition by "Doc" Hewitt and Melvin Howard, well-known Coney Islanders, and the fame of his exit with burning mane and his flight through the crowd brought in a small harvest to the enterprising taxidermists. The police had had it that it was Black Prince that had gone on the rampage, but it was explained yesterday that that animal had been ill for several days before the disaster and was hardly able to walk when it came.

"The fact is," said Frank J. Wilstach, Dreamland's press agent, "the poor brute had never seemed himself since he bit that Spaniard a few weeks ago. I don't know how it was, but it didn't seem to agree with him, and it was just like Oliver Goldsmith's mad dog. 'The dog it was that died.' We hardly expected Black Prince to live through Friday night, anyhow, and so he had no chance of escaping."

The carcass of one lion was found among the ruins yesterday morning, and the relic hunters scrambled for his claws and teeth. Harry Smith, who is employed by Ferari, declared that so keen was the competition that a policeman took a hand in it and got some of the claws himself, driving Smith away when he claimed a certain proprietorship. [. . .]

Dreamland may perhaps have some kind of a regular show in order within a week, Mr. Gumpertz said yesterday:

"Of course, it all depends on what the Directors decide at their meeting to-morrow, but I hope that we shall clear a street right through to the ocean and install immediately old-time Coney Island shows. That would carry us through the season, and we should not have any of the tremendous expenses that the old park had to carry. Moreover, it would give employment to the 1,600 people we had on our wage sheet." [. . .]

So as fast as temporary arrangements can be made Coney will improvise means to meet the situation. Already yesterday a man balanced a piece of board on a box, displayed a handful of damaged curios on it, and announced, "The 5 and 10 cent store is now open." The concessionaires put tables in front of the brick ovens, all that remained of prosperous restaurants, lit the fires, and sold frankfurters. At tables balanced on half-burned beams, on chairs distorted by heat, it was possible to drink beer, of course accompanied with a sandwich. [. . .]

A roaring trade was done yesterday on the Iron Pier Walk in certain half-burned photographs of "Little Hip," the performing elephant which was burned. They were sold as bona fide relics of the fire. They appear to have been genuine enough pictures of the elephant, but some one wandering through the wreckage came across a small boy crouched behind a pile of timber with a candle on one hand and a photograph in the other. He was singing [sic] the edges of the photograph and preparing it for the market.

THE NICKEL EMPIRE: CONEY IN TRANSITION, 1912–1948

BOARDWALK, CONEY ISLAND, JULY 4, 1936. (BROOKLYN PUBLIC LIBRARY, BROOKLYN COLLECTION)

THE TINGLING, TANGLING TANGO AS 'TIS TRIPPED AT CONEY ISLE

Djuna Barnes

Djuna Barnes (1892–1982) was born near Cornwall-on-Hudson, New York. Barnes led a bohemian lifestyle, first in Greenwich Village (in the 1910s) and then in Paris (in the 1920s and 1930s). She was an important figure in the modernist movement, writing avant-garde poetry, fiction, and drama. She is especially known for the novel *Nightwood* (1936), notable for its early depiction of homosexuality. While living in New York City, Barnes wrote for several newspapers and magazines, including the *Brooklyn Eagle*, the *New York Press*, the *Morning Telegraph*, and *Vanity Fair*. Several of her pieces for the *Press* and the *Eagle*—such as "The Tingling, Tangling Tango as 'Tis Tripped at Coney Isle," published in the *Eagle* on August 31, 1913—are about Coney Island. Its free-spirited qualities appealed to Barnes, and she was particularly interested in the dance palaces and the women who frequented them. To read more of these sketches, see *New York* (1989).

ONCE, TWICE, THRICE THE CUP OF LIFE has been emptied; once, twice, thrice the wheel has ceased to spin and run down; once, twice, thrice a girl, leaning across a polished table top, has learned that only a strip of wood separates her from the garden of love. And each time the cup has been refilled, and each time the wheel has been set in motion once more, and each time the maid finds that the garden has tears upon its flowers instead of dew; and yet over and over the same scenes are thrown upon the screen that is the heart.

So, at Coney, the night in a fashionable hotel sees the same play out to the end. Beneath the glare of the electric lights, under the seductive charm of the band behind the palms, the straight black eyes of Therese glow; the large, red mouth is smiling; the low-coiled hair gives to those eyes the magic that the undertow gives to the swell of the wave.

With her chin upon her jeweled hand, she watches the gliding, attentive waiters, the sense of the colored goblets, the red and purple and gold, slowly removing her gloves as manifold women remove theirs in the great mirrors. A queen in black, with a hat of a thousand feathers, she scarcely looks at what is laid before her. Her fingers never close over the stem of the wine glass; she holds it easily because she is certain of it, as one holds accustomed affection. Her eyes drift over the vivid red splashes of silent sea crab laid out upon its bed of green—the sea and the land united in their fruitfulness; the color scheme that art with hunger wrought.

But never one step did she lose of the dancers clinging, gliding, twisting, losing grip, coming together, mocking gravity with jeering feet, caressing with slurring slide, the man bowed above the little woman held close, like a butterfly pinned to his breast.

"What a gown," murmurs Therese above her glass, leveling her languid eyes, noting the bright spots among the smoking men, the telltale, high-thrust feather that shows some woman has consented to be someone's partner for the dance.

"See that glide," the man behind the lights advises.

Semiprofessional, the dancers who specialize for the company are matched against the dancers who may have had some experience before the public. They are daring, yet within the bounds of propriety because they are daring with averted head; they make the dip in gowns that are meant for strolling and, because they see nothing, are aware of nothing.

Sometimes the proprietor walks close, and a couple learns that there are limits. So Therese learns, as with scornful steps she masters the wonder of the tango.

"Shan't we order a dinner?" he suggests, to get out of the uncomfortable position of a person who has been stopped in the excess of a wonderful motion; the catch in the music that makes the feet move. Therese nods, puts her hair back with crinkled white fingers, and moves among the drooping figures of women scattered through the room, hardly more substantial, hardly more resistant than the chiffon in which they are gowned. The cloth begins its mission just below the white throat and ends just above the jeweled slipper, the lace peeping out softly in sheltering folds. There are the sounds heard nowhere but at a pleasure resort: the popping of corks and the guarded, high laugh of the bored beauty, touches of vivid lightning striking across a shifting scene to the low thunder of the laugh of a man.

The professional dancers go back to their places and order refreshments. Those four old women admire the man dancer's dark face while he, with conscious eyes, sips sarsaparilla, one black pump just behind the other; trim, self-possessed, aware that adulation is being poured at his feet. The middle-aged women who have motors and painted cheeks are going to spoil him if they can; they lean upon his table, throwing back cloaks that reveal wondrous evening creations, and try to charm. The dancer, becoming bored, arises, walks among them a bit, drops a comforting word in this ear, smiles into that face, passes one white hand over the other, bows and steps out into the open as the band strikes up. Somehow the pink-gowned girl who dances with him comes to him, as a sunset comes over and claims the mountain, and is borne away upon the shining floor.

"To think that he is a prize," murmurs Therese, who follows him with her eyes. "To think that in a moment the old woman in black and green will be dancing where that lovely young thing is now. Ah, here they come."

And come they do. The man behind the lights smiles, but he is not thinking; few people get a chance to think on such an evening.

"Shall we take a stroll?" inquires he, but she shakes her head. "I think I'm going to order some—" Her voice trails off as she listens to the bit of gossip behind her: "Gone to the mountains, won't be seen here for some time; ran off, you know, with the stenographer or something. . . . They say that she is thirty if she's a day, and yet she comes here. . . . The only man in the place who does not use perfume. . . . He's only here to get life on the wing. . . . Don't drink any more, you'll be sick." Therese shrugs her shoulders and thinks that perhaps her own conversation would make an interesting feature among those others. She throws this out as a starter:

"You have never taken me down the walk, where the spray reaches clear across. I think you are afraid."

"Afraid of what?" he insists.

"Afraid of getting—wet."

"I'm not afraid of anything," he says boldly. "I'm not afraid of spiders or policemen, of gowns with thirty thousand hooks up the back, or of the society notes in the evening papers; why, I'm not afraid of the floor manager."

She shrugs once more. "Give me my wraps," she says languidly and turns her eyes upon the room.

Perhaps the most interesting part of the evening comes in with the tired couples who have done the vulgar end of Coney and have been done by Coney in the end. Tired of the hurly-burly of the amusement parks, tired of the popcorn and the candy, tired of the moving pictures, sated with the sand and the sea, dragging listlessly, they come in, search out a table, languidly, with one hand, pushing the loop over the button of their evening wraps; the man just behind, turning his head from side to side; the child hugging its tiny doll. Utterly played out, they gamely drift across the floor, drop into chairs, and say something about "Oh, my, I'm fagged out!" Fumbling for matches follows, "What will you take, dear?" The light flutters, and smoke issues from a mouth already drooping from fatigue. "I could blow pillows instead of rings," he murmurs, and she orders soup. She is almost too weary to take interest in the gowns on show but not too weary to notice one or two of the most startling ones. The purple crepe with the red sash and the red-heeled slippers catches her eye; she is being soothed, without knowing it; fashion is reviving her spirits, and his, too. He crosses his legs, leans back, and watches the dancers. It is the logical end of a day that has been too full.

The late arrivals get more out of it than these who are in for the opening notes of the orchestra, because they are conscious only of the contentment that comes after entrance and the worry of ordering the dinner and the removal of wraps; they are in on the dessert, as it were.

Half past twelve comes, and everyone is drifting toward the door: the stout woman on whom pearls are wasted, for they are lost in the folds of her neck; the thin, tall woman, who adds sharpness to her figure by steel buckles and diamonds; the men who are conscious that they paid for it all, aware that they are a part of the changing life at Coney, the Coney which a few years ago tolerated nearly any kind of dance and which now tolerates nothing that borders on the sensational.

"Let us walk in the moonlight upon the sand," Therese suggests, "where the waves look like sheer strips of broken beer bottles."

The old Coney is closing down; not stopping, mind you, but changing. We are tremendously interested to see what the evolution is going to be; we are interested to know how shocking society is going to become when it's proper.

NEW COSMOPOLIS

James Huneker

....

James Huneker (1857–1921), although little remembered today, was considered one of the great music critics of his time. A native of Philadelphia, Huneker was a classically trained musician. He moved to New York City in 1886 and lived there for the remainder of his life, writing music reviews for such newspapers as the *Musical Courier* and the *Sun*, both published in New York. Huneker was also a critic of art and literature and was an early appreciator of modernism. Coney, however, to Huneker, pandered to the lowest taste, as he explains in *New Cosmopolis: A Book of Images* (1915). The people who frequented it were "half child, half savage." Still, Huneker admitted that it had an appeal he could not fully comprehend or appreciate.

CONEY ISLAND

BY DAY

I know that you can't make the public enjoy the more refined pleasures of a beach free from vulgarity and rapacious beach-combers, male and female, unless it so wishes. Even mules will not drink unless thirsty. The Montessori method applied to an army of excursionists would be ludicrous; it's a sufficient infliction on children. In a word, it is not a question of restriction but of regulation; decency, good taste, and semibarbarism should not be allowed to go unchecked. Coney Island to-day, despite the efficiency of the police, is a disgrace to our civilisation. It should be abolished and something else substituted. [. . .]

What I can't understand is the lure of the Island for the people who come. Why, after the hot, narrow, noisy, dirty streets of the city, do these same people crowd into the narrower, hotter, noisier, dirtier, wooden alleys of Coney? Is the wretched, Cheap John fair, with the ghastly rubbish for a sale, the magnet? Or is it just the gregariousness of the human animal? They leave dirt and disorder to go to greater disorder and dirt. The sky is bluer, but they don't look at the sky; clam chowder is a more agreeable spectacle; and the smacking of a thousand lips as throats gurgle with the suspicious compound is welcome to the ears of them that pocket the cash. [...]

If the worthy ladies and "uplifters" of indeterminate sex (chiefly old women in trousers) would turn their attention to making the seaside beautiful, or if not beautiful then decent, they would justify their civic existence. Here is where the busy female, with or without a ballot, can come in. A new and attractive Coney Island should be their slogan. But the public likes to be fooled, swindled—alas! [...]

AT NIGHT

As cruelty is proscribed among highly civilised nations to-day—the game of life being so vilely cruel that the arena with its bulls and tigers is unnecessary—our play-instinct finds vent in a species of diversion that must not be examined too closely, as it verges perilously on idiocy. Coney Island is only another name for topsyturvydom. There the true becomes the grotesque, the vision of a maniac. Else why those nerve-racking entertainments, ends of the world, creations, hells, heavens, fantastic trips to ugly lands, panoramas of sheer madness, flights through the air in boats, through water in sleds, on the earth in toy trains! Unreality is as greedily craved by the mob as alcohol by the dipsomaniac; indeed, the jumbled nightmares of a morphine eater are actually realised at Luna Park. Every angle reveals some new horror. Mechanical waterfalls, with women and children racing around curving, tumbling floods; elephants tramping ponderously through streets that are a bewildering muddle of many nations, many architectures; deeds of Western violence and robbery, illustrated with a realism that is positively enthralling; Japanese and Irish, Germans and Indians, Hindus and Italians, cats and girls and ponies and—the list sets whirring the wheels of the biggest of dictionaries. [...]

Everything is the reflection of a cracked mirror held in the hand of the clever showman, who, knowing us as children of a larger growth, compounds his mess, bizarre and ridiculous, accordingly. There is little need to ponder the whys and wherefores of our aberrancy. Once en masse, humanity sheds its civilisation and becomes half child, half savage. In the theatres the gentlest are swayed by a sort of mob mania and delight in scenes of cruelty and bloodshed—though at home the sight of a canary with a broken wing sets stirring in us tender sympathy. A crowd seldom reasons. It will lynch an innocent man or glorify a scamp politician with equal facility. Hence the monstrous debauch of the fancy at Coney Island, where New York chases its chimera of pleasure. [. . .]

Then Coney Island, with its vulgarity, its babble and tumult, is a glorified city of flame. But don't go too near it; your wings will easily singe on the broad avenue where beer, sausage, fruit, pop-corn, candy, flapjacks, green corn, and again, beer, rule the appetites of the multitude. After seeing the aerial magic of that great pyrotechnic artist Pain, a man who could, if he so desired, create a new species of art, and his nocturnes of jewelled fire, you wonder why the entire beach is not called Fire Island. The view of Luna Park from Sheepshead Bay suggests a cemetery of fire, the tombs, turrets, and towers illuminated, and mortuary shafts of flame. At Dreamland the little lighthouse is a scarlet incandescence. The big building stands a dazzling apparition for men on ships and steamers out at sea. Everything is fretted with fire. Fire delicately etches some fairy structure; fire outlines an Oriental gateway; fire runs like a musical scale through many octaves, the darkness crowding it, the mist blurring it. Fire is the god of Coney Island after sundown, and fire was its god this night, the hottest of the summer.

HUMAN NATURE WITH THE BRAKES OFF—OR: WHY THE SCHOOLMA'AM WALKED INTO THE SEA

Edward F. Tilyou

The Tilyous were a family born with Coney Island sand in their shoes. As far back as 1882, Peter Tilyou had established the Surf Theater. His son George then built Steeplechase Park. After George's death in 1914, his eldest son, Edward (1896–1944), who was only seventeen at the time, took over the management of the park. Edward expanded Steeplechase, for example, by acquiring the Parachute Jump and other attractions from the New York World's Fair (1939–1940). Together with his two brothers, George and Frank, he operated the park and other family properties until his death at the young age of forty-eight. In "Human Nature with the Brakes Off," published in the *American Magazine* in July 1922, Tilyou clearly expresses the family philosophy concerning amusement parks. A major attraction of such parks, according to Tilyou, is that they satisfy the desire of the public to "cut-up"—that is, "cut loose from their usual repressions." He gives the example, reflected in the title of the piece, of the prim-looking schoolteacher who walked into the ocean at Coney, "fully clad in her street clothes." Amusement parks also give people an opportunity to play a role different from that of their usual life, to experience excitement, and to watch other people in embarrassing positions. Tilyou concludes his discussion with the words: "As an amusement man, I thank heaven that we Americans never really grow up."

IN THE HEIGHT OF LAST SUMMER'S HILARITY at Coney Island a prim-looking Pennsylvania schoolma'am stirred up one of our daily ripples of excitement by walking into the ocean, up to her neck, fully clad in her street clothes.

This sort of performance is not new at Coney, but it is usually given by women too poor to buy bathing suits. Afterward they sit on the beach and "dry out." The teacher, however, was very evidently not of this class; so the police arrested her. She was brought before a group of examiners, who found her to be as well balanced mentally as any human being you would want to meet.

"But, my dear young woman, why did you walk into the ocean with all your clothing on?" asked one of her inquisitors.

"Because I couldn't resist the impulse to 'cut up,'" the teacher replied. "It has been a hard year at school; and when I saw the big crowd here, everyone with the brakes off, the spirit of the place got the better of me." [. . .]

There are five hundred amusement parks in the United States. At least two hundred and fifty of them are limited editions of Coney Island, with the same sort of fun-making devices, only fewer of them. I have visited many of these parks and have found people pretty much the same everywhere.

Our main advantage at Coney Island is in the size of the crowds. Often we have half a million people here on a Sunday or a holiday. In the course of the season the visitors are said to total between twenty-five and thirty millions. In all the parks of the country, I suppose the seasonal attendance would exceed the total of our national population. These parks, therefore, furnish a gigantic laboratory of human nature—one which psychologists cannot afford to overlook. They would be especially interested in the way people cut loose from their usual repressions.

For instance, there was one amusement which took Surf Avenue, the main street of Coney, by storm several years ago. A number of "ballyhoo" men set up booths with shelves in the rear of them. These shelves were covered with imitation china dishes. In front of each booth was a liberal supply of missiles, and a sign reading:

> If you can't break up your
> own home, break up ours!

There wasn't a single prize offered. People paid their perfectly good money just for the savage joy of smashing dishes. They took an unholy glee in it—as if they were trying to make up for all the times they had felt like throwing things at home and had decided that the gratification of their desire would be either ill bred or too expensive. The sport got so popular that the owners of the booths had to have their wall shelves set in panels that swung around like a revolving door. That was the only way they could get fresh supplies in fast enough.

Theoretically, I suppose, an amusement park is an instrument for the *common people,* to use a phrase we frequently hear. But my observation has been that the more cultivated a person is the more relaxation he finds in letting loose his play impulses. The clerk or truck-driver hasn't so much make-believe personality to shed. The bustle and jostle of the park is closer to his everyday life. [. . .]

I have often thought a statistician or a historian could sit in the midst of the throng at an amusement park and figure out pretty accurately what was transpiring in the world at large, and whether the country was in a state of business prosperity or adversity. One unfailing sign of a business depression, such as we have recently passed through, is the separation of men and women in amusement parks. When everything is prosperous, almost the entire crowd seems to be made up of couples. When money is scarce, however, men are not entertaining the girls so generally. One amusement man recently declared that although attendance was well up to normal, not half as many couples were seen as had been the rule in boom times. On a certain Sunday one of his electrical gate machines recorded two thousand single admissions and not a single double. This was a very extreme case, but it was in line with the trend of the times.

Women in an amusement park are much more economical than men. The average man probably spends twice as much as the average woman. But women carry money more generally and plentifully than they used to. I remember back in 1912 when the lights of Coney suddenly blinked out at nine-thirty in the evening. In the confusion that followed, a number of ladies were separated from their escorts. The result was that the police had to "stake" a good many of these to their car fare home. The same thing wouldn't happen to-day.

I have noticed that girls and women at an amusement park have a queer way of "bluffing" about their station in life. I suppose it is all part of the general game. The little factory girl on an outing talks loudly about "the office," and her work as a "stenographer," or "private secretary." The stenographer, on the other hand, will pretend that she is an executive or a business woman—and so on up the scale. Often I have listened to the happy chatter of a group of girls, manifestly from some garment shop or factory, as they waited in line to take their turn at some of our fun-making devices.

"Hey, Mame!" one of them would call out, holding her blue combination ticket up in the air. "Guess we'll keep these to show at *the office* in the morning!"

"Sure thing! . . . Say, Sade, how many weeks y'going ter spend in the Adirondacks this summer?"

"Long's I like, I guess!"

All this talk would be carried on in loud tones, evidently for the benefit of the crowd round about. It was part of the popular game of make-believe, and the players evidently thought that they were getting away with it.

In like manner, the hard-working woman who owns a small shop on a Brooklyn side street, or in New York's Ghetto, shuts up her store on Saturday afternoon, dons a black satin dress, a hat with an imitation bird of paradise waving in front, her diamonds—real or make-believe—and a silver mesh bag. Then she sets out for Coney Island. Now she is no longer the tradeswoman, but the *grand dame*. She moves with assumed dignity through the jostling crowds. You can spot her as far as you can see her.

Amusement park men often smile over these propensities of women—particularly shop and factory girls—for acting. In their workaday environment the make-believers are what they *are;* no camouflage can change their status. But when they are out for a good time, with several hundred thousand other people similarly inclined, they can put on their best clothes and assume any part at will. They may not fool the rest of the world as much as they think, but they have their own fun out of the rôles.

Men, so far as I have noticed, seldom indulge in this sort of pretense about their stations in life. The matter seems to make little difference to them personally, and they assume that it makes little difference to anyone else.

Women are also inclined to be more critical than men are. Frequently they get angry at being involved in some of the thousand and one ridiculous situations that are the chief stock in trade of an amusement park. Their escorts probably laugh at the same thing. People who operate the side shows and other flamboyant attractions of the "Midway" say that women make up four out of five of the very few folks who complain that they have been *buncoed*.

For instance, a woman with two youngsters may pay thirty cents to see some musical phantasy advertised with flaring posters and a blatant "barker." Certainly she has no right to expect Paris costumes, an [Joseph] Urban background, or Ziegfeld chorus girls. Yet when the chorus comes on, she may turn to the woman back of her and exclaim in a loud voice:

"Did you ever see anything so terrible?"

Such instances, of course, are exceptions. The average woman, like the average man, is a thoroughly good give-and-take sport. It just happens, however, that women form the greater percentage of the deviations from the rule.

Cupid is always lurking around the corner to take advantage of the general loosening of emotions that accompanies the excitations of an amusement park. Many a visit there has had its climax in a wedding. Every year a considerable number of couples coming to Coney are married before they start home again. A minister who has presided at many of these weddings says the larger share of them is the direct outcome of excursions from smaller cities and towns in New York, New Jersey, and Pennsylvania.

The "Tunnel of Love," an attraction found at many amusement parks, has been responsible for a surprising number of proposals. In this and similar devices, couples are allowed to drift through dark or semi-dark underground caverns, usually in a boat or gondola borne on an artificial stream of water. These places fill the same need for couples who have no "beau parlor" that English busses fill for the London youth. There is an English rhyme running:

> And many a miss will be missus some day
> Through riding the top of the car.

The same thing applies to the romantic rides at our American amusement parks. Their dim interiors often give a bashful young man the opportunity to propose. [...]

I have heard people complain that amusement parks are speeding up more every year in glitter and racket. If that is true, it is because you people demand it. You respond instantly to incandescent cupolas, the blare of music, the slam of scenic railways, the beating of tom-toms; and we give you what you want. The most popular shows are those which give the keenest excitement. The tenseness of modern industry and business competition has keyed your nervous organism to such a pitch that you seek a sharp stimulus.

In making a scientific study of this "urge," a group of Cleveland researchers selected as a subject a girl worker in a garment factory who had always patronized an amusement park much on the order of Coney Island.

She was taken to another park, given over for the most part to quieter and less exciting amusements.

"Why don't they have more lights here? Gee, this place is dead!" was her first comment; and she was soon bored to extinction.

This was merely another proof that it takes something more stimulating than an ordinary public park to satisfy the recreational demand of youth worn out by long hours of hard work.

You can't subdue a big crowd of human beings on holiday bent. During the Mardi Gras week carnival at Coney, the island may be plastered with signs stating:

> Arrest Will Follow the Use of Ticklers,
> Paper Dusters, Fuzzy Dogs,
> Slapsticks or
> Stuffing Confetti in People's Mouths

But all these things are going to happen—despite the vigilance of the police.

Most people want their fun at nights, when the lights are bright. The glitter and glare of electrical displays put them in the holiday spirit. Consequently, amusement parks are one of the few institutions around New York, Boston, and other cities to which daylight saving has not been an advantage.

Those of us in the amusement business have studied your psychology, and tried to build our business on a few simple fundamentals. We know, for instance, that most people look back on childhood as the happiest period of their lives. They may be mistaken, but this is the mental attitude they like to adopt. So when they are out for a good time they get infinite joy out of acting like children again. That is why the slides, hobby horses, toy locomotives, and carrousels are always crowded at amusement parks.

Another thing we know is that the average person likes to have a share in making his own fun, instead of having attendants or mechanical contrivances do it all for him. People prefer to steer their own craft on the "Witching Waves," pilot their own airships, hold the reins of their own hobby horses, and find their own way out of the labyrinth.

Folks also take great glee in seeing other folks in embarrassing positions. Not only does it seem funny to them, but it stirs up a soothing complacency that *they* are not the victims. Spectators will stand for hours in front of the "Barrel of Fun," a revolving cylinder in which passengers are likely to be rolled off their feet, or they will watch with equal intentness a narrow wooden lane which suddenly becomes movable, threatening to topple barrels from either side down onto the heads of luckless victims. [...]

I have never quite been able to fathom the psychology of the people who stand in front of the "illusion mirrors" for half an hour or so at a time. These are the mirrors that show you in grotesque caricatures of yourself: perhaps elongated to great height and unbelievable emaciation, or flattened down to the tubbiness of a dwarf heavy-weight. Perhaps the folks who group in front of these glasses are congratulating themselves that they really look so much handsomer than they might look if the reflections were actual likenesses.

Most amusement parks are built beside salt or fresh water beaches, and it is here that we have noticed a gradual but marked change in the habits of human beings. A few years ago the men at the beaches far outnumbered the women. To-day there is about an equal division.

Most of us can remember the time when women were not expected to do any real swimming. They dressed for the *beach,* not for the *water.* Satin beach slippers were quite the vogue. Such women as ventured into the waves were usually led by a protecting male hand. To-day all this has changed. Most girls prefer the rôle of mermaid to that of beach flower. They dress suitably for real swimming, and they are not afraid of getting wet, or sunburned, or even dirty. [...]

Beach bungalows, rented for the summer season, have come into extraordinary demand during the past five or ten years. This is particularly true in the case of people who cannot afford to take the usual summer hotel or boarding-house vacation. We have miles of such bungalows around Coney. Many of them are literally spilling over with human beings—due to the fact that the family taking the original lease is not able or willing to pay the entire rent. Every room that can possibly be dispensed with is sublet. [...]

One eminently desirable change along our Eastern beach fronts is the absence of the old-time three-card-monte man, with his one-legged table stuck into the sand and the inevitable grease spot on one of his cards. Indeed, the day of confidence men and sharpers in amusement places is practically over. Even fortune-telling is no longer legal at Coney Island.

Deliberate swindling at amusement places may be dead, but the harmless hoodwinking of the side shows will always live. People love to listen to the exaggerated promises of the "ballyhoo" man, and they enter his tent prepared to believe almost anything. There have been enough *original* "Wild Men of Borneo" to man a battleship.

"Only a dime, ladies and gentlemen, for the ravishing vision of Fatima, the beautiful Egyptian princess—direct descendant of Cleopatra!" shouts the "barker." You troop in, happy and unquestioning as children. Five minutes later you are rushing across the street to see the "Fire-Eating Fiji Islander."

"Show is about to begin! You'll have to hurry!" shouts another "barker." Experience may have taught you that shows begin only when tents are full—but there is always the nervous rush to the door. You are children again, the same sort of children who used to pay "Five pins—no crooked ones taken!" for a peep through the hole in the mysterious chest guarded by some youthful P. T. Barnum. As an amusement man, I thank heaven that we Americans never really grow up.

CONEY

Giuseppe Cautela

Giuseppe Cautela migrated to the United States from Italy at the age of sixteen. He became a barber, a trade that he practiced for the rest of his life along with his writing. Cautela was a frequent contributor to H. L. Mencken's magazine *American Mercury*. He published one novel, *Moon Harvest* (1925), which tells of the tensions of assimilation in an Italian immigrant family in the United States. In "Coney," published in the *American Mercury* in November 1925, Cautela describes a visit to Coney Island with his wife and children. For Cautela, as with Walt Whitman, Coney represents American democracy, tolerance, and freedom. Races mingle, the beach is filled with lovers and children, and "the garments of Puritanism are given a kick that sends them flying before the winds." Swimming at Coney is like bathing "in the American Jordan," in "holy water." Coney is also a magical place because there an adult becomes a child and "dreams become tangible."

WE GOT OUT, or rather we were pushed out [of the train]. The courage of all these people in the face of the hot sun is really admirable. Humanity, I suppose, was made for the outdoors. All the efforts of Progress to segregate and stifle it within four walls have failed. As long as there is a beach or a meadow left people will gather their bundles and migrate there. That is why Coney Island is a place where man in shackles breaks his bounds. Here he becomes himself. Here he finds that natural expression which makes him kiss his wife or his sweetheart. Here he becomes beautiful, because the sun is not denied him. [...]

New buildings to meet the exigencies of the times have hastily gone up. We found a new order and cleanliness that does credit to the shopkeepers if you consider the crowd they serve every day. And here also huge capital has jumped at the opportunity to establish new, sanitary bathhouses in place of the wobbly shacks of a few years ago. A little to the left of us we saw the municipal baths. Well frequented. Too well, indeed, for all the long lines of people waiting in the hot sun. [. . .]

When you bathe at Coney Island you bathe in the American Jordan. It is holy water. Nowhere else in the United States will you see so many races mingle in a common purpose for a common good. Democracy meets here and has its first interview skin to skin. The garments of Puritanism are given a kick that sends them flying before the winds. Here you find the real interpretation of the Declaration of Independence. The most good for the greatest number. Tolerance. Freedom in the sense that everyone minds his business. In no place have I seen so many lovers as on this beach. On no beach so many wonderful children. Muscles that develop from labor, and beauty that sweats in factories meet here. [. . .]

We bathed, we frolicked, we stretched out on the sand. Toward evening, when the beach began to look quiet and alone again, the sea gave me an impression of being tired. The waves rolled slowly and reluctantly. After a day's work Neptune takes a rest. How old he looks! How weedy! How gray, with patches of white!

Michele, my [. . .] boy, up to now had been as quiet and silent as a mouse. Upon returning to the boardwalk he clutched me. "Papa, I am hungry," I heard him say with his bird-like voice.

"Of course, we shall all eat, Michele. I am taking you to a restaurant presently."

But Michele does not like restaurants. "I hate restaurants," he told me.

"This is very promising; you are beginning to hate very early," I said.

Michele is seven years old. As a sort of retort he tried to arrest my progress. I quickly saw the cause of his prompting. Right in front of us, like so many petards about to go off, sizzled a grill of frankfurters.

"Ah," I gasp, "the plague!"

"No," responds Michele. "They are frankfurters."

"Yes, Pa," mewl the others in chorus.

It's a critical moment. I am determined to hold fast. And I don't look at Michele. If I do, I know it means surrender. You cannot look in Michele's eyes and say no. [. . .] Suddenly he steps in front of me; he catches my eye; I capitulate. What is worse, I join the party. What, indeed, is a visit to Coney Island without a frankfurter?

The magic of Coney Island is such that one becomes a child. This is not easy for many men to do. Most of us lose our primeval sense of life, which is a sense of divinity. But Coney Island brings it back. There you meet your grandfather and your grandmother and they tell you all about fairyland. When it gets dark some goblin, by pushing a button, lets all the stars from heaven drop to earth. And for once in your life you taste that perfect bliss of existence where dreams become tangible. Your body swings in the ether. You climb to dizzy heights and touch the gods with your finger.

You are shown all the punishments of sin and all the rewards of virtue. You become forgetful of both, and your body, taking on wings, flies through the air with the speed of a meteor. You lose all sense of distance and space. You are shaken, you are tossed, you are whirled, you are pinned, and then, almost senseless, you plunge to earth once more. Shrieks, giggles, laughter of every sound and meaning tell you that man is still supreme. Forget, brother, the uncivil strife! The panting rush! Escape the crush of the subway! Damn the telephone, and the blow at close quarters!

Here the planet Luna awaits you. She comes down close to flirt with you. In the far distance she was cold, mysterious and silvery charming. Many a night she disturbed your thoughts. She made you restless and sleepless. But tonight she has consented to meet you and lead you by the hand. She will show you the battle of the gods for the throne of wisdom. And the many men she has charmed by her beauty. What strange faces they have! What gorgeous costumes! Look at the colors! You are filled with light. She gives you the freedom of her house. You may sport and refresh yourself in a limpid pool, or dance as only we mortals can dance. The hours go by. You refuse to leave. You have forgotten the world of yesterday. You begin to pity your boss for his lack of humor. His pounding tomorrow will slide over you like water that doesn't wet you. Beyond lies hell with all its burning ugliness. But here is release. The shackles of toil have gone to the bottom of the ocean.

This is not the same crowd that came with us from the subway and elevated train. All the faces have relaxed. They have a softer expression, and some of them show nobility. Their imagination has soared, and from now on they will talk differently.

BEACH AT CONEY ISLAND, CA. 1940. (BROOKLYN PUBLIC LIBRARY, BROOKLYN COLLECTION)

CONEY ISLAND

E. E. Cummings

Edward Estlin Cummings (1894–1962), one of the most popular American poets of the twentieth century, was born in Cambridge, Massachusetts. His poetry is often characterized by unconventional punctuation, idiosyncratic syntax, and lower-case letters. Cummings wrote a series of essays for *Vanity Fair* from 1924 to 1927, of which "Coney Island," published in June 1926, is one. Cummings had a lifelong affection for circuses and amusement parks—in particular, Coney Island. In Coney, Cummings saw the blending "of the circus and the theatre." He also enjoyed the amusement area's ability to allow everyone to become a performer and thus a source of art—much as George C. Tilyou had intended. As critic Patrick B. Mullen observes: "The audience participates by doing circus tricks themselves, by riding the death-defying roller coasters and loop-the-loops" ("E. E. Cummings and Popular Culture," *Journal of Popular Culture* 5, no. 3 [1971]: 511).

THE INCREDIBLE TEMPLE OF PITY AND TERROR, mirth and amazement, which is popularly known as Coney Island, really constitutes a perfectly unprecedented fusion of the circus and the theatre. It resembles the theatre, in that it fosters every known species of illusion. It suggests the circus, in that it puts us in touch with whatever is hair-raising, breath-taking and pore-opening. But Coney has a distinct drop on both theatre and circus. Whereas at the theatre we merely are deceived, at Coney we deceive ourselves. Whereas at the circus we are merely spectators of the impossible, at Coney we ourselves perform impossible feats—we turn all the heavenly somersaults imaginable and dare all the delirious dangers conceivable; and when, rushing at horrid velocity over irrevocable precipices, we beard the force of gravity in his lair, no acrobat, no lion tamer, can compete with us.

Be it further stated that humanity (and, by the way, there is such a thing) is most emphatically itself at Coney. Whoever, on a really hot day, has attempted to swim three strokes in Coney Island waters will be strongly inclined to believe that nowhere else in all of the round world is humanity quite so much itself. (We have reference to the noteworthy phenomenon that every Coney Island swimmer swims, not in the water, but in the populace.) Nor is this spontaneous itselfness, on the part of Coney Island humanity, merely aquatic. It is just as much terrestrial and just as much aerial. Anybody who, of a truly scorching Saturday afternoon, has been caught in a Coney Island jam will understand the terrestrial aspect, and anybody who has watched (let alone participated in) a Coney Island roller coaster will comprehend the aerial aspect, of humanity's irreparable itselfness. But this means that the *audience* of Coney Island—as well as the *performance* given by that unmitigated circus-theatre—is unique.

Ask Freud, he knows.

Now to seek a formula for such a fundamental and glorious institution may appear, at first blush, presumptuous. Indeed, those of our readers who are dyed-in-the-wool Coney Island fans have doubtless resented our using the words "circus-theatre" to describe an (after all) indescribable phenomenon. We hasten to reassure them: Coney for us, as for themselves, is Coney and nothing else. But certain aspects of this miracle mesh, so to speak, with the theatre and with the circus; a fact which we consider strictly significant—not for Coney, but for art. We repeat: the essence of Coney Island's "circus-theatre" consists in *homogeneity*. THE AUDIENCE IS THE PERFORMANCE, and vice versa. If this be formula, let us make the most of it.

Those readers who have inspected the International Theatre Exposition will realize that the worldwide "new movement" in the theatre is toward a similar goal. Two facts are gradually being recognized: first, that the circus is an authentic "theatric" phenomenon, and second, that the conventional "theatre" is a box of negligible tricks. The existing relationships between actor and audience and theatre have been discovered to be rotten at their very cores. All sorts of new "theatres" having been suggested, to remedy this thoroughly disgraceful state of affairs – disgraceful because, in the present writer's own lingo, *all genuine theatre is a verb and not a noun*— we ourselves have the extraordinary honour to suggest: Coney Island. [...]

And now, a few parting words as to the actual Coney Island, in which it is to be hoped that all readers of this essay will freely indulge at the very earliest opportunity.

Essentially it remains, as we have said, indescribable. At best, we may only suggest its invincible entirety indirectly, or through a haphazard enumeration of the more obvious elements—than which process, what would be more futile? How, by depicting a succession of spokes, may we hope to convey the speed or essence of a wheel which is revolving so rapidly as to be spokeless? No indeed; the IS or Verb of Coney Island escapes any portraiture. A trillion smells; the tinkle and snap of shooting galleries; the magically sonorous exhortations of barkers and ballyhoomen; the thousands upon thousands of faces paralyzed by enchantment to mere eyeful disks, which strugglingly surge through dizzy gates of illusion; the metamorphosis of atmosphere into a stupendous pattern of electric colours, punctuated by a continuous whisking of leaning and cleaving ship-like shapes; the yearn and skid of toy cars crammed with screeching reality, wildly spiraling earthward or gliding out of ferocious depth into sumptuous height or whirling eccentrically in a brilliant flatness; occultly bulging, vividly painted banners inviting us to side shows, where strut and lurk those placid specimens of impossibility which comprise the extraordinary aristocracy of freakdom; the intricate clowning of enormous deceptions, of palaces which revolve, walls which collapse, surfaces which arch and drop and open to emit spurts of lividly bellowing steam—all these elements disappear in a homogeneously happening universe, surrounded by the rhythmic mutations of the ocean and circumscribed by the mightily oblivion-coloured rush of the roller coaster.

LANDSCAPE OF A VOMITING MULTITUDE (DUSK AT CONEY ISLAND)

Federico García Lorca

Translated by Greg Simon and Steven F. White

Federico García Lorca (1898–1936) is one of the greatest Spanish poets and dramatists. His plays include *Blood Wedding* (1932) and *The House of Bernarda Alba* (1936). "Landscape of a Vomiting Multitude" was first published in the literary magazine *Poesía* (Buenos Aires) in November 1933 and later included in *Poet in New York* (1940). Lorca was studying English at Columbia University in 1929/1930, and it is likely that he visited Coney Island on July 4, 1929. The sight of the amusement park, with all its attractions, was "simply too much" for the young writer. Although he had visited Coney in the height of its season, he wrote about it at the dying of the year, on December 29 at twilight. The off-season setting is more appropriate to the tone of the poem, with its bleak atmosphere. The sight of the grotesque fat woman intrigued Lorca, which is reflected in his making her a central character in the poem.

> The fat lady came first,
> tearing out roots and moistening drumskins.
> The fat lady
> who turns dying octopuses inside out.
> The fat lady, the moon's antagonist,
> was running through the streets and deserted buildings
> and leaving tiny skulls of pigeons in the corners
> and stirring up the furies of the last centuries' feasts
> and summoning the demon of bread through the sky's clean-swept
>   hills
> and filtering a longing for light into subterranean tunnels.
> The graveyards, yes, the graveyards,

and the sorrow of the kitchens buried in sand,
the dead, pheasants and apples of another era,
pushing into our throat.

There were murmurings from the jungle of vomit
with the empty women, with hot wax children,
with fermented trees and tireless waiters
who serve platters of salt beneath harps of saliva.
There's no other way, my son, vomit! There's no other way.
It's not the vomit of hussars on the breasts of their whores,
nor the vomit of a cat choking down a frog,
but the dead who scratch with clay hands
on flint gates where clouds and desserts decay.
The fat lady came first
with the crowds from the ships, taverns, and parks.
Vomit was delicately shaking its drums
among a few little girls of blood
who were begging the moon for protection.
Who could imagine my sadness?
The look on my face was mine, but now isn't me.
The naked look on my face, trembling in alcohol
and launching incredible ships
through the anemones of the piers.
I protect myself with this look
that flows from waves where the dawn would never go,
I, poet without arms, lost
in the vomiting multitude,
with no effusive horse to shear
the thick moss from my temples.
But the fat lady went first
and the crowds kept looking for the pharmacies
where the bitter tropics could be found.
Only when a flag went up and the first dogs arrived
did the entire city rush to the railings of the boardwalk.

NEW YORK, DECEMBER 29, 1929

A DAY IN CONEY ISLAND

Isaac Bashevis Singer

Translated by the author and Laurie Colwin

Isaac Bashevis Singer (1904–1991) is one of the masters of twentieth-century fiction, particularly the short story. He won the Nobel Prize in Literature in 1978. Due to the threat of Nazism in Poland, Singer migrated to the United States in 1935. He settled initially in Sea Gate (in Coney Island) and worked sporadically for the *Forward*, a Yiddish newspaper. Although he lived for most of his life in America, he wrote largely of the life and culture that he had left behind in the Jewish shtetls of Poland. In contrast, "A Day in Coney Island" is a semi-autobiographical story about his early struggles in America, particularly finding steady work as a writer. His mixed feelings about Coney may be reflected by Herman Broder, a Holocaust survivor in the novel *Enemies, a Love Story* (1972; film adaptation, 1989). Herman praises Coney's "richness of color, the abundance, the freedom," but he also acknowledges that it is ultimately "cheap and shoddy," a false promise. An excellent film, *Isaac in America: A Journey with Isaac Bashevis Singer* (1986), features a reading of "A Day in Coney Island" by Singer and the actor Judd Hirsch (of *Taxi* fame).

TODAY I KNOW EXACTLY what I should have done that summer—my work. But then I wrote almost nothing. "Who needs Yiddish in America?" I asked myself. Though the editor of a Yiddish paper published a sketch of mine from time to time in the Sunday edition, he told me frankly that no one gave a hoot about demons, dybbuks, and imps of two hundred years ago. At thirty, a refugee from Poland, I had become an anachronism. As if that were not enough, Washington had refused to extend my tourist visa. Lieberman, my lawyer, was trying to get me a permanent visa, but for that I needed my birth certificate, a certificate of morality, a letter saying that I was employed and would not become a public charge, and other papers I could not obtain. I sent alarmed letters to my friends in Poland. They never replied. The newspapers were predicting that Hitler would invade Poland any day.

196

I opened my eyes after a fitful sleep, full of nightmares. My Warsaw wristwatch showed a quarter to eleven. Through the cracks in the shade a golden light poured in. I could hear the sound of the ocean. For a year and a half I had been renting a furnished room in an old house in Sea Gate, not far from Esther (that's what I'll call her here), and I paid sixteen dollars a month for it. Mrs. Berger, the landlady, gave me breakfast at cost.

Until they deported me to Poland, I was enjoying American comfort. I took a bath in the bathroom down the hall (at that time of day, it was not occupied), and I could see a huge boat arriving from Europe—either the *Queen Mary* or the *Normandie*. What a luxury to look out my bathroom window and see the Atlantic Ocean and one of the newest and fastest ships in the world! While shaving, I made a decision: I would not let them deport me to Poland. I would not fall into Hitler's paws. I would stay illegally. I had been told that if war broke out I had a good chance of becoming a citizen automatically. I grimaced at my reflection in the mirror. Already, my red hair was gone. I had watery blue eyes, inflamed eyelids, sunken cheeks, a protruding Adam's apple. Although people came from Manhattan to Sea Gate to get sunburned, my skin remained sickly white. My nose was thin and pale, my chin pointed, my chest flat. I often thought that I looked not unlike the imps I described in my stories. I stuck out my tongue and called myself a crazy *batlan*, which means an unworldly ne'er-do-well.

I expected Mrs. Berger's kitchen to be empty so late in the morning, but they were all there: Mr. Chaikowitz; his third wife; the old writer Lemkin, who used to be an anarchist; and Sylvia, who had taken me to a movie on Mermaid Avenue a few days before (until five o'clock the price of a ticket was only ten cents) and translated for me in broken Yiddish what the gangsters in the film were saying. In the darkness, she had taken my hand, which made me feel guilty. First, I had vowed to myself to keep the Ten Commandments. Second, I was betraying Esther. Third, I had a bad conscience about Anna, who still wrote me from Warsaw. But I didn't want to insult Sylvia.

When I entered the kitchen, Mrs. Berger cried out, "Here's our writer! How can a man sleep so long? I've been on my feet since six this morning." I looked at her thick legs, at her crooked toes and protruding bunions. Everyone teased me. Old Chaikowitz said, "Do you realize that you've missed the hour of morning prayer? You must be one of the Kotzker Hasids who pray late." His face was white and so was his goatee. His third wife, a fat woman with a thick nose and fleshy lips, joined in. "I bet this greenhorn hasn't even got phylacteries." As for Lemkin, he said, "If you ask me, he was up writing a best-seller the whole night."

"I'm hungry for the second time," Sylvia announced.

"What are you going to eat today?" Mrs. Berger asked me. "Two rolls with one egg, or two eggs with one roll?"

"Whatever you give me."

"I'm ready to give you the moon on a plate. I'm scared of what you may write about me in your Yiddish paper."

She brought me a large roll with two scrambled eggs and a big cup of coffee. The price of the breakfast was a quarter, but I owed Mrs. Berger six weeks' rent and for six weeks of breakfasts.

While I ate, Mrs. Chaikowitz talked about her oldest daughter, who had been widowed a year ago and was now remarried. "Have you ever heard of a thing like this?" she said. "He hiccupped once and dropped dead. It seems something ruptured in his brain. God forbid the misfortunes that can happen. He left her over $50,000 insurance. How long can a young woman wait? The other one was a doctor, this one is a lawyer—the biggest lawyer in America. He took one look at her and said, 'This is the woman I've been waiting for.' After six weeks they got married and went to Bermuda on the honeymoon. He bought her a ring for $10,000."

"Was he a bachelor?" Sylvia asked.

"He had a wife before, but she was not his type and he divorced her. She gets plenty of alimony from him—$200 a week. May she spend it all on medicine."

I ate my breakfast quickly and left. Outside, I looked in the letter box, but there was nothing for me. Only two blocks away I could see the house Esther had rented the winter before last. She let rooms to people who wanted to spend their vacations near New York. I couldn't visit her during the daytime; I used to steal over late at night. A lot of Yiddish writers and journalists lived there that summer, and they were not to know about my love affair with Esther. Since I didn't intend to marry her, why jeopardize her reputation? Esther was almost ten years older than I. She had divorced her husband—a Yiddish poet, a modernist, a Communist, a charlatan. He took off for California and never sent a penny for their two little daughters.

He was living with an artist who painted abstract pictures. Esther needed a husband to support her and the girls, not a Yiddish writer who specialized in werewolves and sprites.

I had been in America for eighteen months, but Coney Island still surprised me. The sun poured down like fire. From the beach came a roar even louder than the ocean. On the boardwalk, an Italian watermelon vendor pounded on a sheet of tin with his knife and called for customers in a wild voice. Everyone bellowed in his own way: sellers of popcorn and hot dogs, ice cream and peanuts, cotton candy and corn on the cob. I passed a side-show displaying a creature that was half woman, half fish; a wax museum with figures of Marie Antoinette, Buffalo Bill, and John Wilkes Booth; a store where a turbaned astrologer sat in the dark surrounded by maps and globes of the heavenly constellations, casting horoscopes. Pygmies danced in front of a little circus, their black faces painted white, all of them bound loosely with a long rope. A mechanical ape puffed its belly like a bellows and laughed with raucous laughter. Negro boys aimed guns at metal ducklings. A half-naked man with a black beard and hair to his shoulders hawked potions that strengthened the muscles, beautified the skin, and brought back lost potency. He tore heavy chains with his hands and bent coins between his fingers. A little farther along, a medium advertised that she was calling back spirits from the dead, prophesying the future, and giving advice on love and marriage. I had taken with me a copy of [Jules] Payot's *The Education of the Will* in Polish. This book, which taught how to overcome laziness and do systematic spiritual work, had become my second Bible. But I did the opposite of what the book preached. I wasted my days with dreams, worries, empty fantasies, and locked myself in affairs that had no future.

At the end of the boardwalk, I sat down on a bench. Every day, the same group of old men was gathered there discussing Communism. A little man with a round red face and white hair like foam shook his head violently and yelled, "Who's going to save the workers—Hitler? Mussolini? That social Fascist Léon Blum? That opportunist Norman Thomas? Long live Comrade Stalin! Blessed be his hands!"

A man whose nose was etched with broken veins yelled back, "What about the Moscow trials? The millions of workers and peasants Stalin exiled to Siberia? What about the Soviet generals your Comrade Stalin executed?" His body was short and broad, as if his midsection had been sawed out. He spat into his handkerchief and shrieked, "Is [Nikolai] Bukharin truly a German spy? Does [Leon] Trotsky take money from Rockefeller? Was [Lev] Kamenev an enemy of the proletariat? And how about yourself and the proletariat—you slum landlord!"

I often imagined that these men didn't stop to eat or sleep but waged their debate without interruption. They jumped against one another like he-goats ready to lunge. I had taken out a notebook and a fountain pen to write down a topic (perhaps about these debaters), but instead began to draw a little man with long ears, a nose like a ram's horn, goose feet, and two horns on his head. After a while, I covered his body with scales and attached wings. I looked down at *The Education of the Will*. Discipline? Concentration? What help would that be if I was doomed to perish in Hitler's camps? And even if I survived, how would another novel or story help humanity? The metaphysicians had given up too soon, I decided. Reality is neither solipsism nor materialism. One should begin from the beginning: What is time? What is space? Here was the key to the whole riddle. Who knows, maybe I was destined to solve it.

I closed my eyes and determined once and forever to break through the fence between idea and being, the categories of pure reason and the thing in itself. Through my eyelids the sun shone red. The pounding of the waves and the din of the people merged. I felt, almost palpably, that I was one step from truth. "Time is nothing, space is nothing," I murmured. But that nothingness is the background of the world picture. Then what is the world picture? Is it matter? Spirit? Is it magnetism or gravitation? And what is life? What is suffering? What is consciousness? And if there is a God, what is He? Substance with infinite attributes? The Monad of Monads? Blind will? The Unconscious? Can He be sex, as the cabalists hint? Is God an orgasm that never ceases? Is the universal nothingness the principle of femininity? I wouldn't come to any decision now, I decided. Maybe at night, in bed ...

I opened my eyes and walked toward Brighton. The girders of the el threw a net of sun and shade on the pavements. A train from Manhattan zoomed by with a deafening clatter. No matter how time and space are defined, I thought, it is impossible to be simultaneously in Brooklyn and Manhattan. I passed by windows displaying mattresses, samples of roofing shingles, kosher chickens. I stopped at a Chinese restaurant. Should I go eat lunch? No, in the cafeteria it might be a nickel cheaper. I was down to almost my last cent. If my sketch, "After the Divorce," didn't appear in the Sunday edition, nothing remained but suicide.

Walking back, I marveled at myself. How could I have allowed my finances to dwindle this way? It was true that a tourist wasn't permitted to work, but how would the Immigration and Naturalization Service know if I washed dishes in a restaurant, or if I got a job as a messenger, or as a Hebrew teacher? It was crazy to wait until you were completely broke. True, I had convinced myself that I could be sustained by the leftovers on cafeteria tables. But sooner or later the manager or cashier would notice a human scavenger. The Americans would rather throw food into the garbage can than let it be eaten without payment. Thinking of food made me hungry. I remembered what I had read about fasting. With water to drink, a man can live for sixty days or so. I had read somewhere else that on an expedition to the South or North Pole [Roald] Amundsen had eaten one of his boots. My present hunger, I told myself, was nothing but hysteria. Two eggs and a roll contain enough starch, fat, and protein for days to come. Just the same, I felt a gnawing in my stomach. My knees were weak. I was going to meet Esther that night, and starvation leads to impotence. I barely reached the cafeteria. I entered, took a check, and approached the buffet counter. I knew those who are condemned to death order last meals; people don't even want to be executed on an empty stomach. This, I thought, was proof that life and death have no connection. Since death has no substance, it cannot end life. It is only a frame for living processes that are eternal.

I had not yet become a vegetarian, but I was brooding about vegetarianism. Nevertheless, I picked out flanken in horseradish with boiled potatoes and lima beans, a cup of noodle soup, a large roll, a cup of coffee, and a piece of cake—all for sixty cents. Holding my tray, I passed tables littered with the remains of meals, but I stopped at a clean one. On a chair lay the afternoon tabloid. Although I wanted to read it, I remembered Payot's words: intellectuals should eat slowly, chew each bite thoroughly, and not read. I glanced at the headlines just the same. Hitler had again demanded the Polish Corridor. [Edward] Śmigly-Rydz has announced in the Sejm that Poland would fight for every inch of territory. The German ambassador in Tokyo had had an audience with the Mikado. A retired general in England had criticized the Maginot Line and predicted that it would be broken at the first attack. The powers that rule the universe were preparing the catastrophe.

After I finished eating, I counted my money, and I remembered that I had to call the newspaper and ask about my sketch. I knew that a call from Coney Island to Manhattan cost ten cents, and the Sunday editor, Leon Diamond, rarely came to the office. Still, I couldn't leave everything to fate. One dime wouldn't change the situation. I got up resolutely, found an empty telephone booth, and made the call. I prayed to the same powers preparing the world catastrophe that the operator wouldn't give me a wrong number. I pronounced my number as clearly as I could in my accent, and she told me to put in my dime. The girl at the switchboard answered and I asked for Leon Diamond. I was almost sure she would tell me he wasn't in the office, but I heard his voice on the line. I began to stutter and excuse myself. When I told him who I was, he said brusquely, "Your story will be in on Sunday."

"Thank you. Thank you very much."

"Send me a new story. Goodbye."

"A miracle! A miracle of Heaven!" I shouted to myself. The moment I hung up, another miracle occurred; money began to pour from the telephone—dimes, nickels, quarters. For a second I hesitated; to take it would be theft. But the Telephone Company would never get it back anyway, and someone who needed it less than I might find it. How many times had I put dimes into the telephone without getting a connection! I looked around and saw a fat woman in a bathing suit and a wide-brimmed straw hat waiting for the booth. I grabbed all the coins, shoved them into my pocket, and left, feeling like a new person. In my thoughts I apologized to the powers that know everything. I walked out of the cafeteria and strode toward Sea Gate. I calculated: if I got fifty dollars for the sketch, I would give Mrs. Berger thirty to cover my rent and breakfasts and I would still have twenty dollars to spend. Besides, I would re-establish credit with her and could stay on. In that case, I should call Lieberman, the lawyer. Who knows, maybe he had news from the consul in Toronto. A tourist could not get a permanent visa while in the United States. I would have to go to Cuba or Canada. The trip to Cuba was too expensive to consider, but would Canada allow me to enter? Lieberman had warned me that I would have to be smuggled from Detroit to Windsor, and whoever took me across the bridge would ask a fee of a hundred dollars.

Suddenly I realized that I had committed not one theft but two. In my elation, I had forgotten to pay for my lunch. I still held the check in my hand. This was certainly the work of Satan. Heaven was tempting me. I decided to go back and pay the sixty cents. I walked briskly, almost running. In the cafeteria, a man in a white uniform was standing next to the cashier. They spoke English. I wanted to wait until they were finished, but they kept on talking. The cashier threw a sidelong glance at me and asked, "What do you want?"

I answered in Yiddish, "I forgot to pay for my meal."

He grimaced and muttered, "Never mind, get out of here."

"But—"

"Get out of here, you," he growled, and then he winked.

With that, I understood what was going on. The man in the white uniform must have been the owner, or the manager, and the cashier didn't want him to see that he had let a customer get by without paying. The powers were conspiring to provide me with one stroke of luck after another. I went out, and through the glass door I saw the cashier and the man in the white uniform laughing. They were laughing at me, the greenhorn, with my Yiddish. But I knew that Heaven was trying me out, weighing my merits and iniquities on a scale: did I deserve to stay in America or must I perish in Poland. I was ashamed at having so much faith after calling myself an agnostic or unbeliever, and I said to my invisible critics, "After all, even according to Spinoza everything is determined. In the universe there are no large and small events. To eternity, a grain of sand is as important as a galaxy."

I didn't know what to do with the check. Should I keep it till tomorrow or throw it away? I decided I would give the money to the cashier without it. I tore it to bits and threw them into the trash can.

At home, I collapsed on my bed and fell into a heavy sleep, where I found the secret of time, space, and causality. It seemed unbelievably simple, but the moment I opened my eyes it was all forgotten. What remained was the taste of something otherworldly and marvelous. In my dream I gave my philosophic discovery a name that might have been Latin, Hebrew, Aramaic, or a combination of all three. I remembered myself saying, "Being is nothing but . . ." and there came the word that answered all questions. Outside, it was dusk. The bathers and swimmers had all gone. The sun sank into the ocean, leaving a fiery streak. A breeze brought the smell of underwater decay. A cloud in the form of a huge fish appeared out of nowhere, and the moon crept behind its scales. The weather was changing; the lighthouse fog bell rang sharply. A tugboat pulled three dark barges. It seemed unmovable, as if the Atlantic had turned into the Congealed Sea I used to read about in storybooks.

I no longer needed to scrimp, and I went to the café in Sea Gate and ordered cheesecake and coffee. A Yiddish journalist, a contributor to the paper that printed my sketches, came over and sat at my table. He had white hair and a ruddy face.

"Where have you been hiding these days? Nobody sees you. I was told you live here in Sea Gate."

"Yes, I live here."

"I've rented a room at Esther's. You know who she is — the crazy poet's ex-wife. Why don't you come over? The whole Yiddish press is there. They mentioned you a few times."

"Really? Who?"

"Oh, the writers. Even Esther praises you. I think myself that you have talent, but you choose themes no one cares about and nobody believes in. There are no demons. There is no God."

"Are you sure?"

"Absolutely sure."

"Who created the world?"

"Oh, well. The old question. It's all nature. Evolution. Who created God? Are you really religious?"

"Sometimes I am."

"Just to be spiteful. If there is a God, why does He allow Hitler to drag innocent people to Dachau? And how about your visa? Have you done anything about it? If you haven't, you'll be deported and your God will worry very little about it."

I told him my complications, and he said, "There's only one way out for you—marry a woman who's an American citizen. That'll make you legal. Later, you can get the papers and become a citizen yourself."

"I would never do that," I said.

"Why not?"

"It's an insult to both the woman and to me."

"And to fall into Hitler's hands is better? It's nothing but silly pride. You write like a ripe man, but you behave like a boy. How old are you?"

I told him.

"At your age, I was exiled to Siberia for revolutionary activities."

The waiter came over, and I was about to pay when the writer grabbed my check. I'm too lucky today, I thought.

I looked toward the door and saw Esther. She often dropped in here in the evening, which was the reason I avoided the café. Esther and I had conspired to keep our affair a secret. Besides, I had become pathologically bashful in America. My boyish blushing had returned. In Poland, I never thought of myself as short, but among the American giants I became small. My Warsaw suit looked outlandish, with its broad lapels and padded shoulders. In addition, it was too heavy for the New York heat. Esther kept reproaching me for wearing a stiff collar, a vest, and a hat in the hot weather. She saw me now and seemed embarrassed, like a provincial girl from Poland. We had never been together in public. We spent our time in the dark, like two bats. She made a move to leave, but my companion at the table called out to her. She approached unsteadily. She was wearing a white dress and a straw hat with a green ribbon. She was brown from the sun, and her black eyes had a girlish sparkle. She didn't look like a woman approaching forty, but slim and youthful. She came over and greeted me as if I were a stranger. In the European fashion, she shook my hand. She smiled self-consciously and said "you" to me instead of "thou."

"How are you? I haven't seen you for a long time," she said.

"He's hiding." The writer denounced me. "He's not doing anything about his visa and they'll send him back to Poland. The war is going to break out soon. I advised him to marry an American woman because he'd get a visa that way, but he won't listen."

"Why not?" Esther asked. Her cheeks were glowing. She smiled a loving, wistful smile. She sat down on the edge of a chair.

I would have liked to make a clever, sharp reply. Instead, I said sheepishly, "I wouldn't marry to get a visa."

The writer smiled and winked. "I'm not a matchmaker, but you two would make a fitting pair."

Esther looked at me questioningly, pleading and reproachful. I knew I had to answer right then, either seriously or with a joke, but not a word came out. I felt hot. My shirt was wet and I was stuck to my seat. I had the painful feeling that my chair was tipping over. The floor heaved up and the lights in the ceiling intertwined, elongated and foggy. The café began to circle like a carrousel.

Esther got up abruptly, "I have to meet someone," she said, and turned away. I watched her hurry toward the door. The writer smiled knowingly, nodded, and went over to another table to chat with a colleague. I remained sitting, baffled by the sudden shift in my luck. In my consternation I took the coins from my pocket and began to count and recount them, identifying more by touch than by sight, doing intricate calculations. Every time, the figures came out different. As my game with the powers on high stood now, I seemed to have won a dollar and some cents and to have lost refuge in America and a woman I really loved.

INTO THE NIGHT LIFE

Henry Miller

Henry Miller (1891–1980) was born in Manhattan but moved to the Williamsburg section of Brooklyn, which is referred to frequently in his works, as a child. From 1930 to 1940, he lived in Paris, where he became the lover of writer Anaïs Nin, who subsidized his living expenses and paid for the publication of his first book, *Tropic of Cancer* (1934). The book contains explicit sexual passages and was banned in the United States on the grounds that it was obscene. *Black Spring* (1936), from which "Into the Night Life" is taken, is not truly a novel, but a collection of vignettes, essays, sketches, and prose poems. Miller does not explicitly discuss Coney Island in this work, but uses it as a metaphor for the "sordid, shoddy, thin as pasteboard" landscape of a dream.

SUDDENLY I AM AT THE SEASHORE and no recollection of the train stopping. No remembrance of it departing even. Just swept up on the shore of the ocean like a comet.

Everything is sordid, shoddy, thin as pasteboard. A Coney Island of the mind. The amusement shacks are running full blast, the shelves full of chinaware and dolls stuffed with straw and alarm clocks and spittoons. Every shop has three balls over it and every game is a ball game. The Jews are walking around in mackintoshes, the Japs are smiling, the air is full of chopped onions and sizzling hamburgers. Jabber, jabber, and over it all in a muffled roar comes the steady hiss and boom of the breakers, a long uninterrupted adenoidal wheeze that spreads a clammy catarrh over the dirty shebang. Behind the pasteboard streetfront the breakers are ploughing up the night with luminous argent teeth; the clams are lying on their backs squirting ozone from their anal orifices. In the oceanic night Steeplechase looks like a wintry beard. Everything is sliding and crumbling, everything glitters, totters, teeters, titters.

Where is the warm summer's day when first I saw the green-carpeted earth revolving and men and women moving like panthers? Where is the soft gurgling music which I heard welling up from the sappy roots of the earth? Where am I to go if everywhere there are trapdoors and grinning skeletons, a world turned inside out and all the flesh peeled off? Where am I to lay my head if there is nothing but beards and mackintoshes and peanut whistles and broken slats? Am I to walk forever along this endless pasteboard street, this pasteboard which I can punch a hole in, which I can blow down with my breath, which I can set fire to with a match? The world has become a mystic maze erected by a gang of carpenters during the night. Everything is a lie, a fake. Pasteboard.

I walk along the ocean front. The sand is strewn with human clams waiting for some one to pry their shells apart. In the roar and hubbub their pissing anguish goes unnoticed. The breakers club them, the lights deafen them, the tide drowns them. They lie behind the pasteboard street in the onyx-colored night and they listen to the hamburgers sizzling. Jabber, Jabber, a sneezing and wheezing, balls rolling down the long smooth troughs into tiny little holes filled with bric-a-brac, with chinaware and spitoons and flowerpots and stuffed dolls. Greasy Japs wiping the rubberplants with wet rags, Armenians chopping onions into microcosmic particles, Macedonians throwing the lasso with molasses arms. Every man, woman, and child in a mackintosh has adenoids, spreads catarrh, diabetes, whooping cough, meningitis. Everything that stands upright, that slides, rolls, tumbles, spins, shoots, teeters, sways and crumbles is made of nuts and bolts. The monarch of the mind is a monkey wrench. Sovereign pasteboard power.

The clams have fallen asleep, the stars are dying out. Everything that is made of water snoozes now in the flap-pocket of a hyena. Morning comes like a glass roof over the world. The glassy ocean sways in its depths, a still, transparent sleep.

It is neither night nor day. It is the dawn traveling in short waves with the flir of an albatross's wings. The sounds that reach me are cushioned, gonged, muffled, as if man's labors were being performed under water. I feel the tide ebbing without fear of being sucked in; I hear the waves splashing without fear of drowning. I walk amidst the wrack and debris of the world, but my feet are not bruised. There is no finitude of sky, no division of land and sea. I move through sluice and orifice with gliding slippery feet. I smell nothing, I hear nothing, I see nothing, I feel nothing. Whether on my back or on my belly, whether sidewise like the crab or spiral like a bird, all is bliss downy and undifferentiated.

NOW AND THEN

Joseph Heller

Joseph Heller (1923–1999) was born in Coney Island, which he wrote about in several of his works. Heller is best known for the semi-autobiographical, antiwar novel *Catch-22* (1961), generally considered to be one of the most significant satires written in the second half of the twentieth century. His other novels include *Something Happened* (1974), *Good as Gold* (1979), and *Closing Time* (1994), a sequel to *Catch-22*. The last work has sections lamenting the decline of Heller's Coney Island home. Coney Island also appears in *Good as Gold* and is the subject of "Coney Island: The Fun Is Over" (1962), included in *Catch as Catch Can: The Collected Stories and Other Writings* (2003). Heller's friend George Mandel, a Coney native mentioned in this excerpt from *Now and Then: From Coney Island to Here* (1998), wrote about the amusement area in his novel *The Breakwater* (1960). Another friend who appears, Mario Puzo, author of *The Godfather* (1969), wrote a somewhat nostalgic essay, "Meet Me Tonight in Dreamland," which was published in *New York* on September 17, 1979. In his autobiography, Heller shares his bittersweet memories of the Coney Island of his childhood and his disillusionment over its present condition.

CONEY ISLAND, with its beaches, crowds, commotion, and couple of hundred entertainments, has always been magical to children and a gaudy magnet for adults. People came from everywhere. Early in this century, even Sigmund Freud dropped in for a look on his trip to the United States; the Russian author Maxim Gorky was a sightseer, too. The milling crowds through the 1930s included soldiers on leave and sailors in port, crewmen in the American and foreign merchant marine. Whole families, sometimes clans of extended families, would journey from Manhattan and the Bronx and other parts of Brooklyn to spend the day and early evening. Those who eschewed the lockers and other facilities of the bathhouses would make camp on blankets under the boardwalk, changing in and out of bathing suits, eating from tubs of cooked foods prepared at home before setting out. The place was better known than we who lived there realized and had been a famous, and notorious, playland and summer resort for longer than we could appreciate. [...]

Even at this late date, people I meet with a large stock of memories of visits to Coney Island still express surprise upon hearing that I grew up there, that families lived there, and still do, and that children were brought up there, and still are.

The single image they retain is of a gigantic, sprawling, fenced-in amusement area with an abundance of games and rides, of sideshows and food stands, that is closed down and locked up at the end of each season until the following spring. In fact, though, the amusement area was perhaps only fifteen blocks long, on a strip only one block deep from Surf Avenue to the boardwalk, in a seaside community that is about two and a half miles long and about half a mile wide and which, by contemporary suburban standards, was densely populated with year-round residents. Even back in 1929, when I entered kindergarten, there were sufficient families with young children living in Coney Island to overcrowd the two elementary schools there—and each of these stood five stories high and a full block wide. One was in the Jewish area, the other in the Italian, but this division into Jewish and Italian was anything but absolute. [...]

While certainly not a slum, Coney Island was in my time a depressed area for its year-round dwellers, except for Sea Gate, and this is even truer today than in the past. It appears to me today a rather squalid scene, and it must have seemed so back then to others better off than we who weren't living there. The older my mother became, the more she detested the place for its harsh and rowdy intrusions, especially in summer, when the streets were constantly filled with people and noise, often late into the night. Screened apartment windows were open at night, for this was before the days when air conditioners were ubiquitous. My mother liked the bathing and, before the accident of the broken hip, would go to the beach on sunny days, taking along an empty milk bottle to fill with ocean water for washing the sand from her feet when she returned. But she was distressed and angered by the vulgar turmoil and ceaseless, turbulent motion, the sheer volume and activity, of the crowds everywhere. Bitterly she would denounce our part of the world as a *"chozzer* mart," a pig market. I might feel secretly chastened when I heard her, but I was also secretly unsympathetic, for I was part of the restless commotion and, once old enough for membership in one of the local social clubs, thoughtlessly helped contribute to the din and disorder of the street with our late-night banter and our club room's outdoor loudspeakers blasting away with "jump" music from the unrelenting record players within.

We were children from poor families, but didn't know it. I don't think I have ever in my life thought of myself as underprivileged, as unfairly deprived of something I might reasonably wish to own and didn't. Although incomes were low, everyone's father did seem to have a job, and later everyone's older brother and sister; finally, we, too, were out of school and working. It was a blessing of our childhood to be oblivious of our low economic state and of how others might regard us. We had our beach and our boardwalk, our safe streets, the food and clothing we needed, and I don't believe the circumstance of moderate poverty was too upsetting to our parents either. Nearly all were immigrants and living on a roughly equal level. This was the nature of life; they had learned that in Europe. It was not stylish to bemoan. They expected life to be hard, and most were living better than they had been able to in the Old World. I doubt that many had known the luxury of running water, central heating, and indoor plumbing before they arrived in America. [...]

I once heard George Mandel, an early friend from Coney Island and the first of the people I knew to succeed in becoming a novelist, present in a television interview a description of Coney Island I wouldn't try to improve upon: If a person did have to grow up in a slum (he used that word *slum* for comic exaggeration) he could imagine no better one. [...]

Scattered everywhere about the Island, mostly in neighborhoods near the beach, were complexes of bungalows and frame buildings called "villas" or "courts" or "esplanades," which might all have been there before we were. Certainly, they were already in place when I came along to notice them, and were still there after the war when I married and moved away to attend college. These wooden structures of various sizes would lie silent and shut for nine months of the year and then teem with families who rented the cramped bedrooms and housekeeping units for the summer and came crowding into them excitedly with their bedding and baby carriages—almost all of them arriving, it seemed, in the same few days. They would pour in from other parts of Brooklyn such as Williamsburg and East New York, and from Manhattan, the Bronx, and New Jersey, to pass the next few months in a bustling proximity to each other that would have been intolerable to people more cultivated and less sociable, and likely *was* intolerable to the generation of young they reared. The summer renters would for the most part spend their months in these quarters happily, for the same families returned with bedding and growing children to the same rudimentary "villas," "courts," and "esplanades" year after year. Some of the boys came to be summer friends; their return was awaited and they grew acceptable enough to play in our card games for pennies or soda-bottle tops, or to qualify for a position on the Surf Avenue punchball team of West 31st Street, especially when we were short of players. [...]

Even before World War II, the Island as diversion and playground had been fading in verve and enterprise, its amusement area persistently shrinking. And since the end of that war, in 1945, with the exception of a few government-financed public housing projects, there has not (to my knowledge) been a single new residential dwelling of size constructed. The amusement area, once as up-to-date as any in the world and with a reputation for being just about the best, has not provided a spectacular new attraction since the Parachute Jump from the 1939–40 New York World's Fair was installed by Steeplechase.

Coney Island still presents a boardwalk that seemed then, and probably still does, the longest, widest, and most splendid boardwalk in the whole world. It has a wide beach of fine sand its entire length, a beach that continues well beyond Coney Island into Brighton Beach and Manhattan Beach. One has only to stumble with shock and lacerated arches upon the shorefronts of Nice or the English Brighton—and remember with a sense of affront that these are also called beaches—to begin to fully appreciate the spacious shorefront of Coney Island as a truly distinguished natural treasure.

And Coney Island also had for us those long, paved streets, almost entirely free of motor traffic except in summer, that were better playgrounds than any recreation engineer has ever devised. [...]

The amusement area of Coney Island—that stretch encompassing the rides and the games, the food stands and the penny arcades—was of greatest interest to us in the cooler days of spring and late summer, or to break the routine even on hot days when one of us would get hold of some free passes to Luna Park or Steeplechase. [...]

Of the two amusement parks, there seemed to be a near unanimous preference for Luna Park, and we were inclined to be contemptuous of anyone, usually someone from someplace else, who raved about Steeplechase. The most we could feel about Steeplechase was that it was "all right"—we couldn't honestly say, "It stinks." [...]

Luna Park, as I've said, seemed to us much the better of the two competitors. Yet Luna Park closed first, a few years after the war ended, following a few fires and some desperate and futile attempts to arrest the critical decrease in customers. A housing project of complex design built by private developers for people of middle income now stands in its place.

Steeplechase held on gamely into the sixties before it gave up the battle and closed shop.

A few years before that, I went there one afternoon with my friends George Mandel and Mario Puzo on what proved to be a final trip. Mario had by then published two novels, *The Dark Arena* and *The Fortunate Pilgrim*, but not yet *The Godfather*. George had published *Flee the Angry Strangers* and *The Wax Boom*. My *Catch-22* had appeared shortly before, in 1961. I had met Mario years earlier through George. It was a lazy, drowsy day, and the three of us had come from the city with our children, I with my two, George with his two, and Mario with one or two of his five.

The very qualities that had disappointed us in the past made Steeplechase now ideal for languid fathers in their forties there with young children. It was clean, it was orderly, it was safe. While the children chased about in gawking exploration and enjoyed themselves first on one ride that moved slowly around in a circle, then on another that did exactly the same thing, the three of us could rest calmly on a bench and talk quietly about such things as publishers, book advertising, advances, and royalties, and that lousy Book-of-the-Month Club that had paid no attention to any of us. Luckily for us, the kids didn't want to go on many rides that would have necessitated our going with them, and we weren't really eager to go on any. Coming in, Mario, who was not from Coney Island and was rather portly, had chanced the Magic Barrel. He sank down slowly to the revolving floor and was unable to right himself, presenting a ludicrous picture as he rolled around there helplessly for a minute, laughing, with an unlighted long, long cigar in his hand, until finally the attendant in crimson coat and green jockey cap walked in and helped him through. After that he wanted no more. The place was very still and rather empty that bright afternoon. After a couple of pleasant hours, we prepared to leave, and a thought about the passing of generations occurred to me as we walked toward the exit: It struck me that if a kid like the one I used to be approached and asked for our tickets, he would have gotten from us three blue ones that were just about complete, except for the number-one ride punched for Mario. The next time I visited Coney Island, Steeplechase was no longer there, and only the red skeleton of the old Parachute Jump marked the spot, like a funeral obelisk.

THE ELECTRIC MICHELANGELO

Sarah Hall

Sarah Hall (b. 1974) was born in England and received her higher education in Wales and Scotland. Her first novel, *Haweswater* (2002), was awarded the Commonwealth Writers' Prize. In 2013, she was cited as one of Britain's twenty best writers under forty by *Granta*. Her second book, *The Electric Michelangelo* (2004), was a Man Booker Prize finalist. The novel tells the story of a tattoo artist, Cyril Parks, in the first half of the twentieth century who spends his early life in England and then settles in Coney Island in 1933. Beginning in the 1920s, Coney became the center of the tattooing trade in the United States, a tradition that continues in an annual festival. Parks provides a foreigner's view of Coney Island at a time when it was beginning to decline. In his view, Coney had lost its novelty and ability to thrill, and people "had become unimpressed." The once-great entrepreneurs of Coney were gone, and "now the place was reduced to the mere business of fake-freakery and fast metal." Parks sees Coney as having "all the desperation of a mistress high on some cheap substance eager to please her lover," but terrified that she can no longer keep his interest. He foresees the eventual death of the island, but "until then the desperate carnival would continue its spluttering, groaning wind down."

THE STRETCH OF SEASIDE CARNIVAL on the southern lip of Brooklyn was the biggest amusement park on earth and for several asylum-spun years Cyril Parks would be one of the cogs of its summer machinery. It dedicated itself to invention and intrigue, hedonistic indulgence, freakery. [. . .] Coney Island offered up inebriation with startling dexterity and precision and for a time it could predict the vulgar thoughts of the masses like a mind-reader, responding with tailor-made surrealities and rides which were pure stimulant. [. . .] Coney could hypnotize the crowds with their own sensual fantasies and squeamishness made external. If they feared the dark they would be inserted into a pitch-black chamber and shaken. If they feared perversion some cage or dank oubliette would produce it. Specialization was everywhere, from the sculptor who carved out wax moulds of famous people and painted their wet eyeballs living then destroyed them over a fiery grill, to the variform deformities of the abnormals once imported from every nation in the world by the legendary [Samuel] Gumpertz, now limping about the parks and breeding with each other. Sword-swallowers guzzled blades, fire-breathers spat flaming rings, twisted females were pierced on beds of nails, shrunken heads hung from walls and adorned pikes, wrongly made people were revealed behind curtains of shame. The sick and the sinister abounded. The crowds could choose their indelicate pleasure or poison. They came, they paid, they saw, and they were entertained. [. . .]

The Island [. . .] was absolute consumer-driven modernism, it was in-vogue anthropomorphism, a swim through the guts and entrails of the world. By the start of every season the repulsive and the breathtaking had regenerated itself. New monsters were found, new tracks spiralled. Money would come from somewhere, some mysterious new location, even after rainy summers or failed business endeavours or massive fires. Paint was fresh and the sideshows were ready to excrete their freakish wares, new rides appeared annually, at the cost of tens of thousands of dollars and bought from the World's Fair, to take people to the moon or to the bottom of the sea, to give them artificial magic environments. And the place revelled in near-perfect macabre entertainment, as if the juice of wacky Victorian society had been stewed up and injected into a Promethean American creation, a new world Moulin Rouge, a blaring creature that was concentrated along a two-mile strip of beachfront on the tip of the hipbone of that most fantastic city ever conceived. Coney could have outdone the rest of America's oddest finds had she pried them out of her vast corners and put them together in a room. Cy could stand at the entrance of Luna Park and forget which direction his booth was seven years after first squeezing his business in. He could walk the corridors and never become accustomed to what he witnessed within, the boggling acts, the sickest tracts, the mucus and prolapse and fistula afflicted.

What was the essence of Coney Island, he often wondered, sitting on the train approaching the station. What was it exactly? Horrific proof that the Victorian era could not invoke and conjure the black soul of the Gothic and eternally suppress its darker energy with mere cages of ornament and primness and order. Proof that it could not tinker around with salivating, mechanical wolf-heads, musical skulls and pictures made from human hair and not be opening a terminal crack in Pandora's Box, a vile vessel containing utter subversion of good behaviour, bodily curiosity, the peculiar viscera of Adam, Eve and all their deformed, stump-legged children. Proof that when the Victorian age collapsed under its own weighty ideals and detail, the dark varnish peeled off and stood up on its own, ghoulishly, and that weird spectre did a clatterbone jig right into the next century.

Cy had heard it said that twenty thousand light bulbs blew out on Coney every day—he himself lost one every month or so. In the first decade of the new century it boasted to consume more power a week than an average American city, and when Cy got there it had only added to itself after the sporadic fires that from time to time took down its magnificently housed attractions. Perhaps it was the smell that characterized the place for Cyril Parks. Not the perspiring adrenalin of its customers or the popped corn, the fry of meat and potato knishes, Nathan's nickel hotdogs, not even the grease on the runners of the newly refurbished Steeplechase, or the salty sea air on the skins of the customers. [. . .] What characterized Coney Island was the bitter, slightly sulphuric odour of lights popping, of electric energy being fundamentally used up and escaping from behind glass.

The day that Lulu died was the day Cy knew with certainty that the place itself was also doomed to expire. Something had belly-flopped hard and was smarting. Some vital ingredient of the Island was curdling. The management was killing one of the park's elephants. It turned out to be blasé amusement, for all its hideous effort. The beast, normally gentle, had accidentally killed a man, backing over him while avoiding a speeding vehicle on the road so that his chest and legs were crushed, and his bones made themselves known to the world through his flesh. Lulu was usually found wearing tassels and twirling batons in the Luna circus. She had spent years carrying excited children in a woven basket on her back. Her execution was advertised in the papers and Cy did not truly know why he attended it but he did so. And he was sorry that he did, sorry with himself and his disgraceful curiosity, and sorry for Lulu, who must have known from the way the eyes of humans had changed from kind to cold when they regarded her after she felt the delicate crickle-crackle of skeleton underneath her foot, that she was no longer loved. And then Cy was sorry for Coney Island, for its maliciously disassociated behaviour and its fate. Lulu had been, at one time, a very popular attraction. She could stand up on her hind legs and balance a person on her head. She could kneel and turn tricks with balls and hula-hoops and blow peanuts into the crowd, catch them in the gripping tip of her trunk when they were thrown back. Nobody seemed to care that the twenty-year-old mascot of the circus was condemned, except for her trainer who was restrained in his house that day and eventually given a sedative by a doctor to prevent him from harming himself or anyone else in an effort to save her. Nobody else shed a tear when the switch was thrown, and maybe that was not so very surprising.

Because the place was going down the tubes. Because it had begun to stink. Because there had been a reduction of reactivity to stimulus lately, for it seemed even in the new world with its distant limits to freedoms, you could only go so far before nothing worthwhile and appealing was left. The people had become unimpressed, like devilish abusers who were filled with ennui, they had molested entertainment, consumed it and driven up their tolerance for being entertained, they wanted bigger, they wanted better, more muck, more magic, and they were not getting it. Cy could see it in the glassy, unblinking eyes of onlookers when Madame Electra took to her mains-fed chair and hit the button, and he knew just what they were thinking.

—So the broad likes to sizzle, so what else is new?

And when Swiss Cheese Man threaded metal hooks through holes in his body and was hoisted up on cables into the roof of the tent where he performed, the applause was staccato, bored. There was a disinclination to ride the chutes more than once, children used to run back for another go, and another, and another, now they whined to their parents for candy instead. Things changed accordingly and rapidly. If a ride didn't appeal and make money it was dismantled. It was out with the old, in with the new, and nobody wanted to put a hand to a brow and squint down the road to the future to see where the artificial replacement would end, at what point there would be nothing left to consume. It seemed that every day when Cy came to work there was something being packed away in crates and something else being unloaded and bolted together. The Island's thrill was diminishing year after year. Movies were now in vogue and cheap and a step further out into an abstract world where fantasy was less touchable, less refutable, wires were less visible when people flew.

As a reward for their dissatisfaction, the public had been given new and more shocking shows, spineless children in wicker baskets, human beings born as if through a washing-mangler, things Cyril Parks, with his moderate sensibilities, had trouble reconciling. But the worst had already been seen and there was not the strange anthropology of Nature's Mistakes any more, which had once educated and delighted New York's citizens, it was simply perpetual titillation, sickness for its own sake, the search for a high. Dreamland itself had burned years earlier and the original dreams of the place were still being eaten by the flames. Gone was the noble entertainment model. The crowds had become hooked on the salacious, that feeling in the stomach, that rush. The once-great inventors and builders of the Island had died or were bankrupt, now the place was reduced to the mere business of fake-freakery and fast metal, the give-them-what-they-want theory. And the crowds knew it. And the workers knew it, and they knew the crest of the wave could not last. It was why everyone talked quickly and at cross-purposes to each other about work, not answering questions about new routines or costumes. It was why the dwarfs in Midget Land grew suddenly concerned with their bank accounts and their retirement plans.

Coney now had all the desperation of a mistress high on some cheap substance eager to please her lover, terrified and motivated by the knowledge that he was becoming less interested in her charms and she could no longer instinctively guess his fetish or cavort to his wishes. So there was a sense that although things continued at an alarmingly intense level of savage entertainment and consumer demand, the full-steam-ahead status quo could not go on. If Coney was the city's whore, the city's narcotic escape, the desperation of her sexual effort was climaxing in some unimaginable and deviant and tragic way.

And so Lulu's death became more of a thrill than her life. And it disappointed. The circus management charged ten cents entry to see her demise. She was led into the ring she had been led into so many times before and though it was not the man she was used to having lead her, she still went. She was about to kneel and begin her act when she felt unfamiliar copper coils placed around her two front legs but she was a trusting animal and she did not protest. She lifted her trunk and showed her crinkled lips to the audience, expecting a cheer. Cy looked around. People were chewing on roast nuts they had bought from a vendor, picking sticky pieces out of their back teeth with their fingernails. After a few seconds of massive voltage Lulu's hide began to smoulder and her eyes rolled back. After years of service, one wrong back-step over a passing pedestrian and she was no better than glue, or four hollow umbrella stands, no better than the profit she represented. She made no sound, not even the bleat of a smaller animal, her mouth was paralysed and unable to vocalize what she felt. But Cyril Parks knew what she felt, or at least he knew in part what she felt. That rigid, disempowering energy that makes every fibre in the thing it touches a slave to its command, that white-hot possession. [...] Her quivers seemed not to match her size, and to Cy that marked the tragedy of the event, the pathos of it—that muted quality, which ultimately failed to please the audience, for their gladiatorial thumbs remained down. Her death throes were just subtle ripples in her great grey body, small ruffles on the vast surface of skin and along her ears. Her trunk straightened a fraction, her softer parts began to blacken. She must have died before the power was knocked off, for she did not stagger and sway before slumping to the side when it was finished. Her life popped. She dropped. She went out immediately like another of Coney's bulbs.

There were a few "oohs" and "aahs," a cough or two at the unpleasant odour produced by the execution. Then a grumble swelled through the big top, as multiple unkind comments about the show were made.

—I expected her to explode! Brought a hat in case of a mess. You ever see a squirrel catch a stray current? Those things 'splode like firecrackers!

—I rode her when I was a child, you know. If I'da known she was a killer elephant I never woulda let my Pappy lift me up on her. When I think how close I musta come to ... well, it don't bear thinkin' about.

—Phew-ee! Smells kinda like liver-mush frying.

Cyril Parks put his head in his hands and rubbed his eyes. Then he softly addressed himself and the grizzling crowds.

—Lancashire or Yorkshire, sir? Meat or fat?

Perhaps only the final show, the death of the Island itself, would give the public a fix large enough to sate their habit, so that the dome of whitish light consuming the horizon on the edge of Brooklyn one night or week or month or decade in the future would once again and for one last time have meaning to it, validity. And until then the desperate carnival would continue its spluttering, groaning wind down. And Cy would just have to choose his moment to bow out.

ATTACHMENT TO LETTER TO MAYOR FIORELLO LaGUARDIA

Robert Moses

Robert Moses (1888–1981) was born in New Haven, Connecticut, but moved to New York City with his family as a boy in 1897. After earning a doctorate in political science from Columbia University, he became interested in reform politics. Moses came to the attention of Governor Al Smith and rose to power with him. With a strong command of law and engineering, Moses was able to use New Deal federal funds to oversee a large number of construction projects in New York City. Although never elected to public office, he became head of various public authorities in the city. He was a controversial figure who was praised by some for building a modern infrastructure for the city, but damned by others who claimed that he preferred automobiles to people, destroyed neighborhoods, and displaced people. Moses was no friend of Coney Island, which he believed was noisy, overcrowded, cheap, and too commercialized. He wanted to build a new resort, focused on bathing and outdoor recreation, with much less in the way of mechanical rides and amusements, and he took steps to try to impose his vision. In a letter to Mayor Fiorello LaGuardia prefacing his planning report, submitted on November 30, 1937, to which this summary was attached, Moses stated, "There is no use bemoaning the end of the old Coney Island fabled in song and story. The important thing is not to proceed in the mistaken belief that it can be revived. There must be a new and very different resort established in its place." It was his belief that "any future plan for Coney Island must be based on the supposition that most of the summer patrons will come by rapid transit; that they will have comparatively little money to spend on mechanical amusements, and that more and more they will come for exercise and healthy outdoor recreation."

THE MOST SERIOUS PROBLEMS AT CONEY ISLAND are overcrowding at the public beach, inadequate play areas, and lack of parking space.

Between Stillwell Avenue and Ocean Parkway the boardwalk is so close to the ocean that practically no beach remains at high tide, and comparatively little at low tide. Here it is proposed to acquire land ranging up to a depth of 400 feet of frontage north of the boardwalk, to move the boardwalk back a maximum of 300 feet, to retain about 100 feet north of the boardwalk for games and protection, and to widen the beach with new fill. [. . .] If this plan is carried out, this most congested portion of the beach will be more than doubled in area. The new beach supplied will amount to about 15% of the total beach at Coney Island, and will afford accommodations for thousands of people, and the present congestion will be greatly relieved.

As to the area east of the Municipal Bathhouse, it is proposed to develop it in the same way as the playground to the west. As to parking, it is proposed to acquire ten acres for a parking field north of Surf Avenue at some location not involving frontage on the main highway, but accessible to main streets. This parking field will bring a substantial return to the city, and will help pay the cost of the operation of the beach. It is possible that this parking space may in part be provided by cooperating with the Board of Transportation, which has planned a station for the city-owned subway at Coney Island.

The above plan offers some solution of the bad conditions prevailing today at this beach. If anything is really to be accomplished, a strict enforcement of police, building, fire and health regulations on the beach and adjacent areas must be provided.

The estimated cost of the land taking above outlined is $2,850,000 and for parking spaces above $1,000,000[,] the cost of demolishing the old buildings on this property, relocating the boardwalk, providing recreation areas, and improving the jetties and the beach is $1,500,000.

TO HEAVEN BY SUBWAY

"To Heaven by Subway," published anonymously in *Fortune* in August 1938, gives a balanced, detailed, and fascinating picture of Coney Island near the end of the Depression years. The author describes Coney as being in the era of the "nickel empire," which he or she argues began with the extension of the subway in 1920 and reached its peak in the middle of that decade. By 1910, Coney could have gone in a different direction, emphasizing its "tonier restaurants and exclusive bathhouses," serving as a "convenient summer resort for the well-to-do New Yorker." Instead, it chose the hot dog, roller coaster, and public beach, becoming "the playground of the masses." Compared with the more genteel Jones Beach, Coney "is disorganized, uncouth, and bawdy." The author provides a colorful description of Coney's many attractions and its visitors, discussing such topics as the beach and bathhouses, Feltman's versus Nathan's hot dogs, Dr. Martin Couney's Infant Incubators, Steeplechase Park, the sideshows, and the games along the Bowery. He or she concludes that while Coney may be declining, "it is probably a mistake to sell the nickel empire short."

AT NIGHT SHIPS HEADING IN to New York pick up the lights of Coney Island thirty miles out; and its voice is a muffled bellow that carries a mile and a half offshore. But on a hot, summer Sunday morning fog lies over the lower bay like a damp, too-often-slept-on sheet; and the only sounds are the flat clangings of the bell buoys along the channel. [...]

At close range, in the hard early morning light, Coney Island is almost incredibly banal. Shoddy shows through the tinsel; the shuttered false fronts are frankly two-dimensional; the gaily painted manes of the flying horses of the carrousels are shrouded in canvas; and even the forthright, weedy smell of the sea seems weak and flavorless. At six in the morning Coney Island is like the stage of a very old theatre before the audience arrives—like the empty waiting room of the Philadelphia Broad Street Station. But the voice and color of Coney Island are its people. And at the end of a five-cent subway fare, and less than two hours away, 7,000,000 people are waking to a hot and aimless Sunday.

Coney Island itself wakens slowly. On the sand a few early bathers discard their outer clothing and perform self-conscious calisthenics under a rising sun. Along the Boardwalk men in white sailor suits, from New York's Department of Parks, spear the leavings of last night's mob. Milk wagons and beer trucks rumble down Surf Avenue a block away. And in the Bowery and the side streets concessionaires and ride foremen and spielers and counter men and ticket takers and shills collect in groups . . . and peer anxiously at the sky. [. . .]

Into this fluid mass the subway pours the people of New York and its visitors—young girls with firm high breasts and pretty legs and shrill, discordant voices—hat-snatching adolescents and youths on the make—children in arms and children underfoot and children in trouble—harried, scolding mothers and heavy-suited, heavy-booted fathers—soldiers and sailors and marines—virgins and couples in love and tarts—Gentiles and Jews and the in-betweens—whites and blacks and orientals—Irish and Italians and Poles and Swedes and Letts and Greeks—pushing, plodding, laughing, jostling, shrieking, sweating, posing—shedding their identities, with their inhibitions, in the voice, the smell, the color of Coney Island. [. . .]

As it is, some 25,000,000 people pile into this area in a season—as many as a million on a hot Sunday—leaving behind them a sum estimated at anything from $7,500,000 to $35,000,000. But whatever the amount—and whether derived from the family on relief or from the twenty-dollar plunger and his girl friend—it is an accumulation of the smallest coins of the country; a flow of millions of dollars from the aorta of the city into its most minute capillaries. Coney Island is today the empire of the nickel. [. . .]

The nickel empire, the third and greatest period of Coney Island prosperity, arrived with the extension of the subway and its five-cent fare to Coney Island in 1920. Or perhaps, more accurately, 1920 is a convenient line of demarcation between two periods that dovetail. As late as 1910 Coney Island might have gone in either of two directions. It might have emphasized its tonier restaurants and exclusive bathhouses and become a convenient summer resort for the well-to-do New Yorker—a sort of glorified Atlantic City. Or it might have followed the frankfurter and the roller coaster and the public beach and become the playground of the masses. After 1910 it could still strike a compromise of sorts between the two. But the subway in 1920 forced a decision. Coney Island became the empire of the nickel.

Coney Island economy is founded primarily on weather. Most of its money is earned in a season only fourteen weekends long. Three rainy weekends may mean the difference between profit and loss; five can easily mean bankruptcy. For a summer Sunday cannot be postponed; once lost it is gone forever. The islanders tell you that you can make money by betting against the weather bureau. And because weather is largely unpredictable, and because the cost of rain insurance is prohibitively high, most Coney Island concessionaires roll their shutters up and down with the thermometer as the clouds roll by. And even big Steeplechase park must be prepared to open its gates on a half-hour's notice.

Secondary factor in the nickel empire's economy is the nickel itself—and its abundance in the pockets of the Coney Island customer. The nickel was first a symbol of a new order; it became in time a reality. The mass market slowly forced Coney Island's time-honored price scales downward. The fifty-cent rides became a quarter. The quarter rides became fifteen cents. The ten-cent rides became five. And even the ten-cent frankfurter was by the latter 1920's reduced to a nickel. But until the depression of the early 1930's the abundance of nickels was unaffected by war or panic or depression. In 1907, and in 1914, and in 1921—when business indexes were off from 20 to 40 per cent—the Coney Island take varied practically not at all. And the more enlightened [i]slanders referred to their business as a depression-proof industry. But in the last six or seven years, and more, particularly in the first month and a half of the current season, Coney Island has felt the pinch. The empire of the nickel is frankly worried.

In terms of nickels Coney Island is today three-quarters amusement park and one-quarter beach. But in terms of numbers the position is reversed. And it is on the beach that any properly conducted tour of the island must begin.

It is a fairly good beach, but it includes only fifty-seven acres of sand at high tide. Armed with lunch boxes, water wings, baseballs, harmonicas, hot dogs, diapers, beer bottles, olive oil, and peanuts, and employing every conceivable stratagem for the nominal draping of their more essentially private parts, 600,000 nature lovers, seventy-five million pounds of flesh, black, white, and yellow, converge on this narrow strip on a good Sunday, occupying it to its last square foot of hot dun-colored sand. Perhaps less than a quarter of this army has passed through one or another of Coney Island's bathhouses. More than three-quarters are there through benefit only of the five-cent subway fare. Most of these have worn their bathing suits as underwear—but a few liberated souls have changed briskly on the spot. So, despite the vigilance of the new beach patrol, one of the first and most lasting impressions of Coney beach is not the clothing that is worn— the frankly homemade concessions to modesty, the patched and darned relics of a past prosperity, or the vivid plumage of Davega's, and Macy's basement, and Klein's—but rather the clothing that has been discarded and lies over Coney beach and flutters from Coney jetties and hangs limply on the superstructure of Steeplechase pier.

The one-quarter or less that has yielded to modesty or comfort or convention and has changed its clothes in a bathhouse has had a wide range of accommodations to choose from. There are first the so-called big ten (including Ravenhall, Tilyou, Washington, McLochlin, Ocean Tide, Ward, and Stauch) whose lockers cost some forty to fifty cents a day—a fee that may include the use of a pool, handball and basketball courts, and a solarium for sun-bathing, and that sometimes includes a bathing suit. (Eighty per cent of the customers used to rent suits. Only 20 per cent do today.) Between them these ten bathhouse aristocrats shelter 1,250,000 to 2,500,000 people in a season, collect from $300,000 to $500,000, and account for some 50 per cent of Coney Island's total bathhouse bill. Most of them, however, are doing little better than break even and their take is steadily declining.

Then there are the lesser boardwalk bathhouses, where undressing facilities are as low as fifteen cents, two for a quarter, which do another 20 per cent of the total bathhouse business. And there are the white-elephantine Municipal Baths (one-third closed), now under the supervision of the New York City Department of Parks, which entertained 150,000 people last year at fifteen and twenty-five cents a head—only an estimated 7 per cent of the island's business. And along the side streets are scores of rickety bathhouses, thrown together in alleyways and back yards. And north of Surf Avenue are the dozens of frankly illegal bedroom bathhouses whose dubious proprietors solicit business in the streets and where as many as ten mixed couples may share a single bedroom, hanging their clothes from the mantelpiece and draping them across the bed.

Compared with the relatively genteel Jones Beach, twenty-five miles down the shore, Coney Island is disorganized, uncouth, and bawdy. The Department of Parks, which has just taken over the island's beach and Boardwalk, may hope to turn it into another Jones Beach; but the fact remains that Manhattan families can spend the day at Coney Island with no expenditure other than a ten-cent per person round-trip subway fare, while a day at Jones Beach adds up to several times that sum per person for transportation alone. [...]

And whatever the park department's plans may be it is probable that Coney beach will remain Coney beach for a long time to come. Kosher picnics will litter the sand; youths will chase baseballs across the backs of couples lost in earnest embrace; girls will parade by twos and fours along the water's edge; the physical needs of the youngest generation will be relieved in full sight of God and man; and the fat old women will dog paddle around for hours without being able to swim a lick.

Noon is a scarcely noticeable break in the Coney Island routine. There is simply a slight intensification in the eating that has been more or less general and continuous from early morning and will last until the lights go out—cotton candy, apples on sticks, yellow corn. But now whole families fall to on chunks of rye bread and salami and hot dogs, and in the Negro section in front of the municipal baths there is a certain amount of fried chicken wrapped in oilpaper. As the day progresses, the discards and the leavings and the accidentally dropped portions of these tons of food begin to pile up despite the beach patrol and the numerous but half-empty wastebaskets, and the busy flies.

For those who have not brought their own food supply or who have run short there are many possibilities. There are the small "under the Board-walk" concessions, dark, sunless booths selling hot dogs and ice cream and beer and *knishes*, Jewish potato cakes flavored with onion and *koisha* and fried in deep fat. Further afield, on the side streets toward Surf Avenue, are dozens of small restaurants and stands, kosher and non-kosher—Ru-manian tearooms, pop stands, hot-dog grills, and custard counters. For the very superior there is the chaste dining room of the Half Moon Hotel whose big second-floor windows look out across the Boardwalk and ocean. For the thirsty there are many licensed bars; but hard liquor puts a deep dent in a weekend budget, and beer is the accepted drink of Coney Island.

And then there is Feltman's—Coney Island's largest, most elaborate, and most indigenous eating place. [...]

Feltman's bridged the three periods of Coney Island history, prospered in each, and reached its peak during the big days of the nickel empire. At the height of Coney's boom of the middle 1920's Feltman's employed some 1,200 men, could serve 8,000 meals at one time in its Alpine gardens and frankfurter bars and fisherees, boasted of serving 7,000,000 meals in one year, and illuminated this gargantuan scene with some 42,000 electric lights. Its gross volume and its net profits have never been revealed. But at its peak the gross was probably well above $2,000,000; and the Feltman block is today assessed at $1,200,000.

Unfortunately for Feltman's the ten-cent frankfurter could not be pat-ented, and acts of God have a way of averaging off. What happened to Felt-man's was a newcomer named Nathan who preceded the depression into Coney Island with a frankfurter at five cents.

Today Feltman's puts on a brave front. Its chef is from the Roney-Plaza in Miami Beach; its frankfurters are still stubbornly priced at ten cents; it still serves by far the best food on the island; and it is wooing its lost cus-tomers with a variety of new attractions. A carrousel blares in one corner of the Surf Avenue restaurant. New games and concessions, including a soul-shattering ride called the Boomerang, have blossomed in the long arcade leading to the Boardwalk. And in what was once an Alpine gar-den moving pictures of the past are now shown nightly at ten cents. But Feltman's 1,200 employees have dwindled to 300 or 350. And there is a persistent rumor that the entire property has been offered for sale. Meanwhile less than a quarter-mile away is Nathan's—a corner lunch counter employing perhaps fifty people and occupying only a tiny fraction of Feltman's acres. But the crowd fills the sidewalk fifteen deep, overflows into the street, and blocks the traffic in Surf Avenue—while above its head in endless succession is repeated the magic symbol—5¢—in letters of fire-engine red. [...]

Further along the Boardwalk, just beyond Steeplechase[,] is a white-fronted entrance with a sign above it reading, "Life Begins at the Baby Incubators." Pay your twenty cents and go in; the Boardwalk is only a few yards away, but you are in a miniature hospital—white-walled, immaculate, remote. Along the rear, behind a brass rail, is a row of eight airtight, glass-walled boxes, each with a bubbling oxygen tank beside it, each holding from one to two incredibly minute babies wrapped in fleece. To the left, behind a glass window, is a fully equipped modern nursery. Lined up at the rail a group of self-conscious young couples and wide-eyed elderly women listen to a youngish man who speaks in a low voice with a clipped Liverpool accent.

"Now this little baby came in nine days ago. It weighed only one pound ten ounces and we were afraid we might be too late. It was even bluer than that little fellow over in the other incubator . . . Yes, ma'am, it was a premature birth. About six months . . ."

Baby incubators are one of the major paradoxes that have flowered in Coney Island. They appeal to an unhealthy morbidity; and they have been condemned as rank exploitation. Actually the display is completely humanitarian and has the endorsement of the archconservative American Medical Association. Baby incubators have been the lifework of an astonishing individual, by name Dr. Martin A. Couney, a seventy-year-old physician who combines two diametrically opposed qualities—showmanship and scientific integrity. Dr. Couney developed his first baby incubator in the early 1890's when he was a young interne in a Paris hospital. His funds were limited, and the medical profession was apathetic. Showmanship came to his rescue. He decided to finance his work by direct public subscription in the form of admission fees. His first public appearance, at the

Berlin exposition in 1896, was highly successful. There was, however, one minor embarrassment. The name selected for the new contrivance was *Kinderbrütenanstalt*, or baby breeding-place. And many a literal-minded German was disappointed to find on entering that babies were not being bred at all—merely being kept warm.

Doctor Couney landed at Coney Island in 1904 and has been there ever since—although he has maintained separate establishments at Atlantic City and at the Chicago Century of Progress. In his forty-odd years of work he has saved the lives of some 7,000 prematurely born babies—90 per cent of all those brought to him. These are as a rule children of the poor. Occasionally, however, when all hospital facilities are in use, he takes the children of well-to-do parents; but in no case does he accept a fee. He keeps the babies for from two to three months, then sends them home. To break even, the display must take in $150 a day at twenty cents a ticket. There are the salaries of five registered nurses (one of whom is Doctor Couney's daughter), two wet nurses, and the attendants to be paid—not to mention the cost of equipment, heat, rent, and oxygen. Currently that $150 is not even covered during weekends, and there is a weekly deficit of some $600. But there have been times in the past when things have gone better and following the Chicago exposition Dr. Couney was able to present his entire equipment to the Infant Aid Society and endow it with a $16,000 fund. [...]

Steeplechase believes in a few simple truisms. It believes that most people never grow up and that even adolescents like to escape back into childhood. It believes that half the world likes to show off and that the other and less daring half is perpetually interested in the performance. And it believes that pretty legs, however trite, are never dull, and that ugly ones are always funny. And largely because of these truisms the crowds in Steeplechase park are big and noisy and predominantly young and almost frantically amused, and because of this Steeplechase itself is like all the Sunday-school picnics in the world gathered into a single fifteen-acre park. [...]

The monetary unit at Steeplechase is fifty cents. This covers a combination ticket including admission to the park, the pavilion, the ballroom, and all thirty-one of Steeplechase's rides and attractions. And it is this fifty-cent combination ticket that sets Steeplechase apart from the rest of Coney Island. High enough in price to exclude a vast majority of the Coney Island mob, low enough to attract some 30,000 on a good Sunday, and a fixed charge so that a couple or a family can budget its expenses for an entire day (it takes a good seven or eight hours to try each Steeplechase attraction once), the combination ticket has helped Steeplechase weather Coney Island's first depression and has made it by far the most profitable enterprise on the island.

Steeplechase, which is assessed at more than $2,000,000, is owned by Coney Island's first family—the Tilyous. It was conceived and built by George C. Tilyou, whose father, a French Huguenot, was one of the early Coney Island pioneers. And it is operated today by his sons, Ed and Frank and George C. Jr., who boast that whenever the park is open at least one Tilyou and usually two are there. The park they operate, however, is not the original Steeplechase; that was burned to the ground in 1907—in one of Coney Island's six major fires. And a story the Tilyous like to tell is that before the embers were cool George Tilyou Sr. was selling tickets to the hot ruins at ten cents a head.

The problems of an amusement park begin where those of a more prosaic business end. There are such relatively simple problems as charity; Steeplechase entertained some 5,000 orphans last year free of charge. And there are the problems raised by the involved Coney Island economy of weather and the nickel. But the biggest and the most insoluble problem of all is human behavior—the drunk who won't go home, the spinster who was pinched by a strange man in a cap, and the boy who wants to stand up in the roller coaster. Perhaps that's why the Tilyous get such a kick out of their jobs—why it's so hard to leave the business once you're in it. As Frank Tilyou says, and he has tried both real estate and banking, "Once sand gets in your shoes, you're sunk."

There are three freak shows of a sort at Coney Island, but the islanders will tell you that there is only one showman. That's Sam Wagner of the World Circus Side Show, Inc., who has been in the business thirty-five years. Sam's two boys handle the spieling and inside lecturing. Sam didn't think much of the idea—tried to persuade them to get into something else; but it didn't work.

Sam is discouraged—on a big day he used to draw 20,000 people at ten cents each. Now he thinks he's lucky to get 8,000 on a perfect day, and that 8,000 means a take of only $800. Sam's payroll runs about $1,000 a week and his rent and overhead come to about $600 more; so it takes only a few rainy weekends to put Sam in the red for the year. Sam believes that one reason business is bad is that people just haven't the money to spend any more. Another is that freaks are harder to find. Sam doesn't know why. It may be the competition and it may be just that fewer freaks are born today. Then there are the new regulations of Commissioner [Robert Moses], whose power to issue and revoke licenses is the power of life and death over Coney Island shows. Sam is pretty bitter about the new regulations, which prevent honest outside bally (preview of the show on an outside stand). It's hard enough to get them in off the street with the best spieler in the world.

Sam's present show, and he admits it isn't up to some others he's had, in-cludes: The Spider Boy; Singing Lottie, Fat Girl (O Boy, Some Entertainer); Laurello, the Only Man With a Revolving Head (See Frisco, the Wonder Dog); Professor Bernard, Magician Extraordinary (He will fool you); Pro-fessor Graf, Tattoo Artist (Alive); and his star act, Belle Bonita and her Fighting Lions (Action, Thrills). Last year he had Jack Johnson at a whop-ping big salary but the take wouldn't stand the strain.

But Sam's favorites are his two famous microcephalic idiots, or pin-heads, Pipo and Zipo, whom he dug up in the cracker country nine years ago, after a rumor had sent him scurrying south armed with a letter of in-troduction from Mayor Jimmy Walker of New York to the mayor of Hart-well, Georgia.

Since that time Pipo and Zipo have supported their normal cracker rel-atives with the money Sam pays them for their four months in Coney. (It's $75 a week this year.) In winter they go home for a visit. Pipo is twenty-six, and has the intelligence of an eighteen-months-old baby. His sister, Zipo, is thirty-eight and is much brighter. In fact she is rather horribly smart and winsome. [. . .]

The Bowery runs from the western entrance of Steeplechase into Felt-man's arcade. It is a narrow, congested alley, only three and a half blocks long. But at nine o'clock on a crowded Sunday night its impact is like a hard right hook to the jaw. Only slowly do single voices and smells and faces emerge from the cacophony of the whole. Above the sound of a hundred spielers shouting each other down and a dozen mechanical pianos and radios blasting a dozen different tunes you hear the sudden crash of a roller coaster dropping into space, and high above it all, a short shrill scream. Out of that single complex smell, which has a thick, moist substance of its own, you pick the primary smells of corn and cooking sugar and seaweed and strong perfume. And out of the weaving bobbing sea of faces you catch the quick, primitive technique of the pickup. "Want a ride, baby?" "You want a sock in the puss?" In the Bowery the lifeblood of Coney Island runs rich and red out to its smallest, greediest capillaries. It is the concentrated dis-tillate of all the midways of all the carnivals in America.

There are the games—about evenly divided between those that offer something for nothing and those that provide a chance to show off. Pack-ages of cigarettes and tall thin candy boxes stand alternately on a shelf. You shoot a cork from a popgun. You shoot till you win—but what you win is a tall thin candy box with four gray daubs of taffy, a penny a box by the gross. It's what is known as a gimmick. For the shelf is wide, the cigarettes heavy, the candy light and poorly balanced. But if you know how, you can gimmick the game—slip a thumbtack in the cork.

You throw a baseball at six bottles pyramided on a table—three balls for a dime—and you knock the six bottles down with the first ball. But you can't knock them off. A narrow band extends around the table top and keeps them in place. You may get a bamboo cane anyway. It costs the concession-aire nine-tenths of a cent. [. . .]

And then there are the rides—each going back to one of the old funda-mentals. The roller coasters are frightening (although they are generally among the safest rides of all) but they also bring young bodies into hard, in-timate contact. And the ninety-foot vertical drop of the Bowery's Cyclone is said to be the second highest in America. The carrousels or merry-go-rounds, simplest and oldest rides of all, appeal to the spirit of make-believe. The Wonder Wheel climbing up into the night offers the fear of height and the intimacy of a private seat in the sky. The auto rides and the boat rides with their furious, harmless crashes appeal like the carrousels to the spirit of make-believe but they are also a convenient preliminary to a pickup. The Virginia Reel whirling down a zigzag incline, the Whip cracking around its turns, the long dark tunnel rides, the airplane swing, the fun houses, and the newest rides—the Loop-O-Plane and the Octopus and the Boomerang—the aim of each is to frighten; to color the imagination; or to help boy meet girl.

This nickel empire reached its peak during the middle 1920's. It has been declining ever since. To explain that decline in the depression-proof industry there are a number of theories. There is the theory that people are increasingly interested in active sports—less so in the passive thrills of the midway. There is the theory that the movies and the automobile and the radio are cutting deeply into the whole amusement-park business. And there is the theory that with sixty-mile-an-hour locomotion an everyday matter, the amusement-park business has been signally lacking in imagination. As one Coney Islander puts it, "Nowadays you have to half kill 'em to get a dime."

But whatever the causes of the decline may be and however serious it may seem at the moment, it is probably a mistake to sell the nickel empire short. Amusement parks have lived a long time and have weathered a great many storms. And they still play a vital part in the lives of an enormous number of urban boys and girls. They are what the Caribbean cruise is to the stenographer—what the chance to visit in a strange city is to the small-town girl. They are an escape from the narrow social boundaries of the factory, the block, and the public school. And garish, tawdry, aphrodisiac Coney Island is to a hundred thousand adolescent New Yorkers heaven at the end of the subway.

PARK CIRCUS SIDESHOW, CONEY ISLAND, CA. 1948. (BRAIN MERLIS, BROOKLYNPIX.COM)

CONEY

Amram Ducovny

Writer Amram Ducovny (1928–2003) grew up in the Coney Island area. He is the father of actor David Duchovny, who restored the *h* in the family name. For much of his life, Ducovny earned his living in the field of public affairs. He realized a life dream with the publication of his critically praised novel *Coney* (2000), a semi-autobiographical account of an adolescent's adventures in Coney Island in the 1930s. In this excerpt, the protagonist, young Harry, is sent on an errand to pick up some betting slips from a group of sideshow freaks. Ducovny provides a vivid description of the unusual performers who live together, including a fat lady, a dog-faced boy, and Siamese twins. While Harry is there, the freaks enact a ritual during which they all remove their clothes and invite him to join them, which both excites and repulses him. (Translations from the French are by the editors.)

BY NOON, Harry could no longer wait to grip his new bike. He cut the rest of his classes and sprinted to the bike store. Woody greeted him warmly and handed him the racer, saying, "Ride over to the house of the freaks, pick up the slips and bring 'em back."

Doubled over, clutching the sleek, curved handlebars, Harry pedaled slowly along the boardwalk, admiring his reflection in glass storefronts. A midday sun had called to prayer the ancient sun worshippers who, in a state of sweating grace, were not the audience he desired. When school let out, there would be slit-eyed jealousy.

At Stillwell Avenue he left the boardwalk and stopped at Nathan's for a hot dog, French fries and an orange drink. He remained perched on his bike, a sultan on a throne, mashing the food and liquid into one magnificent taste. He flipped a quarter onto the counter. [...]

Dismounting, he carried the bike up the wooden steps of number 39, pressed the black tit bell and, hearing no ring, tried the door, which scraped the floor as it gave way. He wheeled the bike toward a smell of cooked cabbage and the murmur of conversation.

"*Merde,*" a woman's voice chastised, "you bring tires with ze shit of *chien* [dog] in ze house."

The speaker was Queen Fifi, the fat lady at a sideshow in Coney's Bowery section. Her eyes, nose and lips were tiny islands in a rippling sea of flesh. Yet, rosy coloring on delicate white cheeks evoked Renaissance cherubs. A golden cardboard tiara indented her curly blond hair.

The queen, overflowing a piano bench at the head of a long oblong table, presided over a court of freaks whom Harry recognized from the large posters that lined the Bowery:

Jamie, *the boy with two mouths,* who, lacking makeup, presented a simple hole in his cheek. Olga, *the world's ugliest woman,* whose thickened face and massive shoulders suggested a punch-drunk boxer. Lohu and Mohu, the Japanese Siamese twins, seated in one chair, eating with their outside hands. Jo-Jo, *the dog-faced boy,* a dispirited beagle.

Blue Man, skin glowing as if phosphorescent. Albert-Alberta, *the half-man, half-woman,* bereft of sweater bulges, and Otto, *the strongman,* whose shaved bullet head, bull neck, pendulous purplish lips and filed teeth were, in this company, havens of human familiarity.

Otto strode toward Harry, arms extended, fingers curled to strangle.

"You come see freaks? *Ach,* I show you."

Harry wheeled his bike between them.

"Woody!" he shouted.

Otto stopped.

"Voody?"

"The slips."

"*Ach,* now a boy he sends. You hear Fifi, a boy."

"I like boys," Fifi said, tilting her massive head at Harry. "I like them same like you, Otto."

The diners laughed. The Siamese twins turned toward each other. Harry wondered if they used each other as a mirror. Schnozz said that some Siamese twins were fakes: regular twins yoked together in a tight corset. He scanned Lohu and Mohu, searching for a clue in their identical brown suits, white shirts and green plaid ties.

"Nice boys not stare," Fifi said. "How is your name?"

"Harry."

"'Arry is most pleasurable name. Sit wiz us, 'Arry. We like nice visitor."

Otto placed a chair next to his.

"No, Otto," Fifi said, waggling her index finger, "no under-ze table *dalliance*. Between Albert-Alberta and me will be his place."

Seated, Harry fought a terrible urge to stare. He bowed his head as if partaking in a solemn ceremony.

"Young boy," Olga['s] bass voice boomed, "ven I vass ah beauty I vass ballerina. Nijinsky loffed me. All Moskva and St. Petersburg vass at my feets. Ven is vite nights, I dance in streets. Tsar and tsarina chav see me, invite me to Vinter Palace. Den"—she punched her shoulder—"den dis."

Fifi lip-farted.

"Nijinsky, tsar, hah. Ven you vass ah beauty," Fifi mimicked, "you be a kootch dancer. You slide on ze *fesse* on ze stage and push out ping pong ball from ze *trou* [hole], one after one. One is told zat at zat you ze best. Zoot! like from a cannon. Also lights in zere for ze shining *con* [cunt]."

Olga wiped her lips delicately with a food-soiled paper napkin.

"I not answer fot, degenerate peasant. Vonce I vass ah beauty. Vat vass you effer, but fot stink."

Blue Man stood up and crashed his fist onto the table, rattling plates.

"I not understand," he shouted. "In Prague circus we did not speak so terrible t'ings!"

Fifi cupped one breast with both hands and jiggled it at him, saying:

"But it is all family fight, *monsieur sacre bleu*. It not mean *rien* [anything]. We family. You *envie*?"

"You vood drown him vit dose mountains," Olga said and waited for laughs that did not arrive.

Fifi dropped her chin over her right breast and kissed it loudly.

"Mine are soft, full of life, where armies nurse to *gloire*. You *seins* [breasts] give muscles and sweat. Ze odor of a man."

"And what, pray tell O rotund oracle, is wrong with the odor of a man?" Albert-Alberta said, cocking his head coquettishly. "It is a sign of manhood, just as shit and semen are the smells of a boy."

Otto stood up and flexed his biceps which rose like a camel's hump from the hem of his short-sleeved shirt.

"*Ach*," he said, pointing to Albert-Alberta, "this call itself man. A man has strength. You say you half-woman. I say you all woman."

Albert-Alberta nodded and replied: "Ergo of no possible use to you." He sang: '*Tell me Lord Montague, How many hairy assholes did you screw? Was it one or ninety-two? Oh, tell me, Lord Montague.*"

Fifi applauded vigorously, requiring her to extend her arms so that her palms could collide beyond her breasts.

Harry slowly lifted his head and, receiving no reprimand, swiveled his neck.

Lohu raised his hand and shook it like a schoolboy bursting with the right answer.

"I pity all of you," he said.

His brother added: "All of you understand nothing."

The others took no notice, except for Albert-Alberta, who made the sign of the Cross, and whispered:

"Buddha two, Jesus nothing. But it's a great match, folks."

"But we forget our guest," Fifi said. "'Arry, you like Otto do strong trick for you?"

Harry remembered Mike Mazurki in a movie.

"Could you tear a telephone book in two?"

Everyone laughed. Fifi patted him on the head.

"*Mon petit*, zat is wonderful. *Alors*, Otto, our guest make request."

"Zere is no book in zis shithouse."

Albert-Alberta ran to the foyer and returned with a Brooklyn phone directory. He bounded up to Otto, bowed low and, sweeping his arm grandly in the style of a Shakespearean fop, laid the book on his lap. Otto, staring straight ahead, spread his knees. The book fell to the floor.

Jo-Jo slid off his chair, disappearing under the table, and surfaced back at his seat holding the book. He opened it and, whelping with strain, tore it in half along the binding. Everyone but Otto applauded. Tensing his biceps, the strong man said:

"Yah, yah is funny. Now we go out and lift cars."

"Why is to be ashamed of trick? If not tricks, how we make living?"

Otto chomped on his cheeks.

"'Arry, *écoute* [listen], Otto, he can tear book like in show. But he is like chef. He need time to bake book in oven. Zen is *très simple.*"

"Lie," Otto shouted.

"Fifi," Jamie said, rolling his eyes, "you promised us the Boze Art today."

The room froze. Harry thought of the wax museum. Fifi patted Harry's head.

"*Alors, porquoi pas* [OK, why not], ze boy needs education. I explain:

"'Arry, in *Paris*, once in ze year, we have *Beaux Arts Ball*. All *étudiants* of ze arts invited. At midnight all doors locked and each must remove clothes. Of course one can depart before midnight, but who do such *faux pas*? The doors locked till six *matin* [A.M.]. Not even *gendarmes* can enter, and ze *étudiants* amuse zemself with much pleasure. I tell *mes amis* zis and they have *envie* for Beaux Arts even more zan once in year. You go with us. Zere is no harm, *mon petit*, I promise. Because you ze one *vrai étudiant* [true student] here honor to disrobing *moi, la reine* [me, the queen]."

She turned her palms in a lifting motion. Otto tugged her to her feet. The others savagely tore at their clothes. Shirts, underwear and socks flew and floated over agitated inmates of a madhouse.

Olga, on all fours and gasping like a breath-starved football player, wiggled while accepting leisurely strokes from a kneeling Albert-Alberta, whose hands conducted a symphony orchestra. Spotting Otto sitting sullenly, he pointed to the twins, joined at the hip by what resembled a large fish scale, who were masturbating each other, as if a coxswain were setting a frenetic beat, and shrieked:

"Take a lesson from them, Otto!"

Jamie, seemingly guided by an enormous erection, came to a kneeling rest before Olga, who licked his penis with a pitted tongue.

A lion roared. Olga collapsed.

"Glad to have been of service," Albert-Alberta said, turning his conducting to Lohu and Mohu, who were watching parabolas of semen land like disabled parachutes.

Fifi moved in front of Harry. She was about his height. A white cotton blouse hung loose over a pleated blue ankle-length skirt. Her bare feet, astonishingly small, seemed inadequate to their task.

"*Alors, gentil gosse* [nice boy], is not polite to refuse hospitality. Disrobe me and you, zen do as you wish. No harm will come."

She placed his hand on the top button of her blouse. He unbuttoned her. His penis was stiff. Otto, behind her, removed the blouse. She wore no brassiere. Her skirt fell. Her hand on his head guided him to his knees. He tugged her pink panties to her ankles. She kicked them away. His eyes were level with a tiny patch of blond pubic hair barely visible against the milky dunes of flesh. The odor of Woolworth perfume burned his nostrils like the vaporized mists Bama unleashed to cure his cold.

"Now remove you clothes. Ze *règles* of *fête* [rules of partying]."

Harry piled his clothes before him like a sandbag. His erection throbbed with virginal ecstasy of finally *knowing*, but nausea claimed his stomach.

Fifi turned a sweating face toward Harry, shut her tiny blue eyes, and nodded understanding.

"Such fear, *mon petit*, is only life. You do not wish, you may go now, if zat please you."

Harry grabbed his clothes and ran through laughter. He was desperate to wash. On the steps, wearing only his knickers, he finished dressing. The door opened. Fifi, nude, held out the betting slips. Her other hand gripped his bike.

Harry stretched out his hand to accept the papers. Fifi squeezed it gently.

"Not forget ze *cheval* [horse], brave knight."

He caught his bike as it bumped down the stairs.

STRANGER AT CONEY ISLAND
Kenneth Fearing

Kenneth Fearing (1902–1961) was born in Oak Park, Illinois. In 1924, he moved to New York, where he wrote for the *New Yorker* and was one of the founders of the *Partisan Review*. He also began composing poetry, publishing many of his works in the leftist periodical *New Masses*. Fearing remained committed to Marxist politics throughout his life. In addition to his poetry, Fearing wrote novels, the best known being the mystery *The Big Clock* (1946; film adaptation, 1948). "Stranger at Coney Island" (1948) reflects both Fearing's hopefulness about the ending of World War II and his distress about the increasingly anti-Communist tone in America that would culminate in the McCarthyism of the 1950s.

Not here, but a little farther, after we have passed through the hall of
    mirrors,
Seeing ourselves as ogres, devils, zombies, diplomats,
And after we have entered the dragon's jaws, drifting in our wooden
    boat down a silent river between white, gaping, enormous teeth,
Floating in darkness through grottos of ogres, then plastic devils
    stoking the painted flames of a gospel hell,
Coming safely again into sunlight, and the sound of a band—

To a cavern of echoes, where we hear the fun as strangers rehearse
    and rehearse the surprise they shall give themselves tomorrow,
Watch the signs flash red, and gold, and blue, and green,
"Eat" "Drink" "Be Merry" "At Mike's,"
Where there is no score, in any game, less than a million magic bells
    and a billion electric lights—

Beyond the highest peak of the steepest roller-coaster, in the com-
    pany of persons we do not know,
Through arcades where anyone, even hermits, can have their for-
    tunes told by iron gypsies sealed behind plateglass walls,
Into and beyond the bazaars where every prize is offered, dolls
    and vases, clocks and pillows, miniature closets for the family
    skeleton,
Given freely, with no questions asked, to any, any winner at all—

Until we emerge, sage at last, upon that broad and crowded beach,
To cry aloud: Is there a stranger here?
The stranger we have come so far, and through so many dangers, to
    find?
That one who, alone, can solve these many riddles we have found so
    difficult:—

Who, among us all, is the most popular person?
Whom shall we vote the handsomest, the wittiest, most likely to
    succeed?
What is the name, and the mission, of the embryo so long preserved
    in a jar of alcohol?
How may we ever distinguish between an honest, and a criminal
    face?—

Is this stranger somewhere among you?
Perhaps sprawled beneath a striped umbrella, asleep in the sand, or
    tossing a rubber ball to a child,
Or even now awaiting us, aware of our needs, knowing the very day
    and the hour.

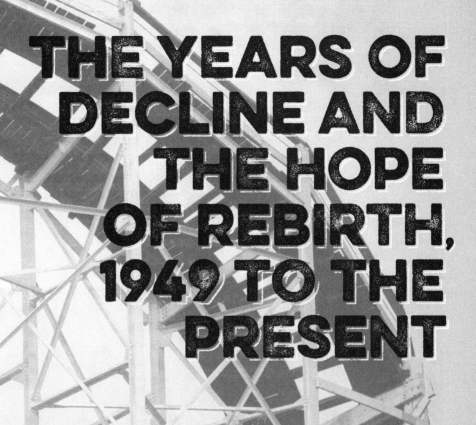

THE YEARS OF DECLINE AND THE HOPE OF REBIRTH, 1949 TO THE PRESENT

PARACHUTE JUMP, CONEY ISLAND, 1950S. (BRAIN MERLIS, BROOKLYNPIX.COM)

A CONEY ISLAND OF THE MIND

Lawrence Ferlinghetti

Lawrence Ferlinghetti (b. 1919) was born in Yonkers, New York. He was one of the founders and leading members of the Beat movement. In addition to the well-known collection *A Coney Island of the Mind* (1958), he wrote many other works, including *Pictures of the Gone World* (1955) and *Open Eye, Open Heart* (1973). Ferlinghetti had a tumultuous upbringing. Following the death of his father and the institutionalization of his mother, Ferlinghetti was raised by his aunt. After graduating from the University of North Carolina in 1941, he served in the navy during World War II. After his discharge, he settled in Greenwich Village and attended Columbia University, from which he received a master's degree in 1947. Ferlinghetti moved to San Francisco in 1953 and, with Peter Martin, founded City Lights Bookstore, still a landmark in the city. The bookstore would become the center of activity for many of the Beat writers—such as Neal Cassady, Jack Kerouac, and Allen Ginsberg—and much of their work would be published under the City Lights imprint. *A Coney Island of the Mind* is not based on an actual Coney Island experience, but is used more symbolically by Ferlinghetti to represent a mythic America, set in contrast to the real America of the 1950s.

20

The pennycandystore beyond the El
is where I first
        fell in love
                with unreality
Jellybeans glowed in the semi-gloom
of that september afternoon
A cat upon the counter moved among
            the licorice sticks

and tootsie rolls
and Oh Boy Gum

Outside the leaves were falling as they died

A wind had blown away the sun

A girl ran in
Her hair was rainy
Her breasts were breathless in the little room

Outside the leaves were falling
and they cried
Too soon! too soon!

THE WARRIORS

Sol Yurick

Sol Yurick (1925–2013) was born in New York City. He is the author of several novels, including *Fertig* (1966), which he considered to be his finest work. However, he remains best known for his first novel, *The Warriors* (1965), and the film version of it. Perhaps no work better symbolizes the decay of Coney Island in the 1960s than *The Warriors*, with its gang violence, drugs, poverty, and crumbling landscape. The nocturnal journey of the Coney Island Dominators (a mix of African Americans and Hispanics) from a pan-gang meeting in the Bronx to their home base in Coney is epic in scope. Their excitement at seeing their familiar "ocean" home is reminiscent of the joy of sailors who sight land after being cast adrift.

JULY 5TH, 5:20–6:00 A.M.

Before going home, Hinton led The Junior and Dewey down the street toward the beach. They followed him; he had become the Father. The morning wind was coming at them from the sea. It was still hot, but every step took them into cooler and cooler areas. It was lighter above the housetops, but still dark below.

They walked toward the boardwalk. When they came to the last block, Hinton halted them before crossing the street. He stood, hand raised, looking up and down. Nothing there but a garbage truck, grinding refuse, yellower than the murky light coming down from the overcast sunrise. The street lights were paling; they had blue, fluorescent edges. Hinton waved his hand the way patrol leaders did; they crossed the street, walking cool, alert for surprises. Far up the street a Headbuster patrolled, his back toward them. They were on their territory now; everything had a tremendous and comforting familiarity. They knew it to its confines, six short blocks by four long blocks. They could cover it in a short time—each brick was completely known, each stain, each sign, each gunmark on the concrete sidewalks, each hiding place. It was like knowing an endless and soul-freeing space where there could be no real threat. There wasn't as much space in the rest of the whole city. They drank it all in, everything from the cracked asphalt to the strutty rise of the roller coaster over the houses. It was there. There. Comforting after their night. They began to walk along the last block before coming to the boardwalk.

Hinton smelled the cool sea wind and began to feel a joyful excitement and quickened his step again. The boys moved a little faster. Hinton began to trot. They trotted after him. He began to shout, shouting nothing, letting the choking in his throat find a wordless opening. He began to run. They ran after him, laughing, silly, unable to control themselves. Was this all there was to being a man, Hinton wondered as he ran? Was this the way you became a leader, a Father? He ran up the ramp to the boardwalk. They ran after him; their feet clattered on the wood, keeping time. A few people strolled along the empty stretch of wooden walk which disappeared along both sides, fading into the morning's red haze. A few fishermen were arriving for early surf fishing. Farther off, a family loaded with blankets and beach equipment crossed the boardwalk, coming to the beach early. The morning sun was balled red in the haze, hanging off to the right. The littered sand and the red-stained water, placid under the wind, lay ahead.

Hinton pointed out and yelled, "The Ocean!"

They yelled, "The Ocean, The Ocean!" and they all laughed hysterically.

Hinton ran down the stairs to the sand and all the way down the beach to the water, veered off sharply to the left, slipping, touching the soft surge of the wave, and feeling the wetness coming in through the rips in his shoe. It was chill-shocking, burning on his abrasions, and then cooling and pleasant. He dipped his scraped hand into the water and shook loose drops into the air.

They ran. They couldn't stop laughing now, trying hard to keep the joy from degenerating into baby giggles. They cackled and made howling, shrieky sounds. A few gulls flew up at their approach; wind blew scraps of paper lightly, lifting them; sand grains sprayed upward as their running feet hit the beach. The wind from the sea was cooling now, almost chilling, and all the air that had stifled them the whole night seemed to be clearing away, and it was as if they were coming loose from a palpable thickness now; every step they took was lighter and they felt hilariously lifted off the ground until they barely felt their exhaustion. Hinton no longer cared that the ruination of his fancy Italian-style shoes that had begun in the park—how far away that seemed, as if it hadn't even happened that day or that week or ever, really—was almost complete now. Where was he going to get another fifteen bucks for shoes like these? It didn't matter. It didn't matter at all. [. . .]

The war party was over. Hinton turned and began to walk back to the [b]oardwalk. The others followed. It was understood. Hinton was now Father.

They walked down the beach for a few blocks. They turned in toward the land and began to walk home. It was close to six o'clock now and it was completely light on the beach. The shadows were still hard and dark in the streets. The seawind blew warm dirt up from the streets. Here the wind smelled of salt, rank weeds, picking up the smells of decaying houses, sour old wood, carrying the garbagy smells of concession-refuse inland.

CONEY ISLAND IN NOVEMBER

Josephine W. Johnson

Josephine W. Johnson (1910–1990) was born in Kirkwood, Missouri, and lived her entire life in the Midwest. Johnson is the author of eleven books of fiction, poetry, and nature writing. She is best remembered for the novel *Now in November* (1934), winner of the Pulitzer Prize in 1935. The stark, powerful novel deals with the devastating impact of the Depression on a middle-class family. "Coney Island in November" (1963), with its attention to Coney's beach, reflects Johnson's skills as a writer of natural settings. The story, set in the off-season, contrasts with the hustle and bustle associated with the resort and depicted in so many of the writings about it. Here, Johnson displays Coney's quieter side, reminding us of its origins as a seaside resort that allows for contemplation and introspection.

SHE THOUGHT OF HER FATHER, walking alone on these grey sands in this hostile season, trying to imagine him, as she often tried to imagine someone she did not know well, nor understand, alone with their own thoughts, having neither to command nor obey, posturing for no one, nor apologizing, without the emperor clothes of command, but alone with the self, whatever it might be.

This craving to see the ocean again had started, Virginia remembered, back in a long dry spell during June, when the wind blew incessantly from the west, or did not blow at all, and the earth dried slowly, and gaped a little here and there. The Illinois land seemed suddenly very flat and wide with no horizons, and all the water stood still in the ponds, or rose up and died in the white, motionless air.

It had become even more urgent to her when she discovered that she was to have another child, and she felt that she must go *this* year or perhaps not at all (having that curiously matter-of-fact perception of death which pregnant women feel, not fearing it, but perceiving it over a long and level period of time). It seemed increasingly evident that she had seen this house she lived in for some time, this yard was known, these mornings of a vast familiarity. The very richness of life had become dry and stale, like a giant coffee cake, aging and crumbling on the shelf, citron and raisin, pecan and orange peel, dusty and turning into stone.

She had wanted to go in July, as she and her sister Nancy and her parents had gone in July thirty years ago to Ocean City, the first time she had ever seen the ocean, and nothing had seemed quite as tremendous and lasting in memory ever since. They had come over the salty marshlands of the Jersey coast, through—or over—the watery swamps full of blooming pink marsh mallows, and far off, along the horizon, the sea had come suddenly into sight, as though suspended above the land, blue she supposed, although she remembered it as gold, and the air smelled of water and salt and living fish.

They had stayed at one of the biggest and newest of the hotels, so new the plaster was still wet in some of the rooms, and there were shocks of incredible gladioli, pink and rose and orange in mammoth vases wherever one went, which gave the hotel a fresh and morning look, in harmony with the smell of plaster, but more fashionable. It was the day of the American Plan, the enormous meal, the white tablecloth to the floor, and the hovering waiter. The nervous busboys filled the glasses with ice over and over until there was no room for water, and everything arrived, still lukewarm, in containers of chipped ice and silver. She and her sister had been urged to eat continuously, since it was all paid for, until meals became a sort of nightmare, and for the first time—she recalled this distinctly—an icecream cone, bought along the boardwalk in a rare, festive moment by her father, had been an ordeal of such proportion, that only by shutting her eyes, and imagining the small mound of greyish white before her as a tremendous mountain of icecream, tall as the hotel, and then opening her eyes to find it just a cone, could she finish its sweet surfeit, and spare herself her father's silent accusation of life's endless criminal waste.

It had not actually been a happy trip. But there had been the ocean, and after dark they sat out on the boardwalk benches alone, because their father went to bed early, this was to be his last trip with the family before he died, and in the dimness watched the breakers pouring along the beach, endlessly, monotonously, beautifully, with that strangely exciting sound, which they had called the "boom[-]wash" as children, and the word still evoked the exact feeling of that lonely, tremendous breaking on the sand.

She had planned to go in July, and then it was not possible and August passed and the autumn, and the emergencies and commitments and the arrangements of family life showed no signs of slackening, and suddenly she said desperately, I will just go *now*. Wasteful, extravagant, running out, leaving her husband to wrestle with house and job and children, she thought grimly, nevertheless, I will go *now*, for though the ocean is ever-lasting, I myself will be no more than a handful of seashells if I wait for the proper time.

So she had come in November to New York where Nancy lived with her husband, a thousand miles from the indiscriminate riches of her life, the arrivals and departures, the incessant work, the eternal wonder and the multiple pains and pleasures of domesticity, and there was the sea again, beautiful and barren, grey and endless, stretching out into the fog and mist where a flock of wild birds flew low above the horizon waves.

"Is it all right?" Nancy and Louis kept asking. Anxiously. Hospitably. "Is it what you wanted to see? We could drive further north, even an hour or so there are better beaches." But she was tired and she did not want to go any farther north, and it seemed appropriate to come to this particular place at last and in this season. She remembered her father's brief letters from New York when he had come here on a winter business trip. Brief and conservative as were all his communications with his family whether present or absent, yet when he had spoken of walking on the cold winter beaches of Coney Island, it had evoked in her mind as a child a perverse de-sire for the strange and the out-of-season, for that something which marks the traveler from the tourist, the grey mist in which Childe Harold to the dark tower came. He had died the year after, and when she thought of him in these later years as she often did for some reason she could not under-stand, it seemed strange to have so few memories, so little knowledge, of one whose hand had been on your life so powerfully, shaping and turning long after the living flesh was over.

It was a grey day, around the thirteenth of November, with a north wind and some mist, but not bitterly cold, more a spring and salty coldness, that at first did not seem to penetrate their winter coats and rubber boots and woolen scarves. From the height of the boardwalk the sea lay before them, silver and stony, fold on fold of it, stretching east into the mist and clouds. The breakers were there, as they had been before, rising and breaking and falling on the grey sand all up and down the coast, night and day, since that time thirty years ago, since time beyond all memory and reckoning.

The grey breakers rose and lifted, driven high by the wind, and broke on the beach into a startling foam, pure white and curling, as though a thousand paws of Chinese dragons ran bodiless across the sand. Flocks of gulls were resting on the beach, their heads motionless and facing windward, and one circled overhead, crying with a beautiful discordant sound. A very old brown gull sat alone and sick on the sand near the grey pier, and when a solitary clam digger wandered near him, the flock of gulls drew around the ancient one in a circle, watching and warning with their cold round eyes.

Here were the long grey beaches where her father had come, clean now as then of the summer carnival, swept completely of the big women and the children sunburned black, and the tired men, and all sound except the sound of the sea. And because of the very presence of the bleached buildings with faded blue and red scrolls and peeling gilt, the presence of the skeleton parachute jump, like a wire sea-nettle suspended in the sky, the great silent Ferris wheel, and the empty boardwalk stretching north and south as far as the eye could see; because these things were here and yet silent, almost grey in the fine mist, harmless and unanimated, without the nervous fiddling of concessionaire or customer, because a great beach could be clean of its vast moving growth and lie quietly under the wind, with only the clean bitter blue of the clam shells, and the feet of gulls, *this* was the place. Not the other beaches where Nancy and Louis, who lived all year round in New York, had wanted her to go. Not the northern dunes, lonely and beautiful, and pure in all the seasons.

"Do you remember," her sister said suddenly, "do you remember Papa writing his *Messages* on the sand at Ocean City? He wrote 'Be Good,' I remember, 'Be Grateful'—and something else, over and over, with circles around them." Nancy laughed, gently and unhappily. "I can't seem to think of that third thing we were never to forget."

"It was 'Never Waste Anything,'" Virginia said. "'Never, *never* waste anything.'"

She stood transfixed by the memory of those circles on those other sands at Ocean City.

"He never seemed to enjoy anything," Nancy was saying. "It was always a lesson . . . or something you had to be grateful for. It would have killed him to think the ocean wasn't there to teach us something. As Browning said – and I guess I'm the only woman my age remembers Browning—'Life will try his nerves / When the sky makes no disclosure / And the earth keeps up her terrible composure . . .'—All that pouring and pouring out there, and he writes us little messages on the sand!"

"I keep wondering," Virginia said, "when he was alone; what did he do when he was alone . . . what did he think about?"

"I don't know," her sister said. "I only know what *I* used to think alone. Those circles around each wrist . . . Be Grateful . . . Never Waste Anything . . . and around my head, Be Good . . . Ahhh . . . !" She grabbed her husband's hand and started to run along the sand. "Come on. Come on. Let's go out on the pier!"

Virginia followed them slowly up the long beach. The sand and her own heaviness made her tired and clumsy. She thought of the winter he was here and knew he was going to die—as much as anyone believes he will ever die, which isn't much, even with death inside as surely and painfully as she had life. Did the "messages," she wondered, powerful and encircling as manacles to his children, broken only by long and painful chafing, sustain *him* to the end, with a sense of orderly fulfillment in the face of the unanswering earth and sky, or was he little and alone and shattered by the mysteries?

They all climbed back up the steps to the walk and then went out onto the pier, where the beating of the ocean against the piles became a roar, and the sound magnified was still the sound of the breakers remembered from the nights in Ocean City, and, she thought surprised, "boom-wash" is still the only word to describe it, desolate and magnificent though an ocean sound should be.

On the pier men and little boys were fishing, unconcerned with the weather and the wind, and the blue crabs escaped from their baskets and scuttled blindly across the wet grey boards. The fishermen opened clam shells with their stiff fingers and baited the lines with the moist white blobs, or selected their bait from rows of small silver fish thrown out on the rainwashed benches. Besides the crabs there were big triangular ray-fish, flopping slowly in death, piled like white, fleshy pancakes on each other.

In their last breathing they made slow susurrations all through their un-divided bodies, and the edges curled and rose and sank with a sea motion to the end. The small, almost obscene mouths seemed to be trying to say something, and the eyes bubbled a little like sea foam.

One fisherman had caught a sea crab, large and thin and moss covered, that walked differently than the blue-green crabs and moved helplessly, but with [a] desperate attempt to escape across the slimy boards.

At the far end of the pier was a coffee stand, glassed in from the wind, but the smell of both dead and living fish was so overpowering, that the cups seemed full of a black and fishy tonic rather than anything that one might think of as coffee at all.

The mist lightened and a pale bruised circle came among the clouds where the sun was moving. Louis wandered off and stood staring up at the frozen arms of the Parachute Jump, his hands clasped behind his back like a little boy. "O perilous seas, O faery lands forlorn!" he said wistfully. "I wish the old Fun House was open now."

"Don't be gruesome, darling," his wife said mildly. "We came out to look at the ocean, so turn around. Mare nostrum . . . *our* sea!"

Down on the beach a child ran, and a man came trotting along, delib-erately and solemnly, dressed only in shorts, and lifting his bare feet high above the icy sand. The man trotted to and fro, swinging his arms, and then plunged suddenly into the breakers, disappeared, came up again, returned and resumed his trotting, emotionless and unquivering as the sand.

"They have Clubs," Louis said, "Polar bear stuff. They sit around and bulge their muscles and compare temperatures they went out in. 'Listen brother!' they say to each other, '*that* beach was nothing! You should have been where I was! Now *that* was really rough weather.' They do it for the sitting around afterward. But why, I wouldn't know."

Does it give them a sense of fleshy well-being, she wondered—a some-thing, a sensation that we have never even remotely known? . . . Or is it just one of the curious goals and hurdles that man sets himself, to make life, already a mass of goals and hurdles, satisfy some devious but definable pat-tern of his own?

The wind became stronger and more cold. It hurled down on them from the north as though determined to clear the sand of all living things and keep the great beaches for the winter and the sea.

"Let's go back," her sister said. "You look blue as the crabs. You'll catch your death if we stay. I know where we can get some hot coffee that tastes like coffee and cake with currants!"

They turned their backs to the wind and hurried south toward the cold, fish-smelling street where they had left the car. But when they reached the top of the steps that led downward to the street, she let them go on and turned back toward the sea.

She stood there a moment in the cold wind, half sheltered by the crumbling walls of the boarded restaurant, and took a long last look at the grey and endless sand. And in that pause she seemed to see her father standing down below on the beach. A middle-aged man with a greying mustache and a black overcoat with a velvet collar and a round black derby hat on his head. He was busy writing on the sand with a long stick. Be Good, he wrote, Be Grateful . . . Never Waste Anything. . . . The tide kept coming in steadily around his polished and solid shoes, but he kept on writing in the sand as though the ocean were far away. He looked lonely and small, and she knew that she would never have any more knowledge of what he had really been thinking in the few years that she had known him; and that it was well that she should leave him, lonely and yet competent and himself, writing his maxims on the sand, somehow magnificent and everlasting in his contempt of the oncoming tide.

MY SON THE MURDERER

Bernard Malamud

Bernard Malamud (1914–1986) was born in Brooklyn, New York. He wrote eight novels, including *The Natural* (1952); *The Assistant* (1957), set partly in Coney Island; and *The Fixer* (1966), which won both the National Book Award and the Pulitzer Prize in 1967. He also wrote numerous short stories, including the collection *The Magic Barrel* (1958), winner of the National Book Award. Many of Malamud's stories display the redemptive power of love, which can transform the characters' bleak existences and lessen their sense of alienation. In "My Son the Murderer" (1968), however, there is no such sense of relief. The story, narrated by both the father and the son, reflects the period in which it was written, a time of race riots, political assassinations, and the escalation of the Vietnam War. In the story, the father's love is unable to help his twenty-two-year-old son, newly graduated from college and on the verge of being drafted into the army. Coney Island, like America, has lost its innocence. It can no longer provide solace from the nation's problems, as it once could. Instead, the bleak, wintery Coney landscape reflects much of the turmoil that exists beyond its borders. It is, as critic Paul Kareem Tayyar states, "a figurative symbol of the innocence, joy, and possibility of not only a youth, but a nation that no longer exists" ("'Because We Could Not Walk on Water': Bernard Malamud's 'My Son the Murderer' and the Limits of Magical Realism," July 2008, *Americana: An Institute for American Studies and Creative Writing*).

HE WAKES FEELING his father is in the hallway, listening. He listens to him sleep and dream. Listening to him get up and fumble for his pants. He won't put on his shoes. To him not going to the kitchen to eat. Staring with shut eyes in the mirror. Sitting an hour on the toilet. Flipping the pages of a book he can't read. To his anguish, loneliness. The father stands in the hall. The son hears him listen.

My son the stranger, he won't tell me anything.

I open the door and see my father in the hall. Why are you standing there, why don't you go to work?

On account of I took my vacation in the winter instead of the summer like I usually do.

What the hell for if you spend it in this dark smelly hallway, watching my every move? Guessing what you can't see. Why are you always spying on me?

My father goes to the bedroom and after a while sneaks out in the hallway again, listening.

I hear him sometimes in his room but he don't talk to me and I don't know what's what. It's a terrible feeling for a father. Maybe someday he will write me a letter, My dear father . . .

My dear son Harry, open up your door. My son the prisoner.

My wife leaves in the morning to stay with my married daughter, who is expecting her fourth child. The mother cooks and cleans for her and takes care of the three children. My daughter is having a bad pregnancy, with high blood pressure, and lays in bed most of the time. This is what the doctor advised her. My wife is gone all day. She worries something is wrong with Harry. Since he graduated college last summer he is alone, nervous, in his own thoughts. If you talk to him, half the time he yells if he answers you. He reads the papers, smokes, he stays in his room. Or once in a while he goes for a walk in the street.

How was the walk, Harry?

A walk.

My wife advised him to go look for work, and a couple of times he went, but when he got some kind of an offer he didn't take the job.

It's not that I don't want to work. It's that I feel bad.

So why do you feel bad?

I feel what I feel. I feel what is.

Is it your health, sonny? Maybe you ought to go to a doctor?

I asked you not to call me by that name anymore. It's not my health. Whatever it is I don't want to talk about it. The work wasn't the kind I want.

So take something temporary in the meantime, my wife said to him.

He starts to yell. Everything's temporary. Why should I add more to what's temporary? My gut feels temporary. The goddamn world is temporary, on top of that I don't want temporary work. I want the opposite of temporary, but where is it? Where do you find it?

My father listens in the kitchen.

My temporary son.

She says I'll feel better if I work. I say I won't. I'm twenty-two since December, a college graduate, and you know where you can stick that. At night I watch the news programs. I watch the war from day to day. It's a big burning war on a small screen. It rains bombs and the flames roar higher. Sometimes I lean over and touch the war with the flat of my hand. I wait for my hand to die.

My son with the dead hand.

I expect to be drafted any day but it doesn't bother me the way it used to. I won't go. I'll go to Canada or somewhere I can go.

The way he is frightens my wife and she is glad to go to my daughter's house early in the morning to take care of the three children. I stay with him in the house but he don't talk to me.

You ought to call up Harry and talk to him, my wife says to my daughter.

I will sometime but don't forget there's nine years' difference between our ages. I think he thinks of me as another mother around and one is enough. I used to like him when he was a little boy but now it's hard to deal with a person who won't reciprocate to you.

She's got high blood pressure. I think she's afraid to call.

I took two weeks off from my work. I'm a clerk at the stamp window in the post office. I told the superintendent I wasn't feeling so good, which is no lie, and he said I should take sick leave. I said I wasn't that sick, I only needed a little vacation. But I told my friend Moe Berkman I was staying out because Harry has me worried.

I understand what you mean, Leo. I got my own worries and anxieties about my kids. If you got two girls growing up you got hostages to fortune. Still in all we got to live. Why don't you come to poker on this Friday night? We got a nice game going. Don't deprive yourself of a good form of relaxation.

I'll see how I feel by Friday how everything is coming along. I can't promise you.

Try to come. These things, if you give them time, all will pass away. If it looks better to you, come on over. Even if it don't look so good, come on over anyway because it might relieve your tension and worry that you're under. It's not so good for your heart at your age if you carry that much worry around.

It's the worst kind of worry. If I worry about myself I know what the worry is. What I mean, there's no mystery. I can say to myself, Leo you're a big fool, stop worrying about nothing—over what, a few bucks? Over my health that has always stood up pretty good although I have my ups and downs? Over that I'm now close to sixty and not getting any younger? Everybody that don't die by age fifty-nine gets to be sixty. You can't beat time when it runs along with you. But if the worry is about somebody else, that's the worst kind. That's the real worry because if he won't tell you, you can't get inside of the other person and find out why. You don't know where's the switch to turn off. All you do is worry more.

So I wait out in the hall.

Harry, don't worry so much about the war.

Please don't tell me what to worry about or what not to worry about.

Harry, your father loves you. When you were a little boy, every night when I came home you used to run to me. I picked you up and lifted you up to the ceiling. You liked to touch it with your small hand.

I don't want to hear about that anymore. It's the very thing I don't want to hear. I don't want to hear about when I was a child.

Harry, we live like strangers. All I'm saying is I remember better days. I remember when we weren't afraid to show we loved each other.

He says nothing.

Let me cook you an egg.

An egg is the last thing in the world I want.

So what do you want?

He put his coat on. He pulled his hat off the clothes tree and went down into the street.

Harry walked along Ocean Parkway in his long overcoat and creased brown hat. His father was following him and it filled him with rage.

He walked at a fast pace up the broad avenue. In the old days there was a bridle path at the side of the walk where the concrete bicycle path is now. And there were fewer trees, their black branches cutting the sunless sky. At the corner of Avenue X, just about where you can smell Coney Island, he crossed the street and began to walk home. He pretended not to see his father cross over, though he was infuriated. The father crossed over and followed his son home. When he got to the house he figured Harry was upstairs already. He was in his room with the door shut. Whatever he did in his room he was already doing.

Leo took out his small key and opened the mailbox. There were three letters. He looked to see if one of them was, by any chance, from his son to him. My dear father, let me explain myself. The reason I act as I do . . . There was no such letter. One of the letters was from the Post Office Clerks Benevolent Society, which he slipped into his coat pocket. The other two letters were for Harry. One was from the draft board. He brought it up to his son's room, knocked on the door, and waited.

He waited for a while.

To the boy's grunt he said, There is a draft-board letter here for you. He turned the knob and entered the room. His son was lying on his bed with his eyes shut.

Leave it on the table.

Do you want me to open it for you, Harry?

No, I don't want you to open it. Leave it on the table. I know what's in it.

Did you write them another letter?

That's my goddamn business.

The father left it on the table.

The other letter to his son he took into the kitchen, shut the door, and boiled up some water in a pot. He thought he would read it quickly and seal it carefully with a little paste, then go downstairs and put it back in the mailbox. His wife would take it out with her key when she returned from their daughter's house and bring it up to Harry.

The father read the letter. It was a short letter from a girl. The girl said Harry had borrowed two of her books more than six months ago and since she valued them highly she would like him to send them back to her. Could he do that as soon as possible so that she wouldn't have to write again?

As Leo was reading the girl's letter Harry came into the kitchen and when he saw the surprised and guilty look on his father's face, he tore the letter out of his hands.

I ought to murder you the way you spy on me.

Leo turned away, looking out of the small kitchen window into the dark apartment-house courtyard. His face burned, he felt sick.

Harry read the letter at a glance and tore it up. He then tore up the envelope marked personal.

If you do this again don't be surprised if I kill you. I'm sick of you spying on me.

Harry, you are talking to your father.

He left the house.

Leo went into his room and looked around. He looked in the dresser drawers and found nothing unusual. On the desk by the window was a paper Harry had written on. It said: Dear Edith, why don't you go fuck yourself? If you write me another stupid letter I'll murder you.

The father got his hat and coat and left the house. He ran slowly for a while, running then walking until he saw Harry on the other side of the street. He followed him, half a block behind.

He followed Harry to Coney Island Avenue and was in time to see him board a trolleybus going to the Island. Leo had to wait for the next one. He thought of taking a taxi and following the trolleybus, but no taxi came by. The next bus came fifteen minutes later and he took it all the way to the Island. It was February and Coney Island was wet, cold, and deserted. There were few cars on Surf Avenue and few people on the streets. It felt like snow. Leo walked on the boardwalk amid snow flurries, looking for his son. The gray sunless beaches were empty. The hot-dog stands, shooting galleries, and bathhouses were shuttered up. The gunmetal ocean, moving like melted lead, looked freezing. A wind blew in off the water and worked its way into his clothes so that he shivered as he walked. The wind white-capped the leaden waves and the slow surf broke on the empty beaches with a quiet roar.

He walked in the blow almost to Sea Gate, searching for his son, and then walked back again. On his way toward Brighton Beach he saw a man on the shore standing in the foaming surf. Leo hurried down the boardwalk stairs and onto the ribbed-sand beach. The man on the roaring shore was Harry, standing in the water to the tops of his shoes.

Leo ran to his son. Harry, it was a mistake, excuse me, I'm sorry I opened your letter.

Harry did not move. He stood in the water, his eyes on the swelling leaden waves.

Harry, I'm frightened. Tell me what's the matter. My son, have mercy on me.

I'm frightened of the world, Harry thought. It fills me with fright.

He said nothing.

A blast of wind lifted his father's hat and carried it away over the beach. It looked as though it was going to be blown into the surf, but then the wind blew it toward the boardwalk, rolling like a wheel along the wet sand. Leo chased after his hat. He chased it one way, then another, then toward the water. The wind blew the hat against his legs and he caught it. By now he was crying. Breathless, he wiped his eyes with icy fingers and returned to his son at the edge of the water.

He is a lonely man. This is the type he is. He will always be lonely.

My son who made himself into a lonely man.

Harry, what can I say to you? All I can say to you is who says life is easy? Since when? It wasn't for me and it isn't for you. It's life, that's the way it is—what more can I say? But if a person don't want to live what can he do if he's dead? Nothing is nothing, it's better to live.

Come home, Harry, he said. It's cold here. You'll catch a cold with your feet in the water.

Harry stood motionless in the water and after a while his father left. As he was leaving, the wind plucked his hat off his head and sent it rolling along the shore. He watched it go.

My father listens in the hallway. He follows me in the street. We meet at the edge of the water.

He runs after his hat.

My son stands with his feet in the ocean.

MAYOR BLASTS TA BRASS ON CONEY ISLAND DEBACLE

George Todd

April 14, 1968, might have marked the low point in Coney Island's history when a racial disturbance broke out between black youths and the police. Several store windows were broken, and the violence spilled over to the nearby Stillwell Avenue subway station, as reported by George Todd in "Mayor Blasts TA Brass on Coney Island Debacle," published in the *New York Amsterdam News* on April 20. Fortunately, no one was killed, but twenty-one people were hospitalized. By the time the police investigation was over, thirty-six people had been arrested, and many stores in the area, including Nathan's, were forced to close early. The incident was another mark on Coney's tarnished reputation. As Charles Denson wrote, "It would take a long time for the general public to forget the images of 1968" (*Coney Island: Lost and Found* [Berkeley, Calif.: Ten Speed Press, 2002], 143).

MAYOR [JOHN] LINDSAY'S BLAST on Transit Authority brass for not being alerted to handle the Easter Sunday mass invasion of Coney Island where disorders erupted, store windows smashed and passengers on Manhattan bound trains scared out of their wits, brought a sharp rebuttal from the TA official.

The Mayor stepped quickly into the fray early Monday demanding immediate steps be taken by William J. Ronan, chairman of the Metropolitan Transportation Authority[,] to prevent a recurrence of the explosive situation. He called for increased trains and buses at Coney Island to get the crowd moving with a minimum of delay[.]

About 5,000 black youths allegedly went on the rampage, leaving the beach community almost in shambles before TA patrolmen managed to get them off the streets and into the Stillwell Ave. station.

NEAR PANIC

A pushing, shoving and shouting crowd caused a near panic in the station. Passengers were terrorized and robbed on the trains, police said, and service was disrupted by the rampaging youths pulling emergency cords on the wild night ride out of Brooklyn.

Police arrested 36 youths on charges ranging from burglary to inciting a riot. More than a dozen persons were injured, among them a patrolman.

In refuting Mayor Lindsay's charge, Walter L. Schlager Jr., executive officer for the Transit Authority, said the agency was "just as concerned that law and order be preserved both on the transit lines and in the city generally."

AVOIDABLE

He conceded that much of what happened could have been avoided, but pointed out that adequate transportation facilities were available. Eighty trains were operating out of Coney Island between 6:30 P.M. and 9:30 P.M. to take care of 100,000 passengers. At the peak of the exodus, 138 patrolmen were on duty, the Authority official said, and 18 arrests were made at the Stillwell station, or on trains.

Angry white residents of Coney Island were still steaming the day after the flareup in their backyard.

THREATS

Several phone calls were received at the Amsterdam News office Monday morning, all expressing outrage over the disorders and threatening violence.

"We're arming ourselves and going to kill all the Negroes out here," declared an unidentified man in a belligerent tone, slamming the receiver down. Most of the calls came from women who were equally stirred up and angry words poured out of their mouths.

KWAN'S CONEY ISLAND

Edward Hoagland

Edward Hoagland (b. 1932) was born in New York City. He is perhaps best known for his travel and nature writing, but he has also written novels and short stories. Hoagland's background prepared him to write on Coney Island, as he spent two summers working at Ringling Brothers and Barnum & Bailey Circus, which he discusses in his first novel, *Cat Man* (1956). "Kwan's Coney Island" (1969) is the story of an immigrant from Hong Kong and his assimilation into the curious melting pot of Coney Island in the 1960s. Hoagland's sympathetic portrait of the outsider may tie in with his own experiences trying to fit in despite his childhood problems with stuttering.

THERE WAS A SAINT IN THE STREETS, a bland silver man about one-fourth-sized who was rolling along on a rubber-wheeled cart while a priest in lace walked in front reading the blessing. Two lines of men gently pulled the lead ropes and behind the saint's cart a large number of women in black carried candles. A uniformed band of fifteen played a salute to anybody who came up with a dollar bill to be pinned to the saint's vestments. "Wait a minute! Wait a minute. Not so fast," said a butcher coming out of his store after the crowd had gone by. He wore a black band on his arm and, holding his dollar, he kept at a sensible step to catch up with them. The band turned, like everyone else, to wait and, when he'd delivered it, did the salute, all the cheeks puffed, the instruments facing him. He got a saint's card from the priest, which his wife kissed.

Kwan nodded familiarly to the marchers. These parades happened almost every month. He followed until the fireworks stage, when a string of firecrackers were laid down for a block and the head man waved his breast-pocket handkerchief a long time, swearing because his assistants at the opposite end couldn't figure out what he meant. Then a shocking great war cannonade went off, filling the air with its smell and smoke. The kids ran the length of the fuse just ahead of the blasts, and yellow and blue and red stains were left in the street which would last till the next occasion. The saint was rolled into a storefront to stay.

Kwan had been downtown for Saturday night and had come back late on the bus. This morning, delightfully logy, he'd lain in bed past eleven o'clock, although he was never a sound sleeper. He lived in the back of his laundry, not to save money so much as because he had gotten to be rather crusty and could do without constant company. He liked company only in short doses. After a get-together he took at least a couple of days to digest whatever he'd heard and several more days to finish enjoying it. He had lived in Pittsburgh for many years, so to live here in New York a few dozen blocks from the central neighborhood of his own people was a luxury. In his block were black men and Puerto Ricans and Sons of Adam, as he called the Hasidic Jews, and Italians as he called the Germans, Poles, Greeks, and Italians, and miscellaneous bums and bearded young scholars. He had a Russian church and a Spanish church alongside his business and, all in all, he could pass in and out with a fine anonymity. Sundays in August now he went to the beach, thinking over the gossip of Saturday night and the fixes his friends had gotten themselves into. Even on a cool day he would go because of the sweltering week he'd put in, as well as the sweltering week to come. He was middle-aged, dressed in his next-to-best suit and a clovered sport shirt, with the mild roundish face of a member of the amphibian family, except for his humorous mouth and firm chin.

The hydrants were going but nobody soaked him as he went past; the Puerto Ricans were after their own. It was a day in the eighties with a marvelous high sky the blue of an organdy robe. He took the subway, reading a Chinese newspaper until the tracks emerged above ground. Having chosen his seat especially, he sat back, his hands clasped in his lap, blinking in the sun, and fanned by a dry city breeze. Although his appearance was staid, he was just as pleased at the holiday as the children who chased back and forth in the car. They were more than pleased—they jumped on the seats, they shoved each other against other passengers and part way out of the window. The train made a great many lackadaisical stops, while Kwan mused down at the street below. At Coney Island the pour of human-kind off the platform and the festival babble and crush got him energetic. There were mynah birds telling fortunes, merry-go-rounds making music, coin-slotted player pianos. On the hurtling rollercoaster, people screamed and screamed. From the pots at Korn's Korn came a scarifying smell like flesh burning, and the teenagers, running in front of the traffic, plunged for the beach. It was all too much, of course, and reminded him of scenes from his boyhood in China, but he was detached and quick on his feet, inconspic-uous, knew what he liked, and liked this contrast with the rest of the week.

He went to his bathhouse establishment. STEAM, the signs said. A lot of the men spent the whole day reading the newspaper in their cubicles. They sunned for a bit on the roof, steamed in the steam room, and never went out on the beach. Kwan sampled the services, getting his money's worth. The fat stomachs on the Italians amused him. Though he was certainly no mus-cle-man, they were so laughably fat that as soon as they took off their belt they had to hold onto their bellies. Their testicles bulged like bunches of onions. To squeeze in for a shower was like having to push through a herd of beach balls. It was always quarrelsome, because most of them weren't alone through the week like he was but were standing up for their rights in some busy business establishment, and they couldn't lay off on Sunday. And the black-white business was tense. Only a handful of blacks came in to change, but today one of them attached on to Kwan to try to get into the showers. He was in the cubicle and he offered Kwan part of a sandwich, struck up a conversation until Kwan left with his towel, and then hurried to swallow and stand up too, more and more nervous about it.

"It's pretty packed, huh?"

"Plenty room," Kwan assured him.

The trouble was that his fear was contagious; for a moment Kwan was afraid to go into that bald gleaming mass of bodies himself, forgetting that nobody ever objected to him. The black man hardly looked at him, he was so busy being nonchalant and looking ahead to the white men's faces.

"Any space?"

Kwan paused beside the Negro, but there were so many people talking that nobody answered. He pushed through to find a spot, the man tagging after, putting a shoulder in Kwan's stream of water and sloshing his front with one hand. It was a crazy room, with shapes such as you never saw on the street, and much genital-fussing and belly-rubbing.

The exit to the beach went under the boardwalk, where the whites were the jittery ones. The shade was dazzlingly striped with thin lines of sun and a good crowd of people had sprawled in the cool twilit sand. Mothers held kids. The passive families with their spraddled-out postures and scraps of food reminded Kwan of a refugee crowd, and the stripes across everything were doubly weird, but the sea glittered peacefully blue. He had on a new bathing suit and his toes had not grown as old or as crooked as some of these fellows' toes. Adding it up, he cut not a bad figure, he thought. Nobody took exception to him.

A bunch of colored children tore by, throwing handfuls of sand. There were drunks with beer cans, tough policemen, and propped, melancholy souls alone on the part of the beach where everyone else was in transit. They lay on one elbow with their lonely detective novel and their plaid thermos bottle and their brown fleabag blanket from home. It was stop-go. A pair of whites would find themselves on a collision course with three blacks and suddenly stop. By the water the hot sand got cold. Jammed family groups whooped it up; screwballs were yelling. The continual verging on violence was tiresome but didn't directly affect Kwan, who picked his way out beside one of the breakwaters until his body was lapped by the waves. Facing the sun, he braced his back against a large rock and dug his heels in, loving the suctioning. This was his favorite time of the week, right now. He wiggled around for the perfect position, worried that soon the day would be gone, that he wasn't happy enough, but he was. The light, multiplied on the water, was a week's worth of sun. He had seaweed to scrub with and salt on his lips. He smiled so much that he wasn't aware he was smiling, and was all the time closing his eyes to enjoy them closed and then opening them to watch the shimmer and action. Probably five thousand kids were being taught how to swim just in the area in front of him, which made for a steady myriad blare, the yeows and shrieks yiping out of it. Jumping, jumping, jumping, jumping — there was scarcely space for the waves to roll in. When the wind cut the hooting, it blew back again. Old-man-in-the-moon faces bobbed up to blow out the water and suck in some air. Horses chased horses. Mothers were teaching by every method, including the drown-

'em-and-laugh-at-'em-cry, if only because they themselves were scared. The lifeguards paddled on little rafts which the fishy kids tried to catch up with, and once they had a shark scare, when the police helicopter started to swoop. A guy clambered out covered with black steamship oil, having swum through a slick. He'd been the shark. In the distance the regular sky-ride screams were like crying dolls squeezed.

Five children crept past after crabs, although the rocks had been hunted clean. Kwan tried to converse with them with avuncular dignity, pretending to peer round his feet in case a crab might be hiding there. He liked their shouts and the teeming water and teeming beach, the women in bouncing bathing suits. While he regretted not having had children, this was not a gnawing or painful feeling because it had never seemed possible. Marriage had never been much of a hope. He'd paid court to several ladies but always as one of so many suitors that the family and daughter had toyed with him, letting him know how privileged he was. Even so, he had various dear memories of the onanist's kind—vigils outdoors, or missing a meal to send flowers he knew that the girl would ignore. Sometimes he'd encountered a colored woman who would come in the back and allow him to tickle her a little instead of charging her for her laundry, and then he had hoped that a permanent amicability might grow up between them. But each time afterwards when he mulled it over, he realized it would only amount to a lot of tickling—no work. If he wanted to share his life with someone, he needed a helper. The flight to Hong Kong to bring back a wife required an enormous sum. To be sure, he had saved toward it, but he was an occasional gambler and he loved his other few pleasures too much.

The mobs were a piece of his childhood, the kids smeared with black sand. He strolled way down to the fishing pier and sat against a green piling. He saw an eel caught and a beer-bottle fight between the men on the pier and the men in the motor boats which were putting about, tangling some of the lines. There was a fight on the beach as well. The white lifeguards in the towers close by had to jump down and help one of their bunch against ten or twelve Puerto Ricans. The police got into it with roaring and clubs and the kids on the sidelines grabbed several girls by the heels and dragged them around, scaring them into hysterics. It was serious for an instant; then it fragmented. The unearthly hordes of people, picnicking, petting, quietly wading, swallowed everything up.

With sharp interest, Kwan watched the ocean-going ships rendezvous with the pilot boat at the mouth of the Narrows. As a boy he had wanted to go to sea and still thought of himself as half seaman, especially because of his one long sea journey. At night in his shop he listened for toots from the harbor, sniffing the salt smells. He liked to walk, so he walked some more, keeping a count of the ships he saw and prolonging the afternoon's activity. When people spat near his feet on the sand he spat back, if not near enough to set off a brawl. The beach was extremely hot. He got up on his toes and trotted under the boardwalk again with the shade-loving crew. The Seashell Bar was there, a whole line of bars, and this was his day for American food. He leaned on the counter as sauerkraut was forked onto his sausage—"Very good stuff. More, man." With big mouthfuls he ate a whole lot. A raving white man kept pulling his trousers off, while the cops attempted to tie them on during the wait for the ambulance. Finally they needed to handcuff him in order to keep them on. He shrieked like a factory whistle and collected a crowd. Kwan scraped with his teeth at a candied apple and winced at the smell of the cooking corn.

The sea was a sizzling, glistening blue. He watched the Parachute Jump, the kids doing stunts. He watched the Diving Bell sink down in its tank where it was nosed by the Porpoise Herd. Couples being jolted out of the funhouse doors at the end of their ride were bloated by mirrors to squeal a last squeal. At the Torture House an elephant was mashing a canvas man underfoot. Santa Claus laughs came up from him. The sign "Chinese Water Torture" intrigued Kwan, since he couldn't guess what that might be. Finally he paid the twenty-five cents. The House was a tent behind a board facade, and the Water Torture was not featured prominently. Both victim and tormentor were yellow as bile, the latter chuckling, apparently. The victim looked up with the face of a calf about to feed, head twisted around to catch hold of the teat. He was papier mâché, and a make-believe faucet dripped on him. Quite accurate characters in a penciled balloon said, "Let me go." Kwan grinned at all this, but some of the other exhibits made him squint; he had squint lines engraved almost like a sun-squint.

There was a live show. A fat man climbed slowly onto the stage. "Folks can come right down close to me where you can see everything and hear everything. No need to be afraid of me . . ." His face was tattooed as if he'd wished to obliterate it, not simply to become a rarer freak. He had a display case of hatpins and needles and two rows of drinking glasses.

"All you good people want to see everything, want to hear everything. That's what you have here, all the odd people," he said, filling the glasses to different levels, and continued in a mesmerizing, biting voice, "My name is Musical Tons." He laughed to get his body shaking, groaning at the discomfort. "I'm fat, but since I'm not as fat as some I'm also musical." He licked his finger and began to rub the glasses' rims. He did "Dixie" and "I Could Have Danced All Night." But the audience grew sarcastic and whistled along. "Mary, to my right, is one of our features. She's going to talk to you about herself in her own words and will be glad to answer any of your questions. Please listen carefully."

"Now you were told outside on the paper that I would show you underneath my dress, and that's what you are seeing," said Mary, who was unbuttoning her dress in mannish haste. The people giggled with whispers. Faint howls drifted from the rollercoaster. She wore a bathing suit. "I am a Christian woman and I do not show you underneath my bathing suit. It is the same. The ladies may feel of anywhere they wish to be convinced that it is real. The gentlemen may feel of anywhere where they would feel their sisters or their mothers. Now I have cards for ten cents which show myself and I will write on them my name Mary in my own handwriting, which is very good."

She spoke fast and she wrapped the dress around her like a towel.

"Now I am called the Crocodile Woman, which is because my skin is like the thick skin or the hide of a crocodile. It is because of a disease, and which is not infectious, do not worry. I am a Christian woman the same as your wife or your mother. Now I have a message for you, which is that God loves you. Enjoy the life which God has given to you, enjoy your skin, be thankful."

"Thank you, Mary," Musical Tons said into the microphone. "May I direct our friends back to myself? I am going to perform what has been called in the newsprint a remarkable demonstration of hardihood. Pay close attention, if you please."

He took his shirt off. There were hooks through his nipples, and he picked up two five-pound weights from the floor with them. "I'd do the heavier ones if we had a bigger crowd." He smiled around. He had separate smiles for the whites and the blacks but in both cases bitter with scorn. As he swung into doing his stuff, what politeness he'd had before peeled away; he was intense.

"What I do mostly is stick these pins through myself. Want me to?"

"Yeah," called the crowd, caustic and mostly young. He grinned at them and they back at him. The Santa Claus *ho's* came from the man being mashed by the elephant outside, and Kwan's squint was well-rooted by now, not much more distressed than a standard sun-squint but limiting the amount that the eyes took in.

"You do?" Turning a bit toward the knot of whites, he dawdled, as if such a personal stunt was humiliating to perform in front of a bunch of Negroes, who were quick to sense this, however. Several pressed in, looking at all those blue bruises.

"Which arm?" he asked.

"Left!" they shouted. And plenty of whites were panting as well, until his contempt grew so delicious to him he couldn't bear it and wheeled around to the blacks again.

"How about both arms?"

People broke into smiles and nodded. He leaned from the stage, stroking the longest hatpins. "You may expect I sterilize these things. No, as a matter of fact, just the opposite." He dropped them and rolled them under his shoe. "The trouble is, a platform like this is never awfully dirty, not the real vicious germs. How about it? Put some on for me, would you? Give me some germs."

Ha! They were startled. Those who didn't freeze up were excited. "You want to get poorly, huh? Over here, babe!"

Musical Tons mixed his colors and took from the young and the old leaning out to give everybody a chance to contribute the smudge off their hands. The women acted as if they were touching a snake, and one fellow had a real brainstorm and licked the pin when it came to him.

"Good. Let's get the worst of it. Give me some more."

He picked a white volunteer to help push the needles through. "You're not much use, are you? Is he, folks?" It was hard going with the first one, particularly on the far side of his arm. The point was dulled so that nothing important inside would be cut. Once the pain started, though, his zest went away; he was deadpan. It seemed like distasteful labor to him rather than pain. Kwan felt twinges penetrating his limbs too.

Anguished figures around the room were painted with blood, but he might have been digging a sewer hole. When he had hatpins sticking through both his arms, "How's this?" he said. "Enough, or do you want 'em through my legs too?"

"Up your old ass, man. Let's see the whole thing!"

He smiled toothily like a dog. "Everywhere? Okay, but your job's the filth. I want all you have. Armpits, that's right, you got the idea."

The racial divisions were gone. It was between those who froze and those who warmed. The pins that were already in obstructed his muscles when he was pushing the new pins through and he looked like a man from Mars equipped for space signals. "How about it?" He pointed to marks on the side of his neck. "Sometimes if I have a big crowd I'll put one through here. Are you people big?"

"Yeah, big. Big as butter," they yelled, with the grins of a gangster movie emptying.

He laughed. "No, you're not. You're too small." He drew out the pins and rubbed the blood drops at each exit point into one of his hands like a powder.

Kwan loafed in a bingo parlor for an hour—a collection of souls who were more his own age. The sun got low. The whistle-pitched roar from the beach subsided. Instead there were drumming parties and bonfires, shouting and stone-throwing. A girl belly-danced. Gangs of kids with handkerchiefs around their heads were swinging clubs. The beach was like a checkerboard, with whites in certain parts and blacks in other parts. Kwan watched the pitching machines pitch baseballs and watched the Scorpion, the Steeplechase. The lights strung over all of the rides went on, and a boy ran along the boardwalk setting the wastebaskets afire. Kwan steamed in his bathhouse again. He sat in a bar, played bingo another half-hour, then saw the jail pen cleared. As this was underneath the boardwalk, an amphitheater was formed around it by the ramps going up. A large crowd gathered, and, since the prisoners came out singly to the paddy wagon, the process was a long one, each fellow making his moment in the limelight just as dramatic as he could. For some it was the last steps of a death march, for some the last steps to the stake. They stalked like concentration camp victims. They wept dementedly and stumbled, protesting, with glances at the sky. Soon afterward the riot that had been brewing finally broke out. It wasn't anything to see, just cobra-mongoose-jumping and strangled yells, figures running dimly and hammering down with their sticks. First the Italians were outnumbered, and then the blacks. New blacks came, more Italians, and then again new blacks, who were sweeping the bench when the cops sirened in.

Kwan wandered through a side alley to get a last feel of the sand. He took his shoes off for the fifth time that day. He couldn't decide whether to go straight home or stop downtown along the way.

He noticed a colored woman who was sitting against a post in the darkness near him. "Hey you," she said. He was cautious—he had started to leave—but turned and edged toward her, kicking ice cream cups and paper plates.

"I'm Chinese," he said.

"I know you're Chinese. Nobody's mad at you. Nobody's going to beat you up." She laughed. The feet on the boardwalk sounded over them.

Lying down, he put his hand behind his head and clasped the post. She fixed a piece of cardboard in the position of a lean-to. Although she was only a youngster, she had a face with glamorous, rich lines, a nose that flared out when she smiled, and very pretty creases in her forehead with which she could pretend surprise.

"I'm Crystal."

He was impatient now. In his old boardinghouse a Cuban girl had tapped along the rows of single rooms each night, being quick and businesslike.

But she insisted. "Say it."

"Clystal."

"Crystal!" she giggled. "No, Crystal. Say it."

"Clystal." He clutched the pole and watched her tongue.

"Crystal. You trying?"

"I hold on," Kwan said.

"Yes, you hold on as hard as you can. First say it, though."

"Clystal."

"Crystal!" she shrieked in giggles, making him wait.

CONEY ISLAND 1969

Edwin Torres

Edwin Torres (b. 1958) was born in the Bronx to parents who were natives of Puerto Rico. He began his poetry career at the Nuyorican Poets Café and was the winner of its first annual prize in 1992. Since then, he has performed his work at many venues, including Lincoln Center, the Museum of Modern Art, and the Guggenheim Museum. He is the author of several poetry collections and has recorded spoken-word CDs. Torres says that his work mingles "the textures of poetry with vocal and physical improvisation, sound elements and visual theater." "Coney Island 1969" is an autobiographical poem, recollecting bittersweet memories of Coney and time the poet spent with his father, who worked at Coney Island in the late 1960s. This version of the poem is Torres's revision of an earlier one read at Parachute: The Coney Island Performance Festival on September 12, 2009.

My father was the manager of Nathan's Hot Dogs on Coney Island
A memory inside a beach ball
My cousin reaching below the surface
Water in my lungs
Gagging
Blue sky
Technicolor white
Where skin should be

My father watched me walk the sidewalk cracks
From our bedroom window
In the Bronx
Asking me
What I thought I was doing

How a line is straight when you walk it
How a man knows exactly where to go

My father took us to Nathan's at Christmas
Company party
Santa
A thousand presents for each and every child
The boardwalk was cold
The rides empty
Coney Island winter
You had to warm your fingers
By hiding them from the ocean

My father gave us hot dogs and fries
Between his affairs
He gave me animals
To show his love
I had a beagle, a turtle, 3 guinea pigs and 2 java rice birds
I loved them
So I loved my father

My father took me and my two sisters to the Statue of Liberty
He told me it was made of Limburger Cheese
I loved him
He never hit me
He never hugged me
I had to walk straight
That's what he told me

When I visit my father
At St. Raymond's Cemetery
I find his gravestone
I have a son I tell him
Winter is our time
When he left
When all those presents at Nathan's were opened
All those families

My father towered over me
Laughing in his eyes
You're my little man he'd say
From up there
The bumper cars
The mirrors
All those reflections

My father had a relationship
With scale
An intuition for location
To remain
Long enough to be found
Calling to catch
What *will*
Does to *weight*

My father was never Coney Island to me
He never knocked on the door
That morning in the Bronx
My mother didn't open
No cops told her nothing
She didn't hide her face in her hands
No silent tears
No floor I play my indians on

No roller coaster tell me no turn
No question come from long legs
No mean kids
No skinny mirror
My father had yoga thumbs
Look what I can do I'd say
Leaning out just far enough
To make you catch me

CONEY ISLAND
Colson Whitehead

Colson Whitehead (b. 1969) was born and raised in New York City. After graduating from Harvard University, he obtained a position writing reviews of television, books, and music for the *Village Voice*. His first novel, *The Intuitionist*, was published in 1999, and he has since written several other widely acclaimed books, including the novel *John Henry Days* (2001). "Coney Island" is from *The Colossus of New York: A City in Thirteen Parts* (2003), a book of essays that has been described as a lyric symphony and a prose poem. Whitehead gives a stream-of-consciousness account of his impressions of Coney on a typical summer day, both the good and the bad. He moves seamlessly from topic to topic, including the "multitude of stenches," people with metal detectors on the beach, the ubiquitous sand, "parts squeezing out of bathing suits," the scene underneath the boardwalk "where they store failed mayoral candidates," and screaming on the Cyclone.

SUCH A MULTITUDE OF STENCHES means it must be summer. It's the baking asphalt that adds that special piquancy. Discomfort without end, surely this planet is hurtling into the sun. Some cavort like idiots in uncapped hydrants, others head for the edge of town. South, to the beach where a broom of briny air sweeps away this miserable funk. So they fall to the bottom of the subway map, settling there like loose change in various denominations. What they will find under their feet will not be pavement but something shiftier.

All tomorrow's sunburns gather in wait. Heads dart to and fro as they seek the right spot. Homestead and land grab. This must be the place. Try to remember your personal formula for comfort on a beach, the whole towel thing. Sizzle on the griddle. How to serve man. Gritty evidence of the last visit to the beach clings to the neck of the bottle of suntan lotion. In unison ask, Can you do my back. The sun sets this melting pot to furious boil, brings it all to the surface, the ancient liaisons, the hidden complexions. That extra seasoning. The struggles of everyone's ancient tribes are reduced to how their descendants fare against ultraviolet. People emphasize particular ideas they have about their bodies via too-tight tops, trunks, and T-shirts. Take it all off and don't forget your favorite scars.

Everything disappears into sand. Objects get lost in sand the way people get lost in streets. There is refuge on the shores of the new world. This is the cozy retirement community for pull-up tabs that have not been manufactured in years, cigarettes butts that have seen better days, limbs of crabs. Wood drifts over from native lands. Naturalized styrofoam bits recite pledges and names of presidents at the slightest provocation. Dirty gulls patrol beats, sidestep seaweed bums and their sob stories. Rumor has it someone over there is eating a sandwich. Scavengers peck away, undertake vain missions. Flies buzz and hop over the dead and the dead-seeming. The crazy guy with the metal detector zigs and zags in efficient search pattern or out of habit to avoid teenagers' thrown projectiles. His take-home pay is quite astounding. The number of house keys lost this day will fall within the daily average of lost house keys. Hypocrites complain about the quality of the sand, as if they are not blemishes on its expanse, and scavengers, too, ripping little shreds of comfort from an afternoon.

Front line in the ancient blood feud between city and nature. What side are you on. Every grain a commando on recon probing for weakness and reporting back. Here are some places sand gets into: eyes, sandwiches, shoes, under beds, scalps, carpets, car floors. Crotches and brainstems and decision-making places. Kids with pails move this bunch of sand from here to there to undo the secret design of tides. Aeons in the making and now it's all ruined. Rule is, violence on purpose and beauty by accident. Their castles rise proudly from soggy plots of real estate, yet despite their enthusiasm a very small percentage of these children actually go on to careers in construction, it's very strange. School's out for the summer but sand is an elementary with lessons. What they shape are cities, no less so for being soft and miniature. Imposition of human order on nature. Sand slips through fingers but no one takes the hint. Our juvenile exercises. What they build cannot last. Fragile skylines are too easily destroyed.

This strip piggybacks one of the world's magic meridians: keep swimming and you'll end up in England, keep digging and you'll end up in China. So they say. Children yo-yo at the tideline, run in when it seems safe and out when a wave approaches. Depressing mechanical regularity. Mimicking parents and ruthless commute. Sometimes a workweek will grind you into sand, pulverize you into particles. Those who live near expressways recognize the sound of waves. The ocean traffics in ebb and flow, that's its business. Parents surge to teach offspring how to swim. Close your eyes. That wasn't so bad now, was it, says mother to child. He spits out seawater. Riptide and undertow are the world's hands grabbing to save you from cities and their influence. The unseen infrastructure of waves. Events a thousand miles away find their final meaning in these gentle little consequences begging at the shore. Do the dead man's float and drop out of society, no sound, no weight, just you and the forces that pushed you here, set you apart. Anchorless. So safe. Is it possible to stay here, renounce the city, swim the other way. The direction of their final strokes this day is an oath of fealty. Look at this pretty shell.

Even out here still too close to neighbors. Horizontal tenement. Loathe neighbors and their loud boorish talk and unfortunate ditties. Envy neighbors on their well-equipped expedition. Yeah, they know how to do it right, with their everlasting cooler and state-of-the-art collapsible seating. What will they pull out next, a Grillmaster 9000 or merely a famous chef. Just when you get settled a breeze or hooligan ruins things. The insult that made a man out of Mack. Please adjust: parts squeezing out of bathing suits, parts having natural reactions to changing temperatures, the bashful edges of the towel, your attitude because it's really getting on my nerves I go to all this trouble why can't you just enjoy yourself for once. Probably not the right time for a sexual reverie but the view argues otherwise. All that stuff they hide when they dress up in civilization. Don't blink or else you'll miss it—that father's annual display of affection toward his son. Seeing this is like looking at the sun. It can blind you.

Out there slow barges cart away tires and exiles, black arrowheads sailing through blue air. Wooden contraptions provide sure footing. Along the top of the pier, fisherman skewer hope on hooks and drop this bait, wait for a little nibble. Along the sides of the pier, barnacles cling with telltale rent control tenacity. Up and down the boardwalk visitors establish their cruising speed. Underneath the boardwalk is where they store failed mayoral candidates. Improbable clam shacks. Hot dog vendor to the world. What was true for citizens a hundred years ago remains so. Generation after generation marvel over the salt air as if they are the first to remark upon it. They keep to themselves the odd feelings brought on by the novelty of a horizon after so many horizonless days. What to do with these notions. Old-timers have seen it all before. We're the reruns they can't help watching. Old-timers will tell ya that every plank on the boardwalk has a story to tell and a secret name. This is in fact untrue. It's just dead wood after all.

Off season this place is dead. Don't tell anyone but the Wonder Wheel is a gear in the great engine of the metropolis and when it stops moving systems fail. Amusement park rides are disguises for other things. Taken medicinally, periodic trips to the bumper cars can prevent road rage. Cherish the fear in loose bolts, statistical inevitabilities, the substance-abuse problem of the operator as suggested by his glassy stare. The ancient metal seats get repainted every season. Dark metal like a stain where people put their hands. They have yet to invent an amusement park paint that can withstand the corrosive agents in fear-sweat. There is no way to avoid it, all must ride the Cyclone. A loop of ribbon lifted by a breeze, sloping down here, twisting up there. Seems so rickety. Struts and girders, toothpicks and straws. The old scares are the best ones. Couples on dates queue up nervously. The country cousin in from the country is egged on by sadistic kin. They make up scary stories about the fatality rate to scare him but when the restraining bar slams shut are swayed by their own fictions.

Too late to back out. Scream if you think it'll help. Clutch my thigh according to plan. Citizens of this new vertiginous city. Up and down. Reel this way and the ocean is upon you in a wave, in beckoning gloom, reel the other way and slam into highrises, into broad brickfaces. A rollercoaster is your mind trying to reconcile two contradictory propositions. Earth and space, cement and air, city and sea. Life and death. Choose quickly. The city and the sea don't get along, never have. Two trash-talking combatants, two old bitter foes. This ride is them throwing punches and you ride on their arms, dip and rise and coast and roll on shifting muscle and sinew. If only they would stop squabbling over us. Dizzy now. Punchdrunk on the view, tide-tossed and beaten, staggering between what is and what could be. Why doesn't the ref do something. It's a massacre. Close your eyes. Relax—it will all be over before you know it.

A CONEY ISLAND OF THE MIND

Katie Roiphe

....

Author and journalist Katie Roiphe (b. 1968), the daughter of well-known feminist Anne Roiphe, grew up in New York City. She teaches journalism and is assistant director of the Cultural Criticism and Reporting Program at New York University. Roiphe is the author of several books, including the nonfiction *The Morning After: Fear, Sex, and Feminism on Campus* (1993) and the novel *Still She Haunts Me* (2001). In "A Coney Island of the Mind" (2008), Roiphe describes a visit to the amusement area with a date. The essay opens with her graphic depiction of a terrifying but thrilling ride on the Cyclone. Four years later, she notes, she will marry her "date in something of the same spirit as that Cyclone ride." She will be taking a risk, one that in the case of her marriage does not work out, but feels "inevitable." Looking back on that visit to Coney, she wants to shout to herself, "Don't do it," but "this is what you can't do." The piece alludes not only to Lawrence Ferlinghetti's *A Coney Island of the Mind*, but to writings by two other authors, Delmore Schwartz's "In Dreams Begin Responsibilities" and Guy Wetmore Carryl's "Marvelous Coney Island."

MY FATHER LEFT FLATBUSH sixty-five years ago with no intention of ever returning, and one brilliant fall day I find myself going back to deepest Brooklyn, to Coney Island, to the last stop on the F train.

My date stops in front of the Cyclone that curls ominously above us. I am astonished that he wants to ride it. I feel twinges of panic on elevators and airplanes, but it somehow seems too early in our acquaintance for him to know that I am too fragile for roller coasters. My date does not give the impression of being afraid of anything. So we end up at the ticket counter. The ticket seller catches a crazy glint in my eyes and says, "Nothing's happened to anyone in the seven years that I've worked here," and we hear the whoops and shouts and rattle of the cars above us, and I look up at my date and wonder how well I know him.

As we climb into the car it feels rickety. The wooden track rising against the sky reminds me of the dinosaur bones in the American Museum of Natural History, which is not a reassuring image. The other passengers are teenagers from the neighborhood who look as if they do things every day that make the Cyclone about as exciting as a crosstown bus.

Once the ride starts, it does not feel safe. It shakes and moans. This is not the sleek modern sound of speed. This is speed from another era. It's the roller-coaster equivalent of reading by gas lamps or sending telegrams. The Cyclone was built in 1927. "Don't worry," my date tells me. How does he know I am worrying? Am I not doing a good job of hiding my worry? "There's a guy who checks every inch of the track every day." But this is hardly reassuring. This seems to me like a fallibly human system. Why should we trust a man checking a track, a man whose mind could be wandering to his girlfriend's erratic behavior the night before, or what he might be having for lunch?

We are pulled into the sky. I feel as if I am nothing but stomach, air, and fear. As we hurtle to the top, I grasp my bag, my date's legs against mine, and I see the rotating water and sky and sand, the crowd milling below us, and it's the greatest view in the whole city, thrill and terror blending into clarity, panic focusing the mind, I feel like I have never seen the ocean before.

Down below us is the boardwalk where my father used to come with his friends in the early thirties to swim and buy Nathan's Famous hot dogs for a nickel. He rode the Cyclone in the brighter, grander, better painted days of its youth. He grew up only a few miles from here, on East Twenty-second Street between Avenue T and Avenue U, in a house that I have never really seen. He drove us there once, on my mother's insistence, but when we got to his block he suddenly put his foot on the gas, and we perceived his childhood house, the house he was evicted from during the Depression, as a blur of color. (Years later, after he dies, I will wish I had gotten him to give me the number of the house; I will wish I had gotten him to talk about the movie theaters where he learned English from Ingrid Bergman, about his parent's marriage, about the Battle of the Somme.) But for now I am a tourist in my father's childhood. I am sailing over the past he wouldn't talk about. I am almost reaching it.

The track dips and the car zips down. My date and I are in our late twenties—he at least seems, ostensibly, to be an adult, but the years are stripped away by wind and fear and we are children again, clutching each other's hands.

It seems as if there is only a small chance that the metal bar will actually hold us in. At any moment we are going to fly out—little dots against the horizon. I imagine us falling through the air, like astronauts in a movie, our hair streaming out in the wind, frozen in a black-and-white photograph the next day in the tabloids.

As we turn the curve, even the teenagers shriek, but I am too scared to scream. It seems as if all of my energy has to be focused on staying alive. In 1911, the Cyclone's predecessor, the Giant Racer, flew off its tracks, killing two women. Picture the tracks bending through the air, the pretty cars careening through the danger they are built to simulate. Think how long it will take the observers to realize that the screams are real.

It feels as if the earth is falling out from under us and I have to close my eyes, no matter what my date will think. We swoop and swerve and finally clatter to a halt. It has been one hundred seconds.

I wonder woozily why I feel so good. I feel sort of bruised and banged up but that feeling is part of the beauty of the Cyclone. It's about terror and the release from terror, about how close dreams are to nightmares, and how easy it is to escape from your life. A journalist from the turn of the century wrote, "Coney Island has a code of conduct all her own," and for the first time I know exactly what he means. The Cyclone gives you the feeling that nothing matters but the second you are in, a feeling worth much more than the four dollars of the ticket. In fact it may be the platonic ideal of dates—a whole journey of risk and reassurance condensed into a minute and a half.

By this point, I am beginning to understand why the city has always had a romantic fixation on this place. Lawrence Ferlinghetti wrote his famous poem "A Coney Island of the Mind" about this too. [...]

As I step onto what seems like solid ground, I feel light-headed and shaky and my date puts his arm around me. We pass a freak show and a dance contest. We walk on the boardwalk in the warm air. My date is tall and quieter than any other man I have ever met. He does not narrate and analyze his inner life in the same compulsive way as everyone else I know. I look back at the Cyclone, arched against the sky. The brightly painted food stands and arcades bear more of a resemblance to the old peep shows in Times Square than to the glamorous architecture of Coney Island's past.

But you can still feel the seediness and greatness of the place, the vague feeling of menace, of leisure and unemployment mixing, along with the elation of a day at the beach.

Four years later, I will marry my date in something of the same spirit as that Cyclone ride. I will be taking a risk that I feel as a risk, and yet it will feel inevitable, as I have bought my ticket and am pulled skyward. Later, when he has moved out, I will go back over time. I will review with some puzzlement what I could have been thinking: Where was that man who checks every inch of the track? What was that man dreaming about when he should have been checking the track?

In Delmore Schwartz's haunting short story "In Dreams Begin Responsibilities," a grown man watches a movie of his parents' courtship. His father wears a tie. His mother wears a hat with feathers. They are trying to impress each other. They ride a streetcar to Coney Island. They ride a merry-go-round, reaching for the brass rings. Then they stand on this same boardwalk, looking out at this same ocean, when his father asks his mother to marry him. Just at that moment the narrator stands up and shouts at this movie screen: "Don't do it. It's not too late to change your minds, both of you. Nothing good will come of it." This is the feeling I have looking at this moment now. Stop the movie, there on the boardwalk. I feel like shouting at myself through the years. But this is what you can't do. *Don't do it. It's not too late to change your mind.*

For now, though, my date buys a large bag of Nathan's French fries, and I wonder how on earth he can eat after what we have just been through, and the crowd is enveloping us with stuffed dogs, and blown-up alligators tucked under their arms, and the sun glistens in the sand, and the sky is as blue as the cotton candy sold by vendors and for now, I am enchanted by the unknown territories of another person, and of the city itself.

CITY PLANNING BEGINS PUBLIC REVIEW ON REZONING OF CONEY ISLAND

New York City Department of City Planning

In 2003, Mayor Michael Bloomberg and the borough president of Brooklyn, Marty Markowitz, formed the Coney Island Development Corporation (CIDC) to formulate plans for the revitalization of Coney Island. Building on the recommendations of a strategic plan initiated by the CIDC in 2005, the New York City Department of City Planning proposed a comprehensive rezoning plan that was approved by the City Council in 2009. The press release "City Planning Begins Public Review on Rezoning of Coney Island," issued by the Department of City Planning on January 20, 2009, provides an overview of the plan, the centerpiece of which "is the preservation and expansion of Coney's legendary amusements" through the creation of a Special District. Zoning was to be modified to encourage a "wide range of amusement and attractions," including water parks, arcades, bowling alleys, performance venues, movie theaters, and restaurants. Hotels would be permitted in the amusement district, but only along Surf Avenue, and would be limited by certain restrictions of location and height. A park would be created, and retail stores and housing would be prohibited in the amusement district. The plan was controversial, and a critical reaction to even a draft version was voiced by the Municipal Art Society, among others.

CITY PLANNING COMMISSIONER Amanda M. Burden today announced the start of public review for a comprehensive rezoning plan that would re-establish Coney Island as a world renowned year-round beachfront urban amusement and entertainment destination. The 19-block rezoning would create an open and accessible 27-acre indoor and outdoor amusement and entertainment district stretching along the famed boardwalk from the Parachute Jump to the New York Aquarium. The district includes a 12-acre boardwalk amusement park area which will be mapped as parkland in order to enable the city to control, expand on and preserve amusement uses in perpetuity. Under the proposed rezoning, an estimated 1.1 million sq. ft. of amusement and entertainment related uses and 800 hotel rooms could be developed in the amusement and entertainment district, creating job opportunities that will last beyond the summer season. New entertainment and amusement uses could include innovative indoor and outdoor rides, dark rides, virtual reality, water parks, IMAX theaters, circuses, performance venues, roller rinks and all varieties of restaurants and catering facilities.

Outside the amusement and entertainment area, the rezoning would catalyze redevelopment of vacant and underutilized land for mixed income housing, a broad range of neighborhood retail and services that the Coney Island community has lacked for decades as well as additional year-round job opportunities. The 4,500 new units of new housing, North of Surf Avenue and West of KeySpan Park, would leverage an estimated 900 units of affordable housing. In addition, in these areas, the rezoning would pave the way for roughly 500,000 square feet of neighborhood retail and the creation of a 1.4-acre neighborhood boardwalk park. This plan is the culmination of an interagency four-year planning effort led by the Department of City Planning and the Economic Development Corporation [EDC] that has engaged residents and stakeholders from Coney Island and beyond during more than 300 meetings since the release of the Coney Island Strategic Plan by Mayor Michael R. Bloomberg in 2005.

Commissioner Burden said, "Our number one goal is ensuring that future generations can enjoy Coney Island as the world's most unique urban amusement destination. Our plan includes a 27-acre year-round open and accessible amusement and entertainment district as well as significant opportunities outside the amusement area for new housing and neighborhood retail. This needs to be a place where families can take mass transit and enjoy a few rides, or just visit the beach, all without paying an entrance fee."

"Certification into the public approval process is a crucial first step towards the rebirth of this iconic New York City neighborhood," said NYCEDC President, Seth W. Pinsky. "Our plan will create a thriving, year-round destination free from the whims of the commercial real estate market, while improving basic infrastructure, providing expanded neighborhood retail and offering new and improved housing opportunities. Coney Island is at an inflection point and it is crucial that all stakeholders come together to ensure that its next century is no less great than its last."

The current C7 amusement zoning is highly restrictive and has prevented new investment in complimentary year-round uses that should be part of an amusement district. This once vibrant area is now nearly devoid of economic activity once the summer amusement season is over. To bring new economic opportunities to the area, the City has developed a comprehensive plan for the revitalization of Coney Island that would foster a total of some 6.8 million square feet of new development. The proposed rezoning covers 19 blocks bounded by the New York Aquarium to the east, West 24th Street to the west, Mermaid Avenue to the north and the Riegelmann Boardwalk to the south.

The centerpiece of the plan is the preservation and expansion of Coney's legendary amusements which will be facilitated in part by an innovative new Special District that responds to the unique character and needs of Coney Island. The Special District will encourage a vibrant mix of year-round, entertainment experiences that would complement the future amusement park and help maintain Coney's singular character. The Special District will also provide for urban design controls to encourage varied building heights and building forms that will respect the iconic landmarked structures such as the Parachute Jump, the Wonder Wheel and Cyclone as well as the beach and the boardwalk. [. . .]

All together, the plan would realize a 44-acre public parkland network along the beachfront—in addition to the boardwalk amusement park—including a new 1.4-acre neighborhood boardwalk park at Highland View Avenue that would serve the surrounding neighborhood and new residents. In addition to the 9.4-acre parkland mapping in Coney East, actions will include a parkland demapping and rezoning of two surface parking lots currently used for KeySpan Ballpark. Developers will be required to incorporate structured parking garages to accommodate adequate parking for the ballpark and new development. Actions related to demapping these parking lots as well as the long term lease of the amusement area to an amusement operator would also require review and approval at the State level.

Integral to this City's overall strategy for Coney Island are major capital investments in open space as well as a community center with affordable housing and streetscape improvements. All told, the rezoning plan, coupled with the city investment in capital improvements, is intended to catalyze private investment of more than $2.5 billion. Over 30 years, the project will create over 25,000 construction jobs and more than 6,000 permanent jobs in industries including amusements, tourism, retail, entertainment, restaurants, and hospitality and generate over $14 billion in economic activity. The City's comprehensive plan for the area builds on the strategic plan for Coney Island announced by the Mayor in 2005 which called for the revitalization of Coney Island as a year round amusement destination and economic engine.

COMMENTS ON THE REVISED DRAFT SCOPE OF ANALYSIS FOR CONEY ISLAND REZONING PROJECT

Municipal Art Society

The Municipal Art Society of New York, a nonprofit organization, was founded in 1893 by a group of architects, painters, and civic leaders. Originally established to create murals and monuments for New York's public spaces, the society took on a larger role after the turn of the twentieth century, becoming involved in broader debates about urban design and historic preservation. It defines itself as a "membership organization that fights for a more livable New York and advocates for intelligent urban planning, design and preservation." In "Comments on the Revised Draft Scope of Analysis for Coney Island Rezoning Project" (2008), addressed to the Office of the Deputy Mayor for Economic Development, the society expressed its concerns, chief among them the criticism that the proposed area set aside for open-air amusements was insufficient. The society believed that open-air amusements "made Coney Island of such unique value—both historically, today and in the future." Although the Municipal Art Society's comments antedate the press release "City Planning Begins Public Review on Rezoning of Coney Island" issued by the New York City Department of City Planning, they do anticipate many of the criticisms that would later be leveled at the rezoning plan.

THE MUNICIPAL ART SOCIETY offers the following comments to the Office of the Deputy Mayor for Economic Development, the lead agency for the review of the Coney Island Rezoning Project.

GENERAL COMMENTS

Coney Island was once one of the greatest amusement districts in the world and remains hugely popular, even iconic, despite years of decline. The area is of vital, unique importance to New York City, representing both one of the most famous brands in the world and a one-of-a-kind opportunity.

We therefore believe that the City's efforts to develop a plan to revitalize Coney Island are vital for the economic, cultural and recreational future of New York City, and we are pleased that the city is focusing its attention on this long-neglected area.

The Society believes that what has made Coney Island of such unique value—both historically, today and in the future—is its open-air amusements. New Yorkers and visitors have other options for entertainment and housing around the city, but only Coney Island can and does offer them amusements in a unique and historic waterfront setting. New Yorkers deserve nothing less than a world-class amusement area from this effort to revitalize Coney Island.

We therefore believe that success of this plan depends on ensuring that we create a 21st century amusement area of sufficient critical mass and size to accommodate and draw visitors from all over the city, the region and even internationally.

The MAS is therefore concerned about the substantial reduction in the size of the area set aside for open-air amusements from 16 to 9 acres in the revised plan released in April. We are not aware of any other amusement areas of a comparable scale that come close to achieving the number of visitors that is the market for a revitalized Coney Island or even Coney Island today. *We are concerned that the proposed area set aside for open-air amusements is of insufficient size and that as a result this revitalization effort will not be successful.*

Our comments are therefore aimed at ensuring that this environmental review studies options and alternatives that would ensure that the City accomplishes the goal of creating an amusement and entertainment area of sufficient size, character and design to truly satisfy the needs of New Yorkers and the city's visitors in the 21st century. [...]

PROPOSED CHARACTER OF AMUSEMENT AREA

The Society believes that ensuring that Coney Island retains and develops the appropriate character is critical to its future success and that of the overall revitalization plan. In particular, we observe that the historical character of Coney Island's Amusement Area had the following characteristics:

- Multiple owners and operators. Traditionally and even today, the Coney Island Amusement Area has been comprised of multiple smaller amusement areas and businesses from Luna Park, Steeplechase Park and Dreamland historically to Astroland and Deno's Wonder Wheel Park today. This has given Coney Island its uniquely heterogeneous, diverse flavor and cultural significance but also has ensured that the amusement area was not dependent on any individual operator for its success, thereby ensuring its long-term survival through multiple economic cycles.
- Range of sizes of different businesses. Coney Island traditionally and today has catered for a range of size businesses from the very largest amusement operators to smaller businesses. This has not only contributed to the diversity described above, but also created a[n] environment that allowed entrepreneurialism and innovation to flourish, as the development of hot dogs, baby incubators and other inventions demonstrates.

In order to ensure these characteristics will remain in the 21st century Coney Island, the EIS [environmental impact statement] should study whether the proposed management structure of the amusement park as well as the zoning text that determines what can be built in amusement or entertainment areas outside of the mapped parkland area will accommodate both multiple operators, owners and different sized businesses, including both independent and corporate ownership.

PROPOSED DESIGN OF AMUSEMENT AREA

In addition, the EIS should study whether the proposed design of the amusement will:

- Retain retail and amusement booths adjacent to the Boardwalk to retain the lively streetscape experience there;
- Contain enough space for new modern rides, especially roller coasters.

CONFESSIONS OF A CONEY ISLAND SIDESHOW PERFORMER

Donald Thomas

Donald Thomas (Donny Vomit; b. 1979) was born in Norman, Oklahoma. He is a classic sideshow performer, entertaining crowds with feats such as sword swallowing, fire-eating, and chainsaw juggling. His specialty, however, is the human blockhead act, hammering six-inch nails up his nostrils. Donny performed at Coney's Sideshows by the Seashore for several years. He has also appeared at Ripley's Believe It or Not in Times Square and at numerous burlesque and vaudeville shows. In "Confessions of a Coney Island Sideshow Performer," written specifically for this anthology, Donny provides two autobiographical sketches, the first a reproduction of the spiel he often gave outside Sideshows by the Seashore to attract customers, and the second a description of his experiences as a human blockhead and the audiences who watch him.

BALLY

C'mon up, folks! Here we go! This is it! This is the one! You've heard about it; you've read about it; you've seen it on TV! Now it's your chance to see it live! The Coney Island Circus Sideshow! Freaks, Wonders and Human Curiosities the likes of which you have never seen. They're here, they're real, they're alive, and on the inside!

Gather round folks, gather round. We are going to do it right here. We are going to do it right now. A little free show, a little free show in front of the freak show. We are going to bring 'em out right now. Sally! Sally, send 'em on out. Send out the Snake Charmer; send out the Rubber Boy. Here they come, folks.

Now just step a little closer. I want you to see this. Now take a look. I want you to take a look above us. Now every thing that you see pictured, painted and advertised on the outside you are going to see live on the inside. And I can tell you about it.

I can tell you about the Fire Eater. This lovely lady is going to eat fire; she will breathe fire; she will lick fire just the same way that you would lick an ice cream cone. Bathe her body in flames! And you are going to see it live.

Then there is the snake charmer, the Amazonian beauty carrying with her the rare Burmese python, thirteen feet long and rounder than a telephone pole! A creature so rare most zoos don't have one. Hell, we don't have one; we have two of them!

I can tell you about the Human Blockhead. He's gonna hammer six inches of solid steel right into the center of his skull and live to laugh and joke about it. There is the sword swallower, swallowing three feet of solid steel from the tips of her lips right down to the bottom of her hoochie pooch!

Just come a little bit closer. Here they come! This here, my friends, is the Indian Rubber Boy. He's gonna bend, twist, curl, curve, and contort his body into positions that most would find physically impossible!

That's right, strange girls! Weird women! We've got the world's tallest midgets and the shortest giants. It's all right here folks. It's all on the inside. The Sword Swallower, The Human Blockhead, The Snake Charmer, Madame Electra! The Rubber Boy, The Escape Artist! I tell you, a true panorama of beauty and splendor will unfold before your eyes! Ten amazing acts to amaze and amuse you! Confound and confuse you!

And I want you to see it; you are in the right place at the right time. It's our first show of the day. Sally! Start that timer! Let me tell you what we're going to do! For the next five minutes we are going to throw out all the adult tickets! You couldn't buy one if you wanted to! We are going to throw out all the adult tickets and let each and every one of you in for a child's ticket! That's right for the next five minutes you are all my children! So follow our acts on in folks because ONE . . . TWO . . . THREE . . . IT'S SHOWTIME!

BLOCKHEAD

I make my living hammering nails into my head.

It wasn't always nails. I have had things such as ice picks, spoons, screwdrivers, power tools, and switchblade knives up in there over the years.

But I always come back to the nails. Right now it is a sixty-penny six-inch spike. I tap it into my nostril, and it slides to the back of the skull and it stops short of hitting my spine. This leaves an inch and a half of the nail still exposed for the audience to see. As I run through my related jokes and observations, I tilt my head up and down, side to side. On a good day, the audiences' eyes lock onto that nail as if it's a ball at a tennis match.

The initial shock of seeing a grown man doing something any child would be smart enough not to do can vary from person to person and crowd to crowd. And there have been many crowds. In the summers, it is at the Sideshows by the Seashore theater in Coney Island. The audiences are tourist and New York families looking to experience some Coney Island tradition. The evenings are in bars and clubs in Manhattan alongside burlesque dancers, comedians, and magicians. In the winter traveling across the states with a Vaudeville Review jumping from town to town with my trusty hammer and nail. I have hammered nails in front of college classrooms, office Christmas parties, bar mitzvahs, and deep-cable television shows. I once even found myself officiating a wedding under the Brooklyn Bridge. The bride and groom took their rings hanging from the nail in my nose. The reactions are always the same.

First, there are the people who are delighted to see something strange and odd. They may have heard about such a stunt being performed by the Fakirs of India or by performers of the past. They could have read about it in the books that romanticize the tent shows of the old carnivals or circuses. Some may have even seen an explanation of the stunt on TV. Now they are seeing it live. They laugh with anticipation and excitement as the nail is tapped into place. Their minds race back and forth with conflicting arguments. They convince themselves that it can't be real, but it must be real, but it can't! When I take the back end of the claw hammer and drag the nail from my face they are cheering and hollering before the nail hits the floor.

Then there are the curious but disturbed. These are the folks who watch the act from between their fingers. The ladies squeeze up against their men. The men grimace and watch out of the corner of their eyes. They squeal and give out nervous laughs. They don't want to watch, but they will. These are the people I can have fun with. I break the patter and try to comfort them in a calm soothing voice. "Trust me; it's not hurting you." This rarely works. They twist and laugh; their reaction becomes the show.

Sometimes I get closer and demonstrate how I can make the tip of the nail twitch and jump at will. Sometimes I even convince them to pull the nail from my face. They hold it with thumb and forefinger at arm's length. They may be slightly repulsed but very entertained.

There are also the fainters. Not a common occurrence but always a memorable experience. It is always the larger men who pass out. The gentleman's body goes limp, his eyes roll back into his head, and he slumps into his seat. This is usually followed by the lady he is with screaming with confusion and fear. I have learned from experience and resist the urge to jump into the audience and help revive. The first thing that you see when you come to should not be me with a nail in my head shaking you awake. The men always say that it was too hot, have a glass of water, and I continue with the show.

Then there are the disgusted, not the fun I-don't-want-to-watch-but-I-have-to! Disgusted but a specific kind that just shuts down. They stare at the ground stone faced. Some will turn around completely if they have the opportunity. They show no emotion except for great concentration, ignoring what is going on. They do not like it, and they never will. I leave these people alone. Maybe I can get a laugh out of them with the next act when I stick my tongue in a mousetrap.

I have learned many stunts in my years as a professional performer. Swallowed swords in the streets of Times Square and warmed up a room eating fire. I got a great workout from juggling a chainsaw and had indigestion from eating too many lightbulbs. I spent a summer hanging from my ankles escaping from a straitjacket and learned a few jokes along the way. But when I am looking for something that is going to stick with the audience, nothing beats the old hammer and nail.

A CONEY ISLAND OF THE MIND

Maureen F. McHugh

Fantasy and science-fiction writer Maureen McHugh (b. 1959) was born in Loveland, Ohio, and is the author of four novels and numerous short stories. She is also a co-founder of No Mimes Media, an alternative-reality game company. "A Coney Island of the Mind" (1993) is set in an unspecified future where people use virtual-reality technology to assume alternative personalities and visit simulated environments of their choosing. In this story, a young man known in the cyber-universe as Cobalt escapes his mundane life in Cincinnati (ironically, a city with its own Coney Island, opened in 1886 and still in existence) by means of this mechanism, visiting the virtual Coney Island and thus making the title of the tale particularly appropriate. In Coney, he meets Lamia, seemingly an attractive woman, who has "diddled the programming" to give herself a not completely human appearance. Her name is a reference to a child-eating female demon in Greek mythology. Cobalt's experience with Lamia suggests both the fascination and the strangeness of Coney Island and its seamy and sexual undertones. Even in the future, it continues to allow for the release of inhibitions.

REALITY PARLOR

He pays his money and goes back to the cubicle with the treadmill and pulls on the waldos, puts on the heavy eyeless, earless helmet. He grabs for the handlebars suspended before him, blind in the helmet that smells intimately of someone else's hair.

Now he can see. Not the handlebars hung from the ceiling on a tape-wrapped cable, not the treadmill. He is the cat with future feet. He sees a schematic of a room; all the lines of the room are in pink neon on velvet black, and in his ears instead of the seasound of the helmet he hears the sound of open space. A room sounds different than a helmet even when there's nothing to hear.

A keyboard appears, or rather a line drawing of a keyboard with all the letters on the keys glowing neon blue. Over it in neon-blue letters is the message, "Please type in your user ID."

"Cobalt," he types, letting go of the handlebars. The waldos give him the sensation of hitting keys, give him feedback. His password is nagasaki.

A neon pink door draws itself in the velvet wall in front of him. The keyboard disappears and the handlebars appear in pink neon schematic until he grabs them. Then they disappear from sight, but he can still feel them, safe in his gloved hands. He starts forward [the treadmill lurches a bit under his blind feet but it always does that at first so he is accustomed to it, doesn't really think about it, just kind of expects it and forgets about it] through the door which opens up ahead of him, pulling apart like elevator doors into the party.

The party isn't a schematic, the party looks real. The party is a big space full of people dressed all ways—boys with big hair and girls with latex skulls and NPC [non-player characters–Ed.] in evening gowns and tuxes— and as he comes out of the elevator he looks to the right, to the mirrors and sees himself, sees Cobalt, sees a Tom Sawyer in the twenty-first century, a flagboy in a bluesilk jacket and thigh-high boots with a knot of burgundy cords at the hips. All angles in the face, smooth face like a razor, a face he had custom-configured in hours of bought-time at the reality parlor, not playing the reality streets, not even looking, just working at his own look. Cobalt eyes like lasers, and blue-steel braids for hair.

Edgelook, whatta-look, hot damn.

Not what he looks like at all in the mundane world of Cincinnati, Ohio, but he isn't in Cincinnati, ho, flagboy, he's not in Kansas any more, he is at *the party*. Here he is, a serious dog, a democratic dog, but he doesn't think he'll spend a lot of time at the party today, looking around he doesn't see anyone he knows. Not that that means they aren't there, because anybody can look like anything, but if they don't have a handle he recognizes and they don't go calling out to Cobalt then they don't want to be the people he knows, right? and anyway, this afternoon the partyroom is full of off-the-racks, look-like-your-favorite-movie-star or take-a-basic-template-what-color-are-your-eyes-your-hair-look-like-a-manikin which he can't abide because he's looking for people with style so he angles over towards the far wall [his real feet, his mundane feet in their grass-stained sneakers that he wears when he mows the lawn just keeping heading straight on the tread-mill, if he angles he'll step off the treadmill, but he turns the handlebars to the left and he's done it so long he doesn't get confused by his feet saying one direction and the handlebars telling him another] to the far wall, full of blank doorways and he stops to read the menu.

It's better now that he's turned eighteen, more choices. Games and Adventures, Simulations, Tanks and Airplanes and Spaceships—but he's not really interested in a lot of that because he's on a treadmill, not sitting down, so back to Games and Adventures, Places To Go and Things To Do, where he is likely to find some people he knows, someone to hang out with; Quixote and Bushman and Taipei.

"Any messages?" he asks out loud.

Soft chime that can be heard over the whole room of the party (except that no one else does). No messages. Nobody in the swim? Then he'll look for a place where maybe he'll meet serious dogs. He almost selects Chi-natown but changes his mind and [left hand lets go of the handlebars and reaches out] pushes the button for Coney Island.

[Feedback through the waldo, it feels like pushing something.]

A line of electricity forms at the top of the door, a forcefield, an edge of static that rolls down like a window shade only draws down an opening on a place.

Black night on the boardwalk with the Ferris Wheel and the para-chute drop all decked out in colored lights off in the distance. Cobalt steps through the door and his feet thump the hollow wood of the boardwalk. The booths spill bright white and yellow light onto the boards. He can hear the ocean. A guy is selling hot dogs. Coney fucking Island.

So he walks down the boardwalk, checking out the crowd, checking out how much is just program—the sailor and his girl at the Toss The Ring who are always at the Toss The Ring every time he comes—and how much is real people. It's a quiet night on the boardwalk.

Maybe he should go back to the party, check out Chinatown. Hey, he's here, maybe he'll just dogtrot on down the boardwalk, out towards the rides, see if there's someone. Then he'll go back to Chinatown.

Moving along the boardwalk, past the cotton candy, past the tattoo par-lor, past the place where the counter is a two-tone Cadillac, dog gone, dog going, into a dog eat dog world.

And the queens (who are mostly black and tall and female and camp, that being the current fashion in queens) are calling "Hey sweetcakes," "Hey, be my blueboy," "Are you hotwired, babyface?" "Are you wired for sound?" Which he's not because he rents time in a fucking public reality parlor (no pun intended) where they aren't going to supply equipment to wire your crotch.

But it's all just noise, white noise, background hiss, the sound of Coney Island and not what he's looking for anyway although who's to say what he'd be looking for if he had the option? But he doesn't, so he isn't, he's looking for his mates, his team, his dogpack. He's checking under the boardwalk behind the Chinese Food place, and watching the mustangs crawl up the street because Quixote like[s] simulations, likes to drive fast cars in crazy places. Watching for spies because Taipei likes adventure games where he fights off attackers, watches for gang members because they all like to play Warriors and Coney Island is where it starts, where they catch the subway to the cemetery in the Bronx.

But the streets are all full of programming, of nonplayer characters, and kids without style, which is to say that this night Coney Island is empty.

So he's thinking that he'll check one more place, maybe take in a movie, or call up the airlock and go on to Chinatown and he stops where he can see the ocean and looks for a moment, the stone dark ocean rolling and making that sound, hypnotizing him and he likes it because there isn't much ocean in Cincinnati, hell, there isn't even much sin in Cincinnati.

She leans next to him with a star hanging off her ear, one lone star in the smoke nebula of her shadow hair, no off-the-rack handle but a costume full of style, like himself, like the dogpack, this woman has taken some time. "Hey blueboy," she says.

"Hey yourself," he says and imagines she smells like perfume, smells like ash. She has full breasts and brown skin in the yellow light. She has yellow snake eyes, not like dice like rattlesnakes and hair that doesn't act like real hair at all but fills some indefinite space, swallows light, absorbs light, no reflections. Soft looking. Nice touch, that. She's a chimera, she's not content to take a strictly human template, she's diddled the programming.

He's a lucky dog.

They make noises in the night, what's your name, Cobalt what's yours? (Rattlesnake, he wonders, or cobra, coral snake, black racer, asp, gila monster, his mind all in a rush before she answers—)

Lamia.

Which isn't what he expected at all and doesn't mean a thing except it sounds liquid. He wishes he had more access, he wishes he had preprogrammed something, an ashen rose maybe, to pull out of the air and give to her, but all he has are things that are useful in adventure games; a smoke bomb, a rope, a bottle that can be broken and used like a knife.

"That's pretty," he says.

She reaches out and takes his hand. And sighs happily.

The ocean rolls in.

"Squeeze," she says in a throaty whisper.

For a moment he doesn't understand but then he squeezes her hand and she half-closes her eyes. "Flagboy," she says, "I think I like you."

"Want to walk on the beach?" he asks.

She shrugs and kneads his fingers, he can feel her hand, all the bones of it and her long fingers, and she can feel his because of the waldos. He pulls her towards the steps and she gives a throaty, gaspy laugh.

She's wearing high heels, spikes with toes like cloven hooves—except that her feet don't look human. Her smoky hair has horns, then it's a halo, a madonna veil, all smoke. She follows him in a clatter across the hollow boards and down the steps into the sand. Their footsteps become silent [it never feels any different, because his feet are still on the treadmill, and his right hand is still on the handlebars, but his left holds the air and the waldos mimic the pressure of her hand].

"Not so tight," she says and he loosens his grip on her hand.

Eyes and hands, eyes and ears and hands. How real is real?

The light from the star in her hair falls on her bare shoulders, on her collar bones. Her clothing has no reason to stay covering her breasts but it does. She wouldn't feel it if he touched her breasts, not unless she's wearing a hotsuit. Could she be wearing a hotsuit, have her whole body wired for touch? Does she have a place at home, a treadmill, the whole bit? Spoiled Fifth Avenue girl? LA girl? Maybe she's forty years old, he doesn't know. Maybe she's ugly.

Interesting thought, that. He looks at her smoky hair and her skin and the hollow leading into her heart-shaped top and squeezes her hand and she sighs. Huuuhhh.

And he sighs too. Maybe she's ugly, or fat, or old. Maybe she is blind, or deformed. Maybe she is married. Wild thought that this beautiful girl can be anything.

His heart is pounding. She stops and they are facing each other, holding hands. If they kissed, there would be nothing but air. Strange to feel her through his palm and fingers, the waldos giving him all the feelings of her hand, and knowing that he could pass his arm through her. She is nothing but light. If he thinks about it he can feel the weight of the helmet on his head.

And her hand. All the bones and tendons and ligaments, the elastic play of her muscle. He finds her fingers, presses them one-by-one. She is watching his with slit-pupiled snake eyes gone from amber to green, although he can't remember when that happened. The ocean roars behind them.

He laces his fingers through hers. "Where are you?" he asks, although it's rude to ask people that.

"On the boardwalk," she says, her voice coming out in a breath. She is watching him, lazily intent, and he is playing with her hand. She closes her eyes and catches her lip in her teeth. Her face is so strange.

"Don't stop," she whispers and he doesn't know what she is talking about and then he realizes it is her hand, her hand in his blue gloved one. Her face is almost empty of expression, but small things seem to be happening in it independent of anything that is in his face.

"Squeeze," she says again.

Confused, he does, and feels her squeezing rhythmically back, pulsing little squeezes, and he realizes in horror just—

[She's hotwired her hand.]

—as she comes. Eyes shut, smoky hair rising in horns, she gasps a little. He jerks his hand away, but she is standing there oblivious, and it's too late anyway.

[You take a hot suit and rewire the crotch so the system thinks it's a hand, then any time someone touches your hand . . .]

He is embarrassed, angry, shocked. He doesn't know if he should just go or not.

[His fingers squeezing her and he didn't know.]

"Blueboy," she says, and sits down on the sand. "Oh Christ, blueboy."

He will go, and he does [turning the handlebars; feet, as always, straight on the treadmill] and starts back for the steps.

"Come on," she says, "what's so awful about it?"

"You didn't tell me," he says, all indignation.

"Prissy little virgin," she says, and laughs behind him.

"Airlock," he says, which is a system command, a gateway back to the party. The line of static starts at the height of a door, and the forcefield rolls down like a window shade.

"Huff on out of here," she says. "Righteous little bitch. Are you a girl?"

"What!?" he says.

Which makes her laugh. [Somewhere in Cincinnati his cheeks are burning.]

"I'm glad," she said, "because I'm not into girls. I just like wearing girl bodies because I like you righteous boys, you sweet straight boys."

He starts to step into the party and stops. "What?" he says.

"Draws you all like moths to a flame," she says. Or he says, or it said.

His first swift thought is that he'll have to change his look, never look like this again, abandon Cobalt, be something else.

She laughs that ashen laugh. "Go on home, blueboy."

And he does, steps back into the party, leaves Coney Island behind. The party, neutral ground, where he shakes his head, dog shaking water off his coat. He blinks in the lights of the party. Thinks of going home, going back to Cincinnati, to thinking about Ohio State in the fall.

Trying not to think about feet like hooves, high heels.

What a frigging nut case!

Bad luck, Quixote is waving across the space. Cobalt doesn't know, just wants to go home.

"Where you been," Quixote says, "you're looking democratic."

Shrugs. What's he going to say, I met this girl—I met this girl and her hand . . . he starts to smile, what a dog story. Quixote is going to be green.

"You won't believe what happened to me in Coney Island," Cobalt says.

He doesn't have to tell everything.

"No way!" Quixote says.

It's a dog eat dog world, sometimes.

APPENDIX
Coney Island in Movies and Music

CONEY ISLAND IN MOVIES

Since its early days, Coney Island has been closely linked to film. It was the home of many nickelodeons and was on the cutting edge of the early film industry. In 1910, it was estimated that more than 450 different motion pictures were playing simultaneously at Coney Island nickelodeons. The Coney Island History Project has held a Coney Island Film weekly series; Coney Island USA organizes an annual film festival. We offer a short list of some films in which Coney plays an important, though sometimes brief, role. Most are available on the Internet and/or on video. For more on Coney Island and film, see Lauren Rabinovitz, *Electric Dreamland: Amusement Parks, Movies, and American Modernity* (New York: Columbia University Press, 2012); John B. Manbeck and Robert Singer, eds., *The Brooklyn Film: Essays in the History of Filmmaking* (Jefferson, N.C.: McFarland, 2002); Michael Immerso, *Coney Island: The People's Playground* (New Brunswick, N.J.: Rutgers University Press, 2002), 118, 176; and "Coney Island—Movie List," http://www.westland.net/coneyisland/articles/movielist.htm (accessed March 13, 2014).

ELECTROCUTING AN ELEPHANT
(EDISON; DIR. EDWIN S. PORTER, 1903)
This silent film records the grisly electrocution of Topsy the elephant, purportedly to demonstrate the dangers of alternating current.

RUBE AND MANDY AT CONEY ISLAND
(EDISON; DIR. EDWIN S. PORTER, 1903)
In this excellent short silent comedy, a country couple enjoys the rides at Steeplechase Park and Luna Park and the sights on the Bowery.

BOARDING SCHOOL GIRLS

(EDISON; DIR. EDWIN S. PORTER, 1905)

Girls from Miss Knapp's Select School go on an outing to Coney Island, including a trip to the beach, in this silent film.

CONEY ISLAND AT NIGHT

(EDISON; DIR. EDWIN S. PORTER, 1905)

This very short film, an early use of night photography, gives a good sense of Coney at the time.

THE VEILED BEAUTY; OR, ANTICIPATION AND REALIZATION

(VITAGRAPH, 1907)

In this silent film, a man pursues a seemingly beautiful woman into Dreamland, only to discover her real appearance when she removes her veil.

MONDAY MORNING IN A CONEY ISLAND POLICE COURT

(BIOGRAPH; DIR. D. W. GRIFFITH, 1908)

This silent comedy was written by and stars Mack Sennett.

A CONEY ISLAND PRINCESS

(FAMOUS PLAYERS; DIR. DELL HENDERSON, 1916)

This silent film stars Irene Fenwick, later the wife of Lionel Barrymore, as Tessie, an exotic dancer whose stage name is Princess Zim-Zim, and Owen Moore, featured in many of D. W. Griffith's films.

CONEY ISLAND

(COMIQUE; DIR. ROSCOE "FATTY" ARBUCKLE, 1917)

Also known as *Fatty at Coney Island*, this pioneering comedy stars the well-known silent-film actors Fatty Arbuckle and Buster Keaton as rivals for the affections of a young woman. The film also features the Keystone Kops and includes great scenes of Coney Island, especially Luna Park.

TILLIE WAKES UP

(PEERLESS; DIR. HARRY DAVENPORT, 1917)

This silent film stars Marie Dressler in one of her many "Tillie" movies of the 1910s, in which she and her henpecked friend, Mr. Pipkins (played by Johnny Hines), each dump their dominating spouses for a day of respite at Coney Island.

THE KING ON MAIN STREET

(FAMOUS PLAYERS-LASKY; DIR. MONTA BELL, 1925)

This silent romantic comedy stars Adolphe Menjou and is set partly at Coney.

THE GIRL FROM CONEY ISLAND

(AL ROCKETT PRODUCTIONS; DIR. ALFRED SANTELL, 1926)

Also known as *Just Another Blond,* this silent film stars Dorothy MacKaill and Louise Brooks.

IT

(FAMOUS PLAYERS-LASKY; DIR. CLARENCE G. BADGER, 1927)

This silent film includes a very brief but excellent segment in which star Clara Bow goes on several Coney rides, including the Human Roulette Wheel and the Giant Slide, with her date. The film established Bow's fame as the "It" girl.

[Other notable films that include brief date scenes set at Coney Island include *Symphony of Six Million* (1932), starring Irene Dunne and Ricardo Cortez; *Manhattan Melodrama* (1934), featuring Myrna Loy and William Powell; *Mannequin* (1937), with Joan Crawford and Spencer Tracy; *Shopworn Angel* (1938), starring James Stewart and Margaret Sullavan; *The Devil and Miss Jones* (1941), with Robert Cummings and Jean Arthur; and *Heaven Help Us* (1985), starring Andrew McCarthy and Mary Stuart Masterson.]

THE CROWD

(MGM; DIR. KING VIDOR, 1928)

Coney Island plays a brief, but vital, role in this classic silent film.

CONEY ISLAND

(FILM BOOKING OFFICE; DIR. RALPH INCE, 1928)

This silent film stars Lois Wilson.

SPEEDY

(HAROLD LLOYD; DIR. TED WILDE, 1928)

After losing his job, Speedy (silent-film great Harold Lloyd) spends part of the day on a hilarious whirlwind visit to Coney Island with his girlfriend. This was Lloyd's final silent film.

MEET ME DOWN AT CONEY ISLE

(FOX; DIR. LOUIS DE ROCHEMONT, 1930)

Short documentary.

SHORTY AT CONEY ISLAND

(PARAMOUNT; DIR. ADOLPH ZUKOR, 1936)

In this brief film, Shorty, a monkey, visits Steeplechase Park. Several slightly different films were also made with Shorty.

CONEY ISLAND

(DIR. WILLIAM CASTLE, 1939)

Positive documentary of the amusement area.

NICKEL HEAVEN

(FORESTER; DIR. PETER HUGHES, 1939)

Lowell Thomas narrates this short documentary, which, despite its enthusiasm for Coney, shows some of the decline that is beginning to settle in.

MEET BOSTON BLACKIE

(COLUMBIA; DIR. ROBERT FLOREY, 1941)

Boston Blackie (Chester Morris) trails a woman (Constance Worth) to Coney Island, where she is struck by a poisoned dart. Before she dies, she tells him to seek a Coney performer whose act is to portray a robot or an automaton. This was the first of fourteen Boston Blackie films.

CONEY ISLAND

(20TH CENTURY FOX; DIR. WALTER LANG, 1943)

This well-known film, starring Betty Grable and George Montgomery, includes such musical hits as "Beautiful Coney Island," but it was not shot at Coney.

CONEY ISLAND USA

(DIR. VALENTINE SHEVY, 1952)

This twenty-minute documentary on one hectic day at Coney is notable for its images inside the Pavilion of Fun in Steeplechase Park. The film is a good depiction of Coney Island after World War II.

THE CLOWN

(MGM; DIR. ROBERT Z. LEONARD, 1953)

In this remake of a boxing film with the same name, Red Skelton, in a rare dramatic role, plays a down-and-out clown who works at Steeplechase Park.

LITTLE FUGITIVE

(LITTLE FUGITIVE; DIR. RAYMOND ABRASHKIN [AS RAY ASHLEY], MORRIS ENGEL, AND RUTH ORKIN, 1953)

This poignant prize winner at the Venice Film Festival is probably the best film featuring Coney Island. A young boy (Richard Brewster) spends a day at Coney, going on many of the rides, and is especially drawn to the pony ride. It was remade with the same title in 2006 by Joanna Lipper.

MURDER, INC.

(20TH CENTURY FOX; DIR. BURT BALIBAN AND STUART ROSENBERG, 1960)

Based on a true-crime memoir, this film stars Stuart Whitman and Peter Falk and features a scene of the death of the gangster Abe Reles at the Half Moon Hotel.

THE COOL WORLD

(WISEMAN; DIR. SHIRLEY CLARKE, 1964)

A Harlem gang leader takes his girlfriend to Coney, where she disappears. The soundtrack includes an instrumental called "Coney Island," written by jazz great Dizzy Gillespie.

CARNIVAL OF BLOOD

(KIRT; DIR. LEONARD KIRTMAN, 1970)

A crazed killer murders and dismembers his victims at Coney Island. The film features a young Burt Young of *Rocky* fame.

THE LORDS OF FLATBUSH

(EBBETS FIELD; DIR. STEPHEN VERONA AND MARTIN DAVIDSON, 1974)

Set in 1957, this coming-of-age movie was filmed in part outside Abraham Lincoln High School in Coney. It stars Perry King, Sylvester Stallone, and Henry Winkler as gang members and Susan Blakely as King's girlfriend.

ANNIE HALL

(UNITED ARTISTS; DIR. WOODY ALLEN, 1977)

This romantic comedy includes a brief but memorable scene of the Thunderbolt roller coaster and the house beneath it, home of the film's protagonist Alvy Singer. The "house" was actually the Kensington Hotel, built in 1895 and incorporated into the structure of the roller coaster when it was built in 1926. Mae Timpano and Fred Moran, son of the owner of the coaster, were longtime residents. The coaster and the hotel were demolished in 2000. An excellent video of Timpano's experiences is "Under the Roller Coaster," www.lilaplace.com/Lila_Place/Under.html (accessed April 2, 2014).

THE WIZ

(MOTOWN; DIR. SIDNEY LUMET, 1978)

Diana Ross and Michael Jackson star in this African American adaptation of L. Frank Baum's *The Wonderful Wizard of Oz*. The Cyclone is the home of the Tinman (Nipsy Russell)

BOARDWALK

(STRATFORD & TRAVELLERS; DIR. STEPHEN VERONA, 1979)

An elderly couple is terrorized by gang members in a decaying Coney Island. The film stars Ruth Gordon, Lee Strasberg, and Janet Leigh.

THE WARRIORS

(PARAMOUNT; DIR. WALTER HILL, 1979)

In this classic adaptation of Sol Yurick's novel, members of a Coney Island gang struggle to return home from the Bronx. The film includes some good shots of the Thunderbolt and Tornado roller coasters, as well as Stauch's Baths (covered in Warriors graffiti). An affectionate parody of the film, *Lost in Coney Island*, was made in 2012.

BRIGHTON BEACH MEMOIRS

(RASTAR; DIR. GENE SAKS, 1986)

Adaptation of Neil Simon's semi-autobiographical play, which opened on Broadway in 1983, about a boy's coming of age in Brooklyn.

THE GOODBYE PEOPLE

(CASTLE HILL; DIR. HERB GARDNER, 1986)

Adaptation of Herb Gardner's play, which opened on Broadway in 1968, about a middle-aged man who reopens a hot-dog stand on the boardwalk at Coney Island. The film stars Martin Balsam and Judd Hirsch.

ANGEL HEART

(CAROLCO INTERNATIONAL; DIR. ALAN PARKER, 1987)

Starring Mickey Rourke and Robert DeNiro, this film features a scene at the Coney Island beach.

ENEMIES, A LOVE STORY

(MORGAN CREEK; DIR. PAUL MAZURSKY, 1989)

Based on Isaac Bashevis Singer's novel about Holocaust survivor Herman Broder (Ron Silver), and also starring Anjelica Huston, who was nominated for an Oscar, this film includes scenes of Astroland, the Thunderbolt, and the Cyclone.

CONEY ISLAND

(STEEPLECHASE; DIR. RIC BURNS, 1991)

This classic documentary, narrated by Philip Bosco, was an episode in the PBS series *The American Experience* and is essential viewing for anyone interested in Coney.

HE GOT GAME

(TOUCHSTONE; DIR. SPIKE LEE, 1998)

Jesus Shuttlesworth (NBA star Ray Allen) is a heavily recruited basketball player from Abraham Lincoln High School in Coney, and Denzel Washington plays his convict father.

THE OBJECT OF MY AFFECTION

(20TH CENTURY FOX; DIR. NICHOLAS HYTNER, 1998)

In this film, starring Paul Rudd and Jennifer Aniston, with a screenplay adapted by Wendy Wasserstein from the novel by Stephen McCauley, the characters visit the amusement park.

WENT TO CONEY ISLAND ON A MISSION FROM GOD . . . BE BACK BY FIVE

(EVENMORE ENTERTAINMENT; DIR. RICHARD SCHENKMAN, 1998)

Two friends seek their buddy, who has disappeared and is rumored to be living a transient life in Coney Island, in a film that was co-written (with Schenkman) by and stars Jon Cryer. It includes some good shots of the Cyclone, Sideshows by the Seashore, and Ruby's Bar and Grill.

REQUIEM FOR A DREAM

(ARTISAN ENTERTAINMENT; DIR. DARREN ARONOFSKY, 2000)

In this adaptation of Hubert Selby Jr.'s novel, Harry (Jared Leto) and Tyrone (Marlon Wayans) operate a drug ring around Coney Island. They victimize Harry's television-obsessed mother (Ellen Burstyn), who lives in nearby Brighton Beach. The film includes some good shots of the boardwalk and the Parachute Jump. Aronofsky also used a Coney setting in *Pi* (1998).

A.I. ARTIFICIAL INTELLIGENCE

(AMBLIN/DREAMWORKS; DIR. STEVEN SPIELBERG, 2001)

Conceived by Stanley Kubick, and starring Jude Law and William Hurt, this futuristic film features a scene with a submerged Wonder Wheel.

TWO WEEKS NOTICE

(CASTLE ROCK; DIR. MARC LAWRENCE, 2002)

In this romantic comedy, lawyer Lucy Kelson (Sandra Bullock) is attempting to save a Coney Island community center from the clutches of a real-estate tycoon (Hugh Grant).

UNKNOWN WHITE MALE

(COURT TV; DIR. RUPERT MURRAY, 2005)

This documentary is about Doug Bruce, who wakes up on a subway at Coney Island not knowing who he is. There has been a debate whether Bruce has a condition called retrograde amnesia or whether the story is a hoax.

ZIPPER: CONEY ISLAND'S LAST WILD RIDE

(DIR. AMY NICHOLSON, 2013)

This documentary is about Eddie Miranda, who operated the Zipper ride in Coney until a real-estate mogul claimed the site.

FAMOUS NATHAN

(DIR. LLOYD HANDWERKER, 2014)

This documentary is about the iconic eatery and its founder, Nathan Handwerker, filmed by his grandson.

CONEY ISLAND IN MUSIC

Coney Island also has had close ties to music since its earliest days, including dance and music halls such as Henderson's and Stauch's. Many marine bands, such as that led by John Philip Sousa, performed at Coney. Sousa, who made annual summer appearances at the Manhattan Beach Hotel, composed "Manhattan Beach March" in 1893. For more on Coney Island and music, see Charles Denson, interview with John Schaefer, in "Ballad of a Brooklyn Beach Front," *Soundcheck*, WNYC, June 22, 2007, http://soundcheck.wnyc.org/people/charles-denson/ (accessed March 13, 2014); Michael Immerso, *Coney Island: The People's Playground* (New Brunswick, N.J.: Rutgers University Press, 2002), 106–123; and "Coney Island in Popular Culture," http://en.wikipedia.org/wiki/Coney_Island_in_popular_culture (accessed March 13, 2014). Many of the songs listed here are available on the Internet (both lyrics and performances). Our emphasis has been on lyrics (and a few instrumentals) that seem to best express the Coney experience.

"A TRIP TO CONEY ISLAND"

(THEODORE MOSES TOBANI, DAVID WALLACE REEVES, C. L. BARNHOUSE, THOMAS H. ROLLINSON, AND ALBERT C. SWEET, 1889)

Serio-comic fantasia instrumental.

"NEW YORK AND CONEY ISLAND CYCLE MARCH TWO-STEP"

(E. T. PAULL, 1896)

This tune reflects the popularity of bicycling, by both men and women, at Coney Island.

"MEET ME DOWN AT LUNA, LENA"

(COMPOSED BY HENRY FRANTZEN, 1905)

Celebration of Luna Park, sung by tenor Billy Murray.

"COMING HOME FROM CONEY ISLAND"

(1906)

Popular vaudeville song, performed by Ada Jones and Len Spencer.

"I'VE MADE MY PLANS FOR THE SUMMER"

(JOHN PHILIP SOUSA, 1907)

Dedicated to Luna Park, this song tells the tale of a girl rejecting her suitor by informing him that she's already made plans for the summer but to ask her again in the fall.

"MY MARIUTCH, SHE COME BACK TO ME"

(HARRY L. NEWTON AND MIKE BERNARD, 1907)

Also known as "Mariutch Make-a the Hootcha-ma-Kootch Down at Coney Island," this comic song was performed in stereotypical Italian dialect by Billy Murray. Used in 1930 in a Max Fleischer cartoon, the piece was also sung by Mae West, among others.

"MEET ME TONIGHT IN DREAMLAND"

(BETH SLATER WHITSON AND LEO FRIEDMAN, 1909)

First sung by vaudeville star Reine Davies and later recorded by such stars as Bing Crosby and Rosemary Clooney, this song was performed by Judy Garland in the play *In the Good Old Summertime* (1949). Whitson and W. R. (Will Rossiter) Williams composed a follow-up song, "When I Met You Last Night in Dreamland" (1911).

"BY THE BEAUTIFUL SEA"

(MUSIC, HARRY CARROLL; LYRICS, HAROLD R. ATTERIDGE, 1914)

Composed on the terrace of the Brighton Beach Casino, this song has been much recorded (by Ada Jones and Billy Watkins, among others) and has appeared in several films, such as *Some Like It Hot* (1959). A Broadway musical with the same title, with songs by Arthur Schwartz and Dorothy Fields, and featuring Shirley Booth, included the tune "Coney Island Boat" (1954).

"MANHATTAN"

(MUSIC, RICHARD RODGERS; LYRICS, LORENZO HART, 1925)

This popular song mentions Coney Island and was first performed in the revue *Garrick Gaieties*. Rodgers and Hart also refer to Coney Island in their hit "The Lady Is a Tramp," from the play *Babes in Arms* (1937).

"CONEY ISLAND WASHBOARD ROUNDELAY"

(MUSIC, HAMPTON DURAND AND JERRY ADAMS; LYRICS, NED NESTOR AND CLAUDE SHUGART, 1926)

Performed by the Mills Brothers and Hoagy Carmichael, among others, this song is about a woman who plays washboard music on the boardwalk.

"YOU'RE THE TOP"

(COLE PORTER, 1934)

Coney Island is mentioned in this popular song from the musical *Anything Goes*.

"GOODBYE, MY CONEY ISLAND BABY"

(LES APPLEGATE, 1948)

This well-known barbershop song is about a man who leaves his lover (whom he apparently met at Coney) in order to avoid marriage. It has been recorded by many artists and was featured on an episode of *The Simpsons* ("Homer's Barbershop Quartet"), sung by the Be Sharps.

"MERMAID'S AVENUE"

(WOODY GUTHRIE, 1950)

Guthrie lived on Mermaid Avenue from 1943 to 1954; his son, singer Arlo Guthrie, was born there in 1947. The song was recorded by the Klezmatics (*Wonder Wheel*, 2006). The British musician Billy Bragg and the American band Wilco recorded three albums of unpublished lyrics by Guthrie, with music written by Bragg and Wilco: *Mermaid Avenue* (1998), *Mermaid Avenue II* (2000), and *Mermaid Avenue III* (2013).

"CONEY ISLAND"

(DON BANKS, CA. 1961)

Lively, light orchestral piece by an Australian musician.

"CONEY ISLAND BABY"

(VINCENT CATALANO AND PETER ALONZO, 1962)

Popular doo wop song performed by the Excellents, a group from the Bronx.

"CONEY ISLAND BABY"

(LOU REED, 1976)

In this title song from Reed's sixth album, of the same name, Coney is mentioned only in passing.

"OH OH I LOVE HER SO"

(JOEY RAMONE, 1977)

Punk-rock love at Coney, performed by the Ramones.

"BONE TO BONE (CONEY ISLAND WHITEFISH BOY)"

(JOE PERRY AND STEVEN TYLER, 1979)

Aerosmith sings about a wild night with a girl at Coney. "Coney Island whitefish" is slang for a used condom found on the beach, and Joan Jett used the same image more blatantly in "Coney Island Whitefish" (1983).

"I REMEMBER CONEY ISLAND"

(JOHN LURIE, 1981)

Upbeat, fast-paced jazz-influenced instrumental performed by the Lounge Lizards.

"CONEY ISLAND STEEPLECHASE"

(JOHN CALE, LOU REED, STERLING MORRISON, AND MAUREEN TUCKER, 1986)

Recorded by the cult band the Velvet Underground in the 1960s, this song was not released until much later.

"CONEY ISLAND MAN"

(ANDY CONNELL AND CORINNE DREWERY, 1989)

Pop-jazz instrumental performed by the British band Swing Out Sister.

"STOP THAT TRAIN"

(MICHAEL DIAMOND AND OTHERS, 1989)

Performed by the Brooklyn-born hip-hop group the Beastie Boys, this segment from the long suite "B-Boy Bouillabaisse" talks of taking a "Coney Island vacation." The group also references Coney Island in their song "Do It" (1994).

"STRANGE POWERS"

(STEPHIN MERRITT, 1994)

Performed by the Magnetic Fields, a synth-pop group, this song contains the memorable image that the number of stars one can see from Coney's Ferris wheel exceeds the number of prostitutes in Thailand.

"CONEY ISLAND GIRL"

(STEPHEN BYRON BORGOVINI, BRIAN LEISER, AND HUEY MORGAN, 1996)

Performed by the New York–based alternative-rock group Fun Lovin' Criminals, this song praises the Coney girl's "swag," but the singer rejects her for another woman.

"SHUT 'EM DOWN"

(ONYX, 1998)

A hip-hop piece, performed by the group with rapper DMX, that refers to a dead rapper washed up on the beach at Coney.

"CONEY ISLAND"

(BENJAMIN GIBBARD, 2001)

Performed by the alternative-rock band Death Cab for Cutie, this song conveys a sense of loss and loneliness through the fate of Coney Island in its declining years.

"CONEY ISLAND BABY"

(TOM WAITS AND KATHLEEN WAITS-BRENNAN, 2002)

Waits's gravelly voice and gritty lyrics perfectly capture the feel of Coney Island from a bygone era. Waits also references Coney in the songs "Take It with Me" (1999) and "Table Top Joe" (2012).

"CONEY ISLAND"

(MIKE ERRICO, 2003)

The seagulls and the sound of the sea help to conjure up Coney in this acoustic instrumental.

"CONEY ISLAND BLUE"

(CURTIS ELLER, 2004)

Vocalist and banjo player Eller demonstrates a nostalgia for the Coney of 1903.

"ELEANOR, PUT YOUR BOOTS ON"

(ALEX KAPRANOS, 2005)

The singer of this song, performed by the Scottish indie band Franz Ferdinand, asks Eleanor to jump across the Atlantic Ocean from the top of the Cyclone to return to Europe.

"MILLION DOLLAR MERMAID"

(JOE MCGINTY, 2007)

Circuit Parade, led by keyboardist McGinty (formerly of the Psychedelic Furs), performed this song about the then imminent closing of Astroland Park, accompanied by a great video mix of Coney sites.

"CONEY ISLAND"

(DAN SCHWARTZ, 2008)

Performed by the acoustic group Good Old War, this song expresses the desire to return to New York City, especially Coney Island.

DREAMLAND

(BRIAN CARPENTER, 2008)

This concept album by the Massachusetts-based alternative-rock band Beat Circus includes such songs as "Gyp the Blood," "Coney Island Creepshow," and "Hell Gate."

"CONEY ISLAND"

(ANTJE DUVEKOT, 2009)

Duvekot, a German-born, American-based folk-pop artist, describes Coney as a place to escape.

"CONEY ISLAND"

(LOUISE BASILIEN AND OTHERS, 2009)

Performed in French by the Plastiscines, an all-female French group, this song imagines Coney as a siren calling.

"TOPSY'S REVENGE"

(MAT BROOKE, 2009)

Performed by the Seattle-based indie band Grand Archives, this song describes the events leading to the electrocution of Topsy, told from the elephant's perspective.

"CONEY ISLAND"

(JAMES SKELLY, 2010)

Performed by the British band The Coral, this song reflects a pleasant memory of a day spent at Coney. An acoustic version of the song was issued later in 2010.

LOVE NEVER DIES

(MUSIC, ANDREW LLOYD WEBBER; LYRICS, GLENN SLATER AND CHARLES HART, 2010)

This much-delayed, often criticized follow-up to *The Phantom of the Opera* (1986), set in Coney Island in 1907, opened in London on March 9, 2010. The romantic musical features such songs as "The Coney Island Waltz."

"CONEY ISLAND WINTER"

(GARLAND JEFFREYS, 2011)

This criticism of the New York City government for its neglect of Coney, by a Brooklyn-based veteran musician, is accompanied by a video with many images of Coney.

"CARMEN"

(ELIZABETH WOOLRIDGE GRANT [LANA DEL REY] AND JUSTIN PARKER, 2012)

This song is a sympathetic portrait of an alcoholic Coney Island prostitute. Del Rey also references Coney Island in "Off to the Races" (2012).

PERMISSIONS